# REMEMBERING

# REMEMBERING

Eric Kierans
with Walter Stewart

Stoddart

Published in 2001 by Stoddart Publishing Co. Limited
895 Don Mills Road, 400-2 Park Centre, Toronto, Canada M3C 1W3
180 Varick Street, 9th Floor, New York, New York 10014

*Distributed by:*
General Distribution Services Ltd.
325 Humber College Blvd., Toronto, Ontario M9W 7C3
Tel. (416) 213-1919   Fax (416) 213-1917
Email cservice@genpub.com

05  04  03  02  01  1  2  3  4  5

**Canadian Cataloguing in Publication Data**

Kierans, Eric W., 1914–
Remembering

Includes index.
ISBN 0-7737-3288-8

1. Kierans, Eric W., 1914–  . 2. Canada – Politics and government – 1963-1984.*
3. Cabinet ministers – Canada – Biography.* 4. Politicians – Canada – Biography.
I. Stewart, Walter, 1931–  . II. Title.

FC626.K54A3 2001      971.064'4'092      C00-932845-9
F1034.3.K54A3 2001

*Jacket design:* Bill Douglas @ The Bang
*Text design:* Andrew Smith / PageWave Graphics Inc.
*Page composition:* Joseph Gisini / PageWave Graphics Inc.

THE CANADA COUNCIL | LE CONSEIL DES ARTS
FOR THE ARTS | DU CANADA
SINCE 1957 | DEPUIS 1957

*We acknowledge for their financial support of our publishing program the Canada Council, the Ontario Arts Council, and the Government of Canada through the Book Publishing Industry Development Program (BPIDP).*

Printed and bound in Canada

TO THE FAMILY

*Cathy, psychiatric nurse and lifelong student;*
*Tom, corporate director and public servant;*
*and Terry, who has guided us all through the years*
*while pursuing her own talents in painting and sculpture.*

# CONTENTS

# One

# GROWING UP IN MONTREAL

*In the [city] charter, the wards are not specifically classified as French, English, Irish or mixed, but their boundaries are fixed so as to arrive* de facto *at this very classification, and no change would be permitted which could materially affect the racial character of the representation.*

— *CANADA AND ITS PROVINCES,* 1914

MY EARLIEST CLEAR MEMORY is of the period when my father came very close to death. I must have been about five or six years old at the time. I remember that the First World War had ended not long before, and since I was born in 1914, it must have been in about my sixth year. He had contracted pneumonia after a bout of flu, and in a world before anti-biotics, pneumonia was all too often fatal, even to a young, strong man like my father. One of his brothers did, in fact, die during that outbreak, and suddenly, in our small flat on the ground floor of a tenement on St. Agnes Street in the Saint-Henri district of Montreal, there was, for the first time, an air of tension, of uncertainty. My father was a quiet man, and we loved him, needed him. He was a steadfast point in our little universe, and now he was ill, stricken, confined to bed, and all the world's uncertainties were visited, or so it seemed to me, on my head. I was the eldest, after all.

Well, he recovered. And before too long, the cheerful whistle on the stairs and the quiet word in my ear were back again; but for me the world was never quite the same after that. It now seemed a more complex place than I had imagined, a place where all certainties could be challenged, might even be undone; the eight decades since that time have merely served to reinforce that early lesson.

## TWO ROADS TO CANADA

My parents, like so many Canadians, were immigrants. My mother was born Lena Schmidt, in 1885, in Hamburg, Germany. Her father, Edmond, was a successful plumbing contractor in that bustling port city, and a staunch democratic socialist. Mother had always been well able to take care of herself — and others. Her mother died when she was still in her teens, and as the eldest daughter, it fell to her to run the Hamburg household — everything from the cooking and cleaning to the shopping — a process that enhanced her considerable self-confidence and competence. When, after a few years, her father remarried, she sensibly thought the time had come to move on; one homemaker per household seemed about the right number. She had often seen foreign ships crowding the quays of the port, so it is not surprising that she soon boarded one of those ships and wound up in London, England, where she got a job working in a hospital as an attendant, and later she was employed in household service. At that time, the newspapers were full of advertisements for jobs in the New World — Sir Clifford Sifton's aggressive immigration policies were in full swing — and she decided to move to Canada. It was not that she knew anything about Canada; but she was a venturesome young woman, supremely confident in her own ability to get on in the world, and Canada promised, if nothing else, an exciting change.

She applied for immigration papers and within weeks was bound for Montreal, and domestic service. Her early life had given her a sound training for this, and she was hired, for fifteen dollars a month.

It was while she was working in this job that a friend introduced her to a short, slender, soft-spoken, good-natured Irish immigrant, Hugh Kierans. He had been born in 1884, in County Monaghan, Ireland, just south of the border with Northern Ireland. His father, my grandfather William, described himself as a "pig merchant," which may have been stretching a point; he was not an independent businessman, but an almost illiterate fellow who got along as best he could on whatever came to hand. The small town where he lived, which was also called Monaghan, was bitterly divided — like the country around — by religious tensions. On my grandfather's side of the street, almost every house, including his, was Catholic; across the road, in almost every house, were the Protestants.

At the turn of the century, Monaghan seemed to my grandfather's family a very good place to get out of; poverty and lack of opportunity marked the area. My dad's eldest brother, Jim, was the first to cross the water, and found work as a logger in Vermont. Presently, two other brothers, Tom and Patrick, followed, and as soon as they could afford it, passage was arranged for Hugh. All three of my father's brothers moved to Montreal when it became clear that logging was not only brutal, hard work — they could take that — but vastly uncertain work, with frequent layoffs and down time. Their eyes had turned to the largest nearby Irish community, which happened to be just north of the border, in Montreal. Tom went first, to a job with the city tramway system, and was soon followed by Jim. In those days, it was normal for members of a family or community to elbow out places for relatives and fellow countrymen. There were no more tramway jobs available for my father, but they managed to get a place for him at Canadian Car and Foundry, the company that built the tram cars, as well as train cars — though not engines — in the Saint-Henri district, just south of the Lachine Canal in central Montreal.

The Montreal of my childhood was a booming, changing city. The population went from under 100,000 in 1870 to more than 600,000 in the greater Montreal area by 1911. It was larger than Brussels, Manchester, Cairo, Bangkok, Naples, Pittsburgh, and even Madras, India. It bustled with the workers of five textile mills, three vast bridge- and ironworks companies, Molson's brewery, Ogilvie's flour monopoly, and Redpath's sugar monopoly. There were rows of vast Victorian mansions along Sherbrooke Street, and rows of working-class flats just down the hill. The population — in the language of the time — was divided among three "races": the English, the Irish, and the French. According to the section on Montreal in *Canada and Its Provinces*, a twenty-two-volume survey of the nation published the year of my birth, it was a grim place in which to be born because it was so crowded:

> In all cities the natural tendency is for business to concentrate around the focal district. In this way population too becomes

concentrated, since it is disadvantageous for the worker to live far from his work. The results are density, overcrowding, close and high building, small and inferior dwellings.*

Had I known, I might have refused to make my debut there, but my memories are of a warm, safe, cheerful home, and a neighbourhood dominated by the rituals and pleasing certainties of the parish where we lived.

My father was an electrician at the Canadian Car and Foundry shop — located at the edge of our neighbourhood — although he never passed an official test making him an electrician; he simply learned to do the job and did it. His amiable disposition made him a favourite at the shop, and he rose to become a foreman, and then supervisor, because he got on well with those both above and below him. He awoke every morning at 5:30 — as I learned to do, and still do — and I remember having quiet breakfasts with him and watching him start off to work in the crisp dawn. We often went for walks together; I did most of the talking, when there was talking, while he listened and nodded. We talked about sports, mostly; he was not the kind of father to lay lectures on his offspring to guide them through the world. Or we just walked along in companionable silence.

## I MISS THE CHANCE TO LEARN FRENCH EARLY

There was no English school within the parish when I was ready to begin my education, although one was promised, so my parents decided to send me to the nearest French school. But knowing nothing of the language, I was bewildered and lonely, and begged to be taken out. Regrettably, I was allowed to have my way. I would certainly have picked up French within a few months, but as it was, I grew to adulthood knowing only a few dozen phrases, many of them not suitable for the parish hall. There was certainly tension, even hostility, between the language groups, but my mother wound up with a number of friends among the French

---

* Decades later, when I was a member of the provincial cabinet and a scheme was underway to redevelop Saint-Henri, Lucien Saulnier, then the executive director of the Montreal civic council, noted that it was necessary to "tear down those old and dirty places in Saint-Henri." I received an outraged telephone call from my mother, who instructed me to tell M. Saulnier that "Saint-Henri was the cleanest place where we ever lived." I didn't call Saulnier, but I did tell René Lévesque, "Your pal Saulnier is in big trouble with my mother."

community. That was because her strong German accent, which she did not lose until well into the 1920s, made her the target of taunts among many of the English during and after the First World War. For our French neighbours, this was not an issue. Among the kids, clashes were also inevitable, because of language and religious bigotry. Years later, I told René Lévesque, who grew up in an English-speaking district, that he didn't know anything about discrimination — when I went to school, I never knew if I was going to be pushed around by a French youngster or an English one. He had only one tribe to worry about.

In addition to language, another complication affected my education: you had to be five to begin school, and my birthday, in February, meant that I was well into my sixth year before I was off to the English school, newly built on Convent Street, next to St. Thomas Aquinas Church.

We now lived in a flat on the top floor of 797 Convent Street, directly opposite the school. And we stayed there for most of my primary and secondary education. I did well in school, because I was determined to do so. The fact that the school was across the street from us made it a constant presence in the lives of myself and my younger brothers, Hugh and Plunkett, and sisters, Kathleen and Helen. My mother, of course, was the moving spirit in demanding top performance from all of us, having benefited from the importance that Germany, and Chancellor Otto Bismarck, in particular, had placed on education.

When I was in Grade 4, and at or near the top of my class, two other students were allowed to skip Grade 5 and go straight into Grade 6. When my mother heard about this, she collected her purse, her hat, and her thoughts and marched off to the school to see that I, too, was put ahead. Naturally, she won her way. The principal was astounded when he learned that I was just as old as the two boys who had been leapfrogged ahead; I simply looked younger. And, to top it off, I had better grades.

Although times were constantly getting better for the family during these years, life was still fragile, and we never knew whether my father's pay envelope might contain a dreaded pink slip. Thanks to his conscientiousness, and cheerful hard work, that never happened, even during the dark days of the Great Depression, but it was always there, as a threat hovering in the background.

My father had only one habit that seemed likely to create trouble at the plant — he would not work on St. Patrick's Day, March 17, and nothing could move him from that. Fortunately, his boss was a man named Boyle, an Ulsterman, who understood this aberration. After first threatening my father with dismissal for his intransigence, he grudgingly gave way. They became fast friends. Not that my father was a noisy Irish patriot; in fact, he attended only one meeting of the Hibernian Society, the favourite haunt of the Irish, and he told me that not much went on there but beer drinking and loud talk, neither of which appealed to him particularly. Much talk, he said, centred on the iniquity of the English at something called the Battle of the Boyne, of which he had never heard before he came to Canada. Besides, he was startled to learn that for all the lachrymose spiel, he was the only man at the first meeting who had ever been in Ireland.

## THE LEAP TO LOYOLA

In early 1927, I wrote the exams sanctioned by the Montreal Catholic School Commission for a scholarship to Loyola, the English Catholic college run by the Jesuits in the west end of Montreal. At this time, Quebec had no provincial education ministry and no compulsory attendance rules, and very few of the children, especially the Catholic children of Montreal, went on to high school. Without this scholarship, I might soon have found myself working to help support the family, and it was constantly impressed on me that if at any time I began to slide in school, that was where I was headed. Accordingly, I was excited when I boarded the streetcar — one of two I had to take to get to Loyola — for the ride out to write the exams. There were only three full scholarships available that year, and I won one of them; this meant that, so long as I kept my grades up, I would be able to attend four years of high school and four years of college at very little cost to my parents.

Needless to say, we were all elated at my success, and in September 1927 I set off for Loyola full of high spirits and higher hopes, only to run into the three worst days of my life to date.

## KNOCKING HEADS

My first day, I turned out for the class football team. I had seldom played the game before — our game in Saint-Henri was lacrosse, played on asphalt, a fast, rough sport. Because I was small for my age, I was made an end, with one of my major duties the task of running downfield to cover kicks. In practice on that first day, I was tearing down towards another boy who had just caught a kick, when he raised his hand. At least I was told that was what he did; I neither saw it, nor knew what it meant. In those days, as in American football today, the kick receiver could call for a "fair catch" by raising his hand, which made it a penalty to tackle him. Such subtleties were lost on me, and I ploughed headfirst into him. Although he was larger than I and a far better athlete, he was completely unprepared to receive a bundle of hurtling schoolboy in his midriff, and he was knocked out cold.

The practice was being overseen by a scholastic, a Jesuit in training who was not yet a priest, and he was naturally upset and angry.

"Didn't you see him put his hand up?"

"What hand?"

I was ordered from the field in disgrace, and dismissed from the team on the spot by the outraged scholastic. The boy I had flattened did not turn up for class the next day, but a close friend of his took up his cause in the locker room, crowding me and stepping on my foot deliberately. There was the usual exchange of courtesies — "Oh, yeah? Yeah?" and other witticisms — and then he began to hit me. He was taller, a rangy sort with a long reach, and he would certainly have cleaned my clock, so I put my head down and charged, bashing him into a locker, where he cut his lip and thus had to go to the infirmary.

This led to a messenger being sent from Fr. Raymond Cloran, the priest in charge of school discipline, to the class where I was studying.

"Do you have a fellow named Kierans here?" the messenger asked the teacher. "Tell him he's to go and see Darby first thing tomorrow morning."

That night was one of the longest of my life. I told my mother what had happened; I was terrified I would be dismissed from the school in shame.

"I tell you what," she said. "You come straight home from school every night this month and get to work and come first in your class. They'll never dismiss a boy who stands first."

Next morning, I went to the office of the prefect of discipline and asked, "Is this where I can find Father Darby?" Father Cloran's nickname was Darby, but I was not to know that. The priest pretended outrage. "Who said that?" he thundered. "Who called me that?"

I started to splutter my explanation of the trouble I was in, but he cut me off. "Here you are," he said, "the smallest kid in the college — you have the nerve to call me Darby. You don't look like much, and in two days you've sent two boys to the infirmary. What have you to say for yourself?"

I told him about the football incident and my ignorance, which he dismissed as "a poor excuse, a very poor excuse indeed." I then explained that the aftermath turned out to be a bigger boy hitting me. He wanted to know why I didn't box him.

"I would have lost."

"Humph," said Darby, but he didn't seem outraged. He told me that I would have to mend my ways and not go putting other boys in the infirmary, and work hard. Knowing Montreal better than the scholastic, he accepted my explanation of the tackling incident.

"That's what my mother told me," I replied. "She said I was to come first, and you'd never put me out then."

"Well," said Darby, "I guess there's no great harm done, yet, anyway. I'll tell them to put you back on the football team."

"I can't do that," I said. "My mother says I'm to spend all my time on schoolwork."

"Get out of here," said Darby.

## AN ATMOSPHERE LIKE OXFORD

Loyola was a wonderful place for a youngster who liked to work hard. There were approximately twenty-one scholastics and Jesuits to teach and ride herd on 210 students. We studied intently — or at least we thought we did. Looking back on our old papers, I am not so sure; but we worked closely with our teachers, and the atmosphere was more like, say, Oxford or Cambridge, with their collegial learning, than it was like a regular high school or college.

Every morning after seeing my father off to work, I would catch the streetcar on St. James Street — twenty-five cents for seven tickets — transfer at the Glen for another streetcar that went along St. Catherine, up Victoria to Sherbrooke, and then west through what became open farm country before coming to Loyola, passing the Benny farm, a mile or more west of today's Decarie Boulevard. The college was founded in 1896, thirty-one years before I arrived, by English Jesuits who promised to develop the moral and mental faculties to make good Christians, good citizens, and good scholars. The original school, in downtown Montreal, was replaced by new buildings on farm property in 1916. The walls were brick, with terra-cotta and limestone highlights; there were gargoyles on the central tower, and heraldic shields. I guess — I know little of architecture — the style was Gothic, or some mixture of Gothic; the buildings still have a look of solidity and authority about them.

The original idea was to have Loyola grant its own degrees, but the best endeavours of the Jesuits to bring this about were frustrated by the French archbishop, and the school had to become affiliated with the Université de Montréal to grant degrees. This lack of university status would rise up to bite me decades later.

At the end of my second month, a messenger came to my class with a request for me to go see the dean of the college, Father Gasson. He was an exile from Boston College, a brilliant scholar whose liberal views were not entirely welcome back home in Boston. He asked me if it would be a great inconvenience for me to carry a letter to Monsignor Reid, our parish priest, and I became a sort of mail carrier for the two, who exchanged comments on church and scholastic matters this way.

The accent was on hard work, with tests every week to gauge how we were doing. It was a fiercely competitive environment, and I thrived on it; at the end of most months, I was top of my class. The Jesuits did not welcome a lot of backchat, and there was a good deal of dogma along with the scholarship, but they did encourage and enjoy debate among and between the students, and boys who were thought to likely develop into scholars were certainly kept in mind.

The college originally offered an eight-year program leading to a baccalaureate degree, but this had been changed early in the 1920s to a high school program of four years, followed by a four-year college program and a B.A. degree. I had arrived at Loyola in 1927, after the change.

The major subjects in the high school were Latin, Greek, and mathematics, with the last being closer to simply arithmetic. We also had, of course, studies in geography, history, English literature, French grammar, etc., but these seemed to be of minor importance.

After all this time, one teacher remains solidly in memory. Gerald Lahey, S.J., was a gifted and enthusiastic teacher of English literature. He had written, during an Oxford year, a book on Gerard Manley Hopkins, the troubled English poet and Jesuit. Lahey, with some of the "piercing intensity" for which his subject became known, managed to instill in us an appreciation not only of the meaning of the poetry, but also of its patterns of rhythm and sound. He was the standout teacher of my high school years.

Looking back on my college years, I hazard my major contribution was in the debating arena. Chosen for the Montreal City debating team in my freshman year, I was busy during the fall and winter terms defending or attacking the League of Nations, the virtues or faults of capitalism, Mussolini, and corporatism.

In our first debate, the Knights of Columbus defeated us, using two former Loyola men, then practising lawyers. The subject was "Resolved that the League of Nations is a Failure." We took the negative, that is, in favour of the League. A saving grace was that the chairman of the judges' committee remarked that the youngest debater on the platform seemed to have been the most knowledgeable and best prepared on the topic.

The following year I made the college team and our first debate was at home against Osgoode Hall, the Toronto law school. Again, we stood for the negative on the same proposition that the League of Nations was a failure. This time, I was the second speaker on the negative. The topic was hot at the time because the League (really, the Great Powers) stood by helplessly as Japan, a member of the League, invaded Manchuria. My colleague built our case in defence of the League on its initial success in, among other issues, the Swedish-Finnish border dispute over the Åland Islands. An unfortunate remark by the second speaker on the affirmative side disclosed that he had not really understood the issues, a fact that I was able to make much more important than it really was. This and other points caused me to go on in rebuttal for quite a while, until suddenly the chairman signalled that I had only three minutes left.

"But I haven't started my notes yet," I protested.

Much laughter and handclapping. I summarized very quickly and we did win the debate.

During my four college years, the five debates or more each year meant hundreds of hours of research on the important concerns of the times. At least, it did for me. I loved working evenings at the Mechanics Institute on Atwater Avenue, digging out the material on both sides of the topic confronting me. To be effective and persuasive, I quickly learned, debating had to be based on meaningful content.*

Sports, that is, football and hockey, were not activities in which I had particular skills. I played football for three years, but I made the teams mostly because they needed twenty-four players yet rarely had more than twenty-one or twenty-two candidates. I played intramural hockey for some years, and was drafted in my final year to play for the college because the two regular goalies were disbarred by the college authorities for academic reasons. In a small college, everyone had to contribute; to "let Joe do it" was not an option. There were no Joes.

A recurring theme in Jesuit education is the phrase "What doth it profit a man if he should gain the whole world and suffer the loss of his own soul" (Ignatius to Francis Xavier). The phrase fascinated me. Eventually, I modified it by taking out the transcendental and secularizing the meaning by substituting "suffer the loss of his own living." What kind of contribution was I going to make with my life? That became the key to my thinking. This theme became clear in my debating activities. I was probably the most active debater in Loyola's history. I loved it, and, loving it, wanted to be good at it. Very good at it. Sociology was not a word much in vogue in those days, but in preparing for the debates on the major problems of the day, I read widely — history, politics, economics — for the clues that would help to make my points. Although I did not realize it at the time, this reading was driving me towards a social and political future, not a commercial one. The idea that I was very much a part of the community began to build slowly.

The two outstanding teachers of my college years, who had an

---

* Two years after I resigned from the federal cabinet, a friendly deputy minister told me that Prime Minister Trudeau was heard to say, "I really miss Kierans; he always covered both sides of any issue."

enormous influence on me and became fast friends, were Bernard Lonergan and Eric O'Connor. Originally from Halifax, O'Connor was a talented scholar whom the Jesuits had picked out and sent to Harvard, where he completed a doctorate in mathematics in eighteen months. He taught us physics and mathematics, and gave me a lifelong admiration and aptitude for math. He also encouraged us to think and question in ways that were sometimes frowned on by more orthodox priests. His favourite remark was "What is the question?" He later became the driving force behind the Thomas More Institute, founded in 1945, which did its best to open questions in a church not noted for its openness. Many of us former Loyolans support the institute to this day.

## BERNARD THE DEEP-BROW'D

The first speaker at the first meeting of the Thomas More Institute was Father O'Connor's good friend Father Lonergan, a brilliant philosopher known as "Bernard the Deep-Brow'd" because he was so often lost in thought. He came from Buckingham, Quebec, and he was later to become one of the outstanding theologians of the twentieth-century Catholic Church. I came to know him not only as a teacher, but also as the man responsible for the *Loyola Review.* He promptly named me managing editor, which meant collecting the funds to finance the *Review* from alumni, corporations where alumni worked, and so on. He also helped with advice on our debates.

We debated other schools in Montreal and, later, other universities farther afield, such as Bishop's, near Sherbrooke, and St. Michael's, in Toronto. It was at Bishop's that I first ran into John Bassett, who was later to achieve great fame as a publisher and television mogul. He was a competent, aggressive debater, but my clearest memory of him comes not in this forum but from the football field. He was a large player, not too fast, but strong. During an intercollegiate game, I caught a pass and tore off seventy yards down the field with Bassett close behind me, and the stands went delirious with joy. Apparently the sight of long John pursuing someone considerably smaller whom he could never quite catch was a rich one to behold. The crowd didn't realize that the touchdown I scored was not for the glory of dear old Loyola — I was running for my life!

My first brush with Father O'Connor came during third-year Arts. I was riding a little too high, and he gave me a grade of 50 in physics. When I protested, he told me bluntly that I had not shown the slightest interest or curiosity in the subject, that I had not worked, and that I could not expect to get by on past performance. He brought me down to earth with a thud. After that we became strong friends.

As I remember him in those early days, he was a great one for asking questions, never for giving answers. He was curious about such intellectual interests as we might have had and the careers we were contemplating. This was fearful and uncertain stuff in the early thirties. His curiosity, however, was the expression of his interest, his concern, his attentiveness to those around him and their problems. A volume of his statements, questions, and interviews was called *Curiosity at the Centre of One's Life*\*; its theme was that education was about questioning, choosing, and being responsible. There was not a student who did not appreciate his open door and respect his frankness, even when it hurt. He was a listening post with eyes that did see us, and ears that did hear. He resolutely maintained that education is understanding and that the very best understanding comes from studies that are pursued for their own sake — liberal studies, philosophy, literary criticism, artistic production, psychology, the classics, modern languages, the movement of history, theology, and the physical sciences. This was not the direction that universities were pursuing (even then; they fly from such pursuits today). No one was more aware than he that universities were tending more towards specialization, towards becoming professional schools and technical institutes, and no one was more disturbed than he by this trend.

What I gained from these two men, and indeed from the whole Loyola experience, was a reinforcement of the first lessons of Saint-Henri, the importance of community, the responsibility each of us owes to the society around, not merely in the John Donne sense that "no man is an island," but in a sense both social and spiritual that a civil society depends on the interdependence of its parts, and that when we try

---

\* *Curiosity at the Centre of One's Life: Statements and Questions of R. Eric O'Connor,* ed. J. Martin O'Hara (Montreal: Thomas More Institute, 1987).

to shuck off responsibility — in business, in politics, wherever — we are shucking off humanity.

I was by nature — and this may not come as a total shock to the reader — both competitive and questioning (within the bounds of orthodoxy, usually). I was encouraged in both characteristics by my favourite teachers, but not everyone felt the same way.

In my final year, in a class on theology taught by the dean of the college, we were talking one day about infallibility, a subject with which I had a good deal of difficulty. In the theory, when the pope speaks *ex cathedra*, that is, from the chair of Peter, on matters of faith and morals, his pronouncements are exempt from the possibility of error; this is a gift of teaching from the Holy Spirit. In the same way, definitive pronouncements of an ecumenical council, if ratified by the pope, are also infallible. These rather lofty points of theology have direct human consequences, and, at the time of which I write, the thirties, one of the subjects occupying many of our minds was vivisection.

Did humans have the right to use animals for experimental purposes in order to benefit mankind in — the obvious example — the field of medicine? To my mind, there could be only one answer: they did. If laboratory rats could promote a cure for cancer, they ought to be used that way.

So I rose in my place in class to ask, "What if the pope decides that vivisection is not acceptable to the teachings of the church? Would I be bound to take that view?"

"Yes, you would," said the reverend father, shortly.

"I don't know if I could."

The good father was obviously irritated with me when I persisted in this line of questioning and suggested that I come to his office after class. There, he told me I was not showing leadership by taking these positions, and there was not much I could say to that.

That evening I walked up to my favourite library, the Mechanics Institute on Atwater, near the Forum, and looked up material on infallibility. I discovered three things that surprised me. The first was that the doctrine of papal infallibility was new; it really dated only from the Vatican Council of 1870. The second was that the Curia Romana, the papal administration, had divided on the issue; it was far from clear-cut.

And the third was that the Jesuits had been dead against the whole idea of infallibility.

At the next theology class, I went after the dean and asked how was it that I would have to accept a view I didn't share on the basis of a doctrine that was quite new, that had been passed with some degree of disagreement, and that the Jesuits had been dead against. Well, back I go to his office, and this time he told me that he was not sure that I was the kind of person who deserved to receive a degree from Loyola. He also said he would move to block me from being the valedictorian at our graduation, which was coming up. I pointed out that I had been elected by the class; it was not a question for the faculty, but he said something to the effect that we would see about that. I later learned that when he raised the issue, the rest of the order jumped on him, and that was that. But I had not made a friend for life in the dean.

It seems curious to me now that we took theology, although it was really the study of the catechism, rather than anything a scholar would recognize as theology. As mentioned, we also studied Latin and Greek, but little French. Part of the innocence, ignorance, or unworldliness of the Jesuits, perhaps. Latin and Greek gave me a good handle on my own language, although I always thought the problem with Latin was that there was so little you could say in it, unless you happened to be a general. As a result, I grew to manhood in an increasingly French milieu with little more than just enough of the language to read the back of the cornflakes box, when finally the barriers were lowered enough to permit French on the box.

I blossomed in my eight years at Loyola; went out for tennis, hockey, and football; debated, worked, and played with the same unalloyed enthusiasm I had always had; and nearly always finished at the top of my class. I kept my scholarship, and was able to stay in school right through the depression, although there must have been many times when a second paycheque would have greatly helped the family. There were four of us youngsters, now: me; Hugh, my young brother — who was a first-class scholar and later went into the priesthood as a Jesuit; Kathleen; and Helen. Plunkett had died, very young, in 1924. It never occurred to me until I came to write these words that, for all we thought we were a progressive and forward-looking family, it was the boys who went on in education. In those days, it was accepted that after high school, the boys went to college and the girls took shorthand.

Making ends meet was always difficult. I did spend a couple of summers working at Canadian Car and Foundry, but I was never asked to quit school, although at the end of high school, in 1931, it did seem that I would have to go to work instead. The depression was at its dangerous depth, and it seemed inevitable that my father would be laid off. That summer, for the first time, I had a long search before I was able to land a job; the thirty-five cents an hour I had earned at Canadian Car was no longer available, and that made things worse at home. But my professors knew that times were difficult and did what they could to help by putting me in the way of tutoring jobs that paid. One of my pupils was the son of Andy McNaughton, the distinguished soldier, if undistinguished and short-lived minister of national defence in the King government.[*]

In the summers during the early 1920s, we had rented a cottage at Rawdon, in the Laurentians about forty miles north of Montreal, and it was here that I developed what became a lifelong passion for tennis. The people in the cottage behind us had a court, and I was first hauled in, about the age of eight, to make up a game of doubles. This went on for many summers. Tennis became the only sport I was really good at; I used to climb the hill to Westmount Park and bang tennis balls against the practice wall there until I wore them out. As a result, I won a junior championship in my first year at Loyola, but I was never tall enough to succeed in really competitive tennis; I just enjoyed the game, which in time became a link to René Lévesque, Pierre Laporte, and Paul Gérin-Lajoie.

I joined the Canadian Officer Training Corps (COTC), which aspired to make stalwart, disciplined future officers of college students. It did provide some training, as well as a four-week paid summer camp at the Connaught Ranges in Ottawa in 1934. The experience would later cause me a minor embarrassment.

## I DECLINE AN INVITATION
At the Loyola convocation of 1932, I led the freshman class with an average of 91.3 per cent. There were fourteen academic prizes (mostly

---

[*] King appointed him, but he was twice defeated trying to get a seat in Parliament.

books), and my name was called thirteen times for first prize. Then we came to the fourteenth prize. A pause. The master of the convocation was playing it for all it was worth. Finally, "for French...Michael O'Brien." He got a standing ovation, and I got a boxed mention in the *Gazette* the next day.

I was called in one day by Father Lonergan to discuss what came next. He said he thought I should seriously consider joining the Jesuits, and he would be happy to sponsor me. It was a flattering suggestion, but not really tempting; I had nothing of the inborn call that marks the natural priest. We talked about this for two hours, and then he brought the discussion to a close with "Well, this has been a very good discussion, would you like to continue it?"

I said yes, and went home and thought about it a good deal. Finally, I went back about a week later and explained that while I was very drawn by the offer to join the Jesuits, "my father makes $150 a month; this year, there will be two of us here at Loyola, myself and Hugh, and my two sisters are in convent school, and my responsibility, first and foremost, is to my family, to help them." Joining the Jesuits would not do that, I explained. I also had a responsibility to look after my parents, because in those days your children were your pension fund; there was nothing else, and I felt that duty very keenly. After all, look what they were doing for me.

He understood perfectly, and as we talked it became clear that he was not pressuring me, he was simply making me clarify my own thoughts, explore my own wishes, and consider, of course, the possibility that I might want to spend my life in teaching and the church. He told me that fellow student Bob MacDougall was "going up to Guelph," which is where the first stage of Jesuit training would take place, and then I made a mistake that I have regretted from that day to this.

I said, "Wouldn't it be great for you if both of us went?" and he went dead white and said, "Is that fair?"

And of course, it was not; he was not, and never had been, seeking kudos for himself, only direction for me.

I told my father about these discussions, but he never presumed to tell me what to do. "Be your own boss" is all he ever said, a short phrase that signalled that his life of work under others had not been free from a dread and fear of unemployment and failure.

# Two

# LIFE AFTER LOYOLA

*A full and active business life can never be completely*
*satisfying. The price is usually emotional and cultural atrophy.*
— D.H. MILLER BARSTOW, *BEATTY OF THE C.P.R.*, 1951

DURING MY FINAL YEAR at Loyola, 1935, at one of the few tea parties that I attended, I met a young, bright, vivacious blue-eyed girl who put any thoughts of the priesthood I might have had out of my head. Her name was Teresa Whelan, and sixty-five years later we are still together, madly enjoying our return to Montreal after a fifteen-year sojourn in Halifax.

Her father, Edward Patrick Whelan, along with his wife, Julia (née Cooney), had built one of the first houses out along the western end of Monkland Avenue, not far from Loyola. Here, Terry was raised. The family was Irish and Catholic; her grandfather had landed at Quebec City in the mid-nineteenth century and soon moved to Montreal, where his son went to work for Canadian Pacific Railway (CPR). Edward Whelan stayed there fifty-two years and developed such a reputation for energy and integrity that Sir Edward Beatty, long-time president of the railway, put him in charge of the ticket agency at the Windsor station when rampant corruption was discovered in the accounts there. Terry's father soon had that cleared out.

Terry had an unusual upbringing. An only child — an older brother died shortly after birth — she was educated at home until she was nine years old, when she was sent off to a convent school, where she turned out to be well ahead of her classmates. Two older cousins moved into the Whelan household when their own parents died, and she found a second mother in her cousin Vera, who was fifteen years older than Terry and helped to raise her. Terry has a distinct artistic bent, now represented by striking sculptures and oil paintings around our home, then by a deep and abiding interest in music and all the arts. She had a young man when I met her, a very fine fellow named John Newman, who was a couple of years ahead of me at Loyola. But I was not about to let that stand in my way, and we were soon dating. Our idea of a bounteous evening in those days was that I would scrimp and save until I had enough to take Terry out for a chicken sandwich, and away we would go on a round of debauchery that sometimes included french fries.

As my career at Loyola was winding down, I applied for a Rhodes Scholarship in hopes of being able to continue my studies. I was one of sixty or so young men in the Montreal area to do so, and made it as far as the interview with the selection board — chaired for years by Sir Edward Beatty in his role as chancellor of McGill University. To get to this final stage, all candidates had to write an essay on one of three pre-selected topics. I chose "Socialized Medicine." Then, during the fateful interview in the board of directors' room of the CPR, I made two mistakes. The first was when Sir Edward said, "I see that you have debated socialized medicine; I suppose you gave us your debate?" He meant that I'd rehashed my debate in my paper.

I replied, "No, sir. I was on the negative side in the debates, but I am really in favour of socialized medicine."

He grunted. I quailed.

Then he asked, "What have you been reading lately?"

I replied, "*Empire of Steel*," which was a not particularly flattering book about the battle between CPR and Canadian National Railways (CN). I also mentioned the three-volume memoirs of Walter Hines Page, the American journalist and diplomat who had founded the book publisher Doubleday, Page and Company. That was that. The following winter, I met Professor Corbett of the McGill Faculty of Law, who had been a member of the selection committee. He told me that I had put on a "very good performance — but unfortunately, you hit the chairman the wrong way." Beatty had commented, apparently, "One socialist in my life is enough." No point in saying that I wasn't a socialist. Beatty had been the chair of the committee that had awarded David Lewis, who was an undoubted socialist, a Rhodes in 1932; that was enough for Beatty, he would no longer trifle with the left.*

My politics, as it happened, were liberal, in both the small-*l* and the capital-*l* senses, and indeed I was about to become a spokesperson for the Liberal party — at five dollars per performance. This came about through Colonel John Long, one of our instructors in the COTC at Loyola, who had seen me in action on the debating team and thought I might make a useful recruit for the Liberals. I confess that I was attracted more by the idea that I could make five dollars for a speech than by a desire to see the Liberals triumph, but I quickly agreed. I went to the library, and looked up some of the debates then taking place between Mackenzie King, the Liberal leader of the Official Opposition, and Prime Minister R.B. Bennett, the corporate lawyer who, by this time, was frantically trying to grab policies from Roosevelt's New Deal to make up for the neglect that had been his main instrument for dealing with the depression.

Thus primed, I went out to party meetings to spread the gospel, enjoyed it, and was generally well received. At one meeting in a farm house in Marieville, I was handed a glass of something just after I had spoken.

"What's this?" I asked.

"7Up," said the young lady who provided it. It was a clear liquid but did not have the expected bubbles, so I took a cautious sip. It was straight vodka, and I hastily put it down.

I would sometimes make as many as three speeches in a single day, which meant fifteen dollars, a welcome addition to the finances. At least I was stamped as a lifelong Liberal at five dollars a speech. However, one evening, I did not get to speak at all, although I was scheduled for one of my fifteen-dollar runs. The first meeting, where I was on the card, turned out to be chaired by a fellow student at Loyola whom I had soundly beaten at tennis in a tournament not long before. His father was the candidate, and he was determined to keep me in my chair. Which he did, by calling on a succession of others until it became clear that the

---

* At Lewis's interview, Beatty asked, "Lewis, if you were the first socialist prime minister of Canada, what is the first thing you would do?" Lewis replied, "Nationalize the CPR, sir." Apparently, accepting that remark used up Sir Edward's supply of tolerance.

audience had been spoken to enough, and it was time to call a halt. It was also too late for my other engagements. The next day, I went to my contact at Liberal headquarters and reported what had happened. He insisted on paying me fifteen dollars anyway.

"Not your fault," he said. I knew that I had joined the right party. The Liberals won the subsequent election, on October 14, 1935, in a landslide, but candour compels me to admit that my speeches were possibly not what had turned the tide. At this time, the federal and provincial Liberals were part of the same organization, and indeed remained that way until 1964 — I saw nothing odd in this arrangement then. I did not know enough about politics to realize that this meant that the Ottawa Liberals controlled the Quebec party with an iron hand. This was not a vital factor during this period, but it became so with the *maîtres chez nous* approach of the 1960s. The split became final in 1964, with the establishment of a separate provincial party.

## ACCOUNTING FOR TASTES

It was time now to set about seriously to get a job, to help support my family, and to get on in the world. I had worked at Canadian Car; I had also worked for a few weeks in summers on the order desk at Ogilvie Flour Milling Company, a job obtained through my brother Hugh, who was a good friend of the son of the secretary-treasurer there. However, I was not exactly a strong candidate for a job in the constrained market of 1935. I had briefly thought of going into accounting, and in 1931, when, as we have seen, it appeared that I might not be able to go back to school, I had trudged around to a large number of accounting firms in search of work. They were not interested in anyone with no practical training, and the length of time required to become a chartered account-ant put that right out of the picture. The same logic put a degree in law beyond my reach, another career that appealed to me at the time.

In the fall of 1935, I went down to the offices of the Chartered Accountants Association in Montreal and put my name in for any posi-tion requiring a junior. I reasoned that I could learn on the job. Lo and behold, something came of this stab in the dark; the man who inter-viewed me judged that I had enough knowledge of figures and decided, "Your B.A. should see you through." So I was sent down to Quebec City to work as a junior on an audit there. It paid forty dollars a week, plus expenses to cover our rooms in the Château Frontenac. The accounting firm was based in New York, and the audit we worked on was for the Brown Paper Company of Berlin, New Hampshire, which had mills in La Tuque, Quebec, and offices in Quebec City.

The post led to my further education, this time four intensive months of accounting and learning on the job. In checking through some bills of lading, I came across the following notation: "La Tuque, Quebec, 500,000 cords of wood, ship to Berlin, New Hampshire. Nc." ("Nc." stood for "No Charge.") I brought this to my superior, a Canadian, who whistled and took it to the senior accountant, who was an American and the man in charge of the audit. He told both of us to forget that we had seen this note, which showed how a Canadian subsidiary was being used to create profits outside the country. It was my first experience in the transfer pricing shenanigans of multinational corporations.

The accounting interlude was instructive but did not lead to a permanent job. I had maintained my connection with Ogilvie Flour, and eventually an opening came up in the sales department. That led to an interview, and I was finally hired in July 1936 to go down to Moncton, New Brunswick, to replace the salesman there who had been promoted to Maritime sales manager. I took the train and checked into the Brunswick Hotel, right opposite the CN station in downtown Moncton. A message had been left at the hotel for me from the man I was replacing. He was out playing golf — it was a Sunday afternoon — and would call by after the game. So I spent a couple of hours on the hotel veranda, listening to a fascinating discussion about the possibilities of Maritime union, a subject that then, as now, would bob up every few years to roil the currents for a short time, and then drift out to sea. The arguments I heard at the time that solidly and adamantly opposed any proposal to join the three Maritime provinces together still echo today in exactly the same way.

The man I was replacing turned up after his golf game, and we hit it off very well until he asked me if I could drive.

"A little," I said. I had actually taken three lessons with Terry, who could drive, when I learned that this would be required in my new job.

"A little? You'll be driving all the time!"

Fortunately, there were not so many cars on the roads in those days, and the Model A Ford that served me for two years got me through without major disasters. Most of my time was spent on the road; Ogilvie had in mind expanding their operation against the competition of Robin Hood, the U.S. firm that dominated the market. Ogilvie's strategy seemed to be aimed in large part at getting around competition by buying up bakeries, one at a time, which would then order their supplies from Ogilvie. I didn't know this; I knew only that I was sent out to sell flour, and I gave it my best. I was just twenty-two, a full decade younger than most of the salespeople I met on the road, but I was certainly keen, and within a short time I was exceeding the company's expectations. I worked fourteen-hour days, sometimes seven days a week, and lived in small hotels and boarding houses in Chatham, Bathurst, Newcastle, Tracadie, Richibucto — all across northern New Brunswick, and as far south as New Glasgow and Truro, in Nova Scotia.

I called on local bakeries, trying to sell boxcars of flour manufactured in Montreal. In the evenings, I often played bridge or poker with other travellers, read, or worked on correspondence courses I took continually to improve my bookkeeping and accounting skills. I put an average of 35,000 miles — more than 56,000 kilometres — on the Model A each year, over roads that knew not asphalt, tar, nor even grader. When we hit a stretch of blacktop, we both heaved a sigh of relief.

I was paid by salary and commission, with a drawing account of $125 a month, plus expenses. I always made enough sales to earn much more than that, but bonuses were few and far between.

Besides selling wholesalers carloads of flour and feed, about 50,000 pounds, I did a lot of "detailing" — that is, selling to individual stores, a practice most other sales reps felt was not worth the trouble. I might sell the general merchant in Oxford, Nova Scotia, a carload on condition that I would bring in orders of 150 to 200 bags from smaller stores in the area. Prices for a 98-pound bag of Grade 1 flour at this time were in the three-dollar range.

I liked the job very much; it was a good start. But I was also very ambitious and let it show. I made it clear that I wanted to be a sales manager, with a district of my own, and this led to an offer of a new job from Maple Leaf Mills, at $150 a month, in Saint John. In the small world that then constituted Maritime selling, word soon got back to Ogilvie, and my salary was raised to $150 a month.

I was learning a good deal about business, selling, and people, but I had one experience that taught me something more. In and around Campbellton, which is in north central New Brunswick by the border with Quebec, I detailed a large number of small retailers for my wholesale customer W.T. Cook. The orders came from northern New Brunswick, as far west as Kedgwick, located halfway between Campbellton and Edmundston, in northwest New Brunswick. The problem was that a large food wholesaler in Matapedia, just over the Quebec border, covered the area, too. He began to lose volume, and he complained and asked to see me. He offered to buy three carloads of flour and feed, spaced over three months, if I would detail them for him. I said no, that I had no authority to sell in Quebec. Subsequently, I got a message from Montreal telling me to take this man's salesman, who happened to be his son, around northern New Brunswick for a full day, which I did. Then he gave me orders, which he duly signed, for the three carloads stipulated. But he then tore them up in a rage when he noticed that they were marked "SD/BL," which stood for "Sight Draft, Bill of Lading." This meant that the money was to be paid as soon as the carload arrived, and before it was unloaded. He said that he always paid his Quebec suppliers no sooner than thirty days, and this was usually stretched to ninety days. Montreal okayed the change when I rewrote the orders, and they went through.

In New Brunswick there was no such leeway; when I sold in Campbellton, less than half an hour away, the deal was cash on the barrelhead — Sight Draft, Bill of Lading attached. I was given a graphic proof of the fact that when large central Canadian commercial institutions deal with the Maritimes, the Maritimers usually got the short end of the stick.

As often as I could, I gathered my savings together and took the Ocean Limited train back to Montreal, where Terry and I pursued our romance with all the ardour then permitted by custom. Her father was very much on my side, but I had the feeling that her mother thought Terry could do better for herself than a young man from Saint-Henri who had managed to land a job selling flour in New Brunswick. Still, I persisted, and when her parents were going to New York with Terry for a holiday over Easter in 1938 I took the bus down there and joined them. I gave Terry an engagement ring to the swing and sway music of Horace Heidt and the orchestra, and we were married on November 12, 1938, at Saint Ignatius of Loyola Church in Montreal.

Her father had arranged, through his CPR connections, for us to go on a twelve-day cruise through the Caribbean, and then we hurried back to Moncton, where things were brewing.

### THE LUCKIEST BREAK OF MY LIFE

Ogilvie Flour had decided that its Halifax operation was not doing as well as it should. Sales had been sluggish to dropping for some time, because the company had fired its thirty-year veteran salesman, who had built a solid territory. I believe to this day that the new salesman there, if allowed a little more time, might have turned things around as the economy improved with the drift towards war; but the company decided to send in the "star" from Moncton to see what he could do. As a result, after about a month in Moncton, Terry and I were off to Halifax, where I was soon writing large orders again. By August 1939, domestic sales were back to where they had been and everybody was happy.

The outbreak of war, of course, led to increased economic activity and my sales increased in the Halifax area. Export sales moving through Halifax rose phenomenally, but they had nothing to do with me. With business surging, in November 1940 I wrote a letter to the general sales manager in Montreal, with the recommendation of the Maritime sales manager, asking for a raise based on my performance. What I got back was a letter that gave me the biggest break of my business life. It convinced me I had to work for myself. The general sales manager wrote to say that yes, it was true that sales had improved under me by 84 per cent, but there had been a meeting of senior officers of the company — and he included all the names, among them that of the Hon. Charles Dunning, a former finance minister of Canada and now chairman of Ogilvie; the president; the vice-president of manufacturing; the secretary-treasurer (my sponsor); and himself. This solemn conclave had decided that due to the fact that war had been declared, there would be no salary increases that year. However, they felt they could extend a special recognition to me for my fine work in the territory, and he was pleased to enclose a cheque for seventy-five dollars.

I was in no position to follow my instinct when I received that letter, which was to quit. Terry and I had moved into a new little house just off the St. Margaret's Bay Road in the Armdale section of Halifax. We had little money, it goes without saying, but I had persuaded a very good up-and-coming builder, Walter Havel, to build us a bungalow for $3,800. We had put $300 down and had taken out a mortgage for $3,500. (The last time I checked, about fifteen years ago, this house had just sold for $135,000.) Tommy, our first child, had been born on December 2, 1940; this was not the time to quit in a huff. I knew enough about Ogilvie now to conclude that it was not a company likely to appreciate entrepreneurial initiative or skill. It made more out of its portfolio of securities than it did by manufacturing in its five mills across the country; that is, it was content to watch its shares increase in value with time rather than to put its earnings to work aggressively. If I were ever to rise in the company, it would be through dead men's shoes, not promotions earned through merit.

I sent out resumés and feelers, and applied twice for jobs advertised in the *Financial Post,* but never even received the courtesy of a reply. No one was going to pay for an applicant from the Maritimes to come to Montreal or Toronto, where the only exciting jobs were, for an interview.

I went back to work, determined to prove myself anew. I learned all I could about flour and went on the road to sell it. I concentrated on trying to win over three large bakeries, one in Wolfville, one in Yarmouth, and one in Berwick. I kept calling on them, spent hours sitting on the dough table and chatting with the boys. One night when I was staying in Kentville, I woke up long before dawn, very restless, wondering what I could do, and I decided, what the heck, why not go over to Wolfville — bakers start early. I chatted with them for three hours, and when I got up to leave, the owner said, "My guys like you and think I should give you a break."

I said, "I think so, too."

He ended up giving me an order for three carloads, and later on I landed the two other bakeries, because I had sold him. The bakers were in a very difficult position; they sometimes needed money, and a milling company would lend it to them. Before they knew it, they were in the grip of the company and having to buy from that firm alone at prices set by that firm alone. Really independent bakeries were hard to find, but they were good customers if the quality of your flour held up.

I was learning, on my feet, lessons that are not taught in economics, where that strange and evanescent beast called "perfect competition" determines prices in a market economy. A market economy that exists only in the heads of people who have never sat on a dough table and talked to a baker at 4 a.m.

When the war broke out — and it was no surprise; after Munich, anyone who could read a newspaper could see that there would be no "peace in our time" — I gave serious thought to joining up. But I was a new father, with a new family and a lot of new debts, so I decided to wait a while and concentrate instead on getting back to Montreal, to our roots and families. I told the sales managers (Maritime and Canadian) that I was eager for a promotion and would take anything they had in that line in Ontario or Quebec, but I received no reply or encouragement.*

Terry and I talked it over, as we have always done, and as always she told me to do what I thought was best and that I would hear no complaints from her. After a year of saving and tightening our belts, in late 1941 we sold our Halifax house and cleared all our debts. With a nest egg of $1,000 left over to finance our start in Montreal, we then went back home.

## I JOIN THE VICTORIA RIFLES

Through some of the sales contacts I had made, I landed a job with Ronalds Press, a large printing company, which, not surprisingly, gave me the accounts that nobody else wanted. I wasn't able to do much with them. After a few months, I went to Dewitt Ronald and told him I wasn't earning my keep. He said the company had no complaints about me, but I was not happy doing a poor job, so I went instead to another printing firm, ES&A Robinson. Based out of northern England, this company specialized in promotional material. Here I did rather better.

One of the first things I did after returning to Montreal was to join

---

* About twenty years later when I was director of the School of Commerce at McGill, I ran into Charles Dunning, the former Ogilvie chairman, at a dinner and told him, "I used to work for you." He said, "I know; we made a bad mistake there, letting you go." Cold comfort.

the Victoria Rifles, a reserve regiment. Shortly after our marriage, I had applied for insurance at Manufacturer's Life and been turned down. No reason was given. When I joined the Vics, the medical officer rated me a C, with severe varicose veins. I didn't tell the regiment that I had been in the COTC and had attained the rank of lieutenant. Later, I was told that I had been entitled to officer status the day I joined. I may have been entitled to it, but I had forgotten most of the drill and could have started my new military career by ordering a platoon to make a right turn into an armoury wall.

We lived in a very nice flat on Victoria Avenue, the bottom half of a duplex, for which we paid, as I recall, forty dollars a month. Later, we moved to Hingston Avenue in Notre-Dame-de-Grâce. It was here that our second child, Catherine Anne, was born, and made her views known — as she still does — with crystal clarity. (Catherine, a practising psychiatric nurse today, is also a Ph.D. candidate in the Humanities program at Concordia University. Her thesis-in-progress is entitled "Patient Violence Against Nurses." She now lives in Westmount with her two Kerry Blue terriers.)

I left the printing company to join two other former Robinson men who wanted to build their own sales promotion company and who invited me to sign up with them. What I really wanted was to be on my own — be my own boss, build my own business, take my own risks — but I was not ready for that yet. I was not a partner in the new firm, but I was given all of Montreal as my sales area. I did very well, but the job was bound to be a temporary one, because the two principal partners had made a commitment to a former associate who was set to join them as soon as he got out of the forces at war's end.

I began looking around for opportunities to buy a business of my own, but before I could do so, I learned a lesson about corporations that was as illuminating as a bright light. I had just concluded a large sale to a customer when he suddenly said, "Say, is your company a partnership or a limited corporation?" (In fact, it was a partnership.)

I replied, "What difference does it make?"

"All the difference in the world," he said. "This is a very large order, a large amount of money for me. Suppose your company goes broke; if it is limited, the liability of the owners is no more than the money they put into the shares. If it is not, everything they own may be on the table. Believe me, it makes a difference." He gave me the order anyway, but also much food for thought.

It seemed astounding to me that the responsibility of someone operating in business, whose activities could destroy the lives of others, depended in large part on the way in which that business was incorporated. Later, I learned that there were good economic reasons for limited liability and the corporate idea. What struck me forcefully was that I had been operating in the business world for ten years without knowing very much about how it ran and was governed. I could parse a Latin sentence, quote from T.S. Eliot, and tell you more than you needed to know about flour, but the framework behind the economy was a vague mystery to me. I would have to do something about that.

## GETTING A GRIP ON BULLDOG GRIP

In late 1945 I heard through a friend that a firm called Bulldog Grip Cement Company was in trouble, and likely to plunge into insolvency soon. If it could be turned around, and provided I could get someone else to put up the money, it was exactly the kind of opportunity I was looking for, something small enough to handle. Those were two big ifs, however; but I went after it as hard as I could. I had already examined and rejected a few other companies that were in difficulty, but this one seemed to provide the most promise for someone who knew absolutely nothing about linoleum and tile cement — a product line that was bound to boom, I reasoned, with ballooning postwar housing construction. Just the same, I did know quite a lot about salesmanship. I would sell myself to whoever stood to lose the most if Bulldog Grip went under.

When I had an accountant friend look the situation over, it turned out that the potential big loser would be the Royal Bank of Canada, the largest bank in the land, whose offices on St. James Street resembled a cathedral more than a factory of finance. Bulldog had debts to the Royal that it was not going to be able to pay. After a single telephone call, I was able to arrange a meeting with Morris Wilson, then the president of the bank. (Wilson had returned to Montreal after a stint in Washington, D.C., as Canada's chief purchasing agent of war materials; he had succeeded Arthur Purvis, who had been killed in an airplane crash, as president.) Today, I would be lucky to cross the portal of a freshly minted account manager, but in those days, if you were persistent enough, you could get to the top. I was persistent, if nothing else. I was also very nervous as I entered the sanctum sanctorum. I might have been comforted to know that the land on which the building stood had once been sold for a bottle of rum and two cartwheels, but I didn't know that until later. A history of Montreal I read recently described the historic building as "rich and warm. The effect in the banking room is bright, mellow and sunny, the rough amber glass always giving the effect of sunlight." It did not seem warm to me the day I called on Morris Wilson.

I told him he had an account in the east end of Montreal that was going to turn sour on him, if it hadn't already, and I was willing, with the help of a few friends, to take it over, provided the bank would help with the financing. He listened to me politely, and sent me down to see the general manager, a Ted Atkinson. We had a long talk; he took my accounting information and said that he would get back to me.

Atkinson called me a week later and said the bank had no interest in my proposition because my figures on the assets of the company were out by $55,000. "I can't help you," he said.

It turned out that the bank's valuation of the company was based in part on $55,000 worth of buttermilk powder — a big ingredient in casein glue those days — which was on consignment from the Granby Milk Co-operative. Or to put it bluntly, the bank was counting, as an asset, inventory that the company didn't own. When I mentioned this, I got a sharp indrawn breath, and a promise to call back.

The next day, Atkinson reported that my figures were the correct ones and, "We think we can help you, after all." I went to see him, and he asked, "What do you need?"

I told him that I could round up support of about $11,000; we would offer $23,000 for the company, so I needed $12,000 in financing.

He said, "Do your friends know that you have to have a majority control?"

"Yes."

"I don't know a damn thing about you."

I pulled out the letter the general sales manager at Ogilvie had written about me in refusing my bid for a raise, and after reading about my sales record and the meeting of top executives at Ogilvie he said, "That must have been their busy day."

From then on, he was willing, even anxious, to see me take over Bulldog Grip, and I bought the business, with the help of my friends, for $23,000. Then I started to learn more about it, and soon discovered that a little glue lasts a long time. Bulldog Grip operated out of a plant in the east end of Montreal, an industrial district. The owner was a man who was the head of a French technical school, a nice fellow who often told me how well the company had been doing, when in fact he was losing his shirt. It was essentially an adjunct of a food plant, a manufacturing building at the back end of a chocolate factory, with two garages. Buttermilk powder was used in both businesses; it was processed to produce casein, a protein widely used in cheese, as well as to make adhesives and paints, and for printing textiles and wallpaper. We were able to offload the buttermilk business to Harry Bronfman, Sam Bronfman's brother, for one of his businesses — a dairy.

The next three years passed in something of a blur; I would get up at 5:30, grab breakfast, rush off to the plant, and do whatever needed to be done to keep the business from falling over a cliff. I could stay in business only by cutting costs, which meant making the very best use of everyone and everything within reach. I was the manager, production chief, salesman — whatever it took, I did it.

## AT YEAR'S END, A $500 PROFIT

At the end of the first year, we had made $500; not much, but compared to the steady drumroll of losses in previous years, it showed that we were on our way. My four fellow investors, who did not have my stake in the business and were really just helping me out, let it be known that they would like to be bought out, so I did that. All of them, in turn, started their own businesses. As the firm began to blossom, I changed the name from Bulldog Grip to Canadian Adhesives Limited.

I was a good adhesive salesman, as it turned out, and not a bad entrepreneur. And while we weren't getting rich, it was pretty clear that we were going to be secure — for the first time in my family in a generation — comfortable, and with luck, even well off. Running a business wasn't a science in those days; few business schools were turning out M.B.A.s with braces, cellphones, and one-hundred-dollar hairdos. Hard work and experience gradually gained seemed to do the trick — plus a lot of luck.

But I knew that I did not want to be merely another businessman. Don't misunderstand me, I am not knocking business people in any way, for the work they do, the risks they take, the jobs they provide. I had been spoiled, however, for any life that measured itself merely in money, spoiled forever by Loyola, by Saint-Henri, by the notion of community and responsibility. I hungered to do something that mattered more to me, and I yearned to be able to understand the forces that controlled not only my business but the larger economy as well.

What pushed me into taking action, though, was what I at first thought of as an extended sales trip, in 1947. I had joined the Canadian Manufacturers' Association (CMA) — why not? I was a Canadian manufacturer now — and they were sponsoring a trip that would put their members on two trains, one leaving from Montreal and the other from Toronto, to western Canada. We would go right out to the coast, stopping at Banff, Alberta, for the annual meeting. Canadian Adhesives had very little business in the west, and this seemed an ideal and relatively cheap way to see if I could drum up some more.

The CMA had planned the trip as follows. The Montreal and Toronto trains would consolidate in Sudbury, and from there one train would continue to Winnipeg, arriving in the early morning and leaving travellers to spend the day attending provincial receptions, playing golf, or meeting customers. The train then went on overnight to Regina, then overnight to Calgary; this was followed by a three-day convention stop at Banff and then out to Vancouver and Victoria on the CPR route. We would return to the east via CN. The idea was to give us a full-day stop at every major city, ideal for a travelling salesman. Moving by night, working by day.*

One of the most interesting stops we made was in Saskatoon, where Tommy Douglas, then premier, spoke to the CMA capitalists, and not only made a lot of good sense but had them rolling in the aisles with his

---

* Another manufacturer, representing Hahn Brass, as I recall, would be hanging on the steps as the train pulled into the various towns. The two of us actually called on the same hardware and furniture wholesalers. We laughed as we compared notes, while criticizing all our companions in the train, who preferred playing golf, attending luncheons, etc., to working.

jokes and asides. I gained an admiration for him, which despite our differing political views I never lost.

My only personal indulgence was an excess of baked Alaska served at the provincial banquet in Saskatoon. I had never struck this dessert before, and after I finished my own, my neighbour at the table offered his; I finished that, too. Soon there were three or four desserts in front of me, but I only got partway through the third. Evidently, baked Alaska did not look good to people with a few drinks under their belt! This was one of the few official functions I was able to attend; I spent most of my time building contacts and trying to make sales. Saskatoon being a relatively small town, with only three major possible customers, I even had time to go to North Battleford, about ninety miles northwest; a salesman I ran into on my last call was on his way there, and he offered me a lift.

At that annual meeting in Banff, there was a tremendous amount of discussion that seemed to me to make very little sense. The members wanted the government to stay out of their business — they made that clear, especially when it came to collecting taxes. But they also wanted the government to protect them from foreign competition; supply them with information; finance their foreign forays; and ladle out as many grants, subsidies, and low-cost loans as possible. I remember watching in fascination as the president of Canadian Industries Limited, a wholly owned British firm, deplored the iniquities of chemical imports into Canada — and I thought it wonderful indeed.

We were a small country, these men kept saying, a mere 14 million of us; if only we were 25 million, we could become a real, industrial, competitive country. (I had heard this argument before, in a debate in the early 1930s; then the argument went that Canada, a nation of slightly more than 10 million, needed 14 million to be competitive.) In the meantime, what we needed was lower taxes and higher tariffs, while we awaited the bright new day when competition — for we all believed in the magic powers of competition — would ensure the best possible use of resources for the entire nation. I did get up and argue briefly about what seemed to me the inherent contradiction of salaaming to competition while trying to make sure none of it came sneaking over the border, but the president of Lever Brothers, another wholly owned subsidiary of a foreign firm, slammed me into silence, banging his fist on the table and telling the government that what was needed to make Canadian business the grand thing it ought to be was "cash on the barrel-head." He loved the phrase, and repeated it. I did not see the relevance to my comments, but anyway...

I realized that if I didn't do something about my lamentable ignorance, I could not make the connection between the workings of the economy and the political world. I would wind up in the ranks of so many other business types. It was time to go back to school.

*Three*

————•◦•————

# TEACHING
# AND LEARNING:
# THE McGILL YEARS

*When geometric diagrams and digits are no longer the key to living things...*

— NOVALIS, 1800 (TRANSLATED BY ROBERT BLY)

IN MID-1948, I WENT to see Burton Keirstead, then the chairman of the Department of Political Science and Economics at McGill, who said he would be delighted to welcome as an M.A. student someone who had actual business experience. Keirstead was a Maritimer who had studied at Oxford, an energetic liberal economist who modernized the department, bringing in courses on labour and trade, finance and banking, without diluting the important academic and theoretical studies. He was a disciple of Alfred Marshall, a mathematician whose highly touted *Principles of Economics*, written in 1890, did much to persuade economists that theirs was an exact science and taught them to love equations.

The department was then housed in Purvis Hall, a beautiful old house about halfway up Mount Royal, at the top of Peel Street. It shared quarters in this building with the Faculty of Law. Frank Scott and Maxwell Cohen were prominent members of that faculty, and there was a lively interchange of ideas between them and members of the department.

My classmates, all younger than I, of course, were an exceptionally bright bunch; their numbers included Jack Weldon, who was to become one of my closest friends; Sylvia Ostry, later a national and international economic bureaucrat of note; Tommy Shoyama, who became Tommy Douglas's chief economic adviser, and later a key figure in the Department of Finance at Ottawa; Bob MacIntosh, later a prominent banker and president of the Canadian Bankers Association; and Michael Oliver, who would go on to become vice-president of McGill and then president of Carleton University. Weldon and Oliver were very much to the left, and active in the Co-operative Commonwealth Federation (CCF).

In addition to Burton Keirstead, I became particularly close to two professors — Donald Marsh, formerly of Columbia University, who had written an outstanding textbook on international trade; and Ben Higgins, a strong supporter of Keynesian analysis and policies. All three were well beyond the theory of general equilibrium so much in vogue at that time, with its underlying belief that capitalism was a self-regulating system — in J.B. Say's* sense that supply always creates an equivalent demand, and therefore there could be no depression or mass unemployment. The thirties had killed this naïve approach for all time.

Nevertheless, one had to deal with the argument, by now solidly entrenched in the teaching of economics. By the time I arrived at McGill, economics had reached a high level of abstraction in its search for, and insistence on, a theory of prices as the scientific basis of economics. The prevailing standard was the "theory of marginal utility," a description of the point at which it just pays someone to produce a good that someone else will find worth buying. This point of intersection will determine the price of the commodity under perfect competition. General equilibrium simply meant that if this were good for coffee, it would also be good for tea and all other commodities. Thus, a system of general equilibrium would come into being, connecting all prices in an economy — under perfect competition, of course (this was a little like saying, "in the presence of unicorns, of course"). General equilibrium analysis I found a bit ephemeral.

Industrial studies, forerunners of business schools, had developed "break-even-point analysis," to the point that the graphing of fixed and variable costs displayed the volume at which firms began to make profits and below which, of course, they were likely to go bankrupt.

---

* Jean Baptiste Say, a French translator and disciple of Adam Smith, argued that a competitive economy automatically moved towards full employment of men and resources, because all of the income generated by the economy tended to be spent either by the people who earned the income or by the merchants and factory owners to whom they loaned their savings. This was embodied in the disarmingly simple Say's Law: Supply creates its own demand. I wrote it off by calling it "double-entry bookkeeping."

These were more to my taste. The graphs were particularly useful since they mapped so much that was hidden in pricing diagrams. Because I used this analysis in pricing the products of my own company, it made the abstractions easier to understand. The fact that I continued to run my own company throughout my academic studies meant, on the one hand, that I was almost constantly overworked, and on the other, that I always had concrete examples from the real world of commerce to set beside the abstract theories.

## A NEW WORLD OPENS FOR ME

I took courses in basic economic and monetary theory and political science, and a whole new intellectual world opened for me. I devoured John Stuart Mill, Adam Smith, David Ricardo, and the emerging giant of our own day, John Maynard Keynes. I found much to disagree with, as well as much to admire, but what struck me most about men like Mill and Smith was that they were moralists, not number crunchers. Smith, much quoted but seldom read, was a professor of moral philosophy at the University of Glasgow. John Stuart Mill was a philosopher, as was his father, James, and his sometime mentor, Jeremy Bentham. To these enlightened men, the notion that an otherwise reprehensible action becomes justifiable on the grounds that it returns a profit, or satisfies the demands of the "market," would have been anathema. To such men, the notion that "efficiency" could be defined merely in terms of maximum gain, and that economics is a numbers game in which social, cultural, and political considerations are to be ignored, would have seemed gibberish. So would the notion that economics is somehow beyond politics, and that to attempt to impose social control on the workings of the marketplace is wicked, wasteful, and — oh, deadly sin — uneconomic. Good and evil, right and wrong, justice and injustice were weighed on the scales by these men, whose modern counterparts reject such considerations.

In my second year, Keirstead appointed me to the post of teaching assistant. If a professor gave a course that involved three hours of lectures a week, the assistant would give the third lecture, or a summing up of the first two. The job offered a major boost to the ego, and I enjoyed the teaching as much as anything I had ever done. I took the oral exams at the end of my second year and passed at the doctoral level.

The orals, although much dreaded, turned out to be one of the happier steps in my academic career. Burton Keirstead chaired the board of examiners, and the members were James Mallory, from Political Science, and Donald Marsh and Ben Higgins from Economics. Mallory was not overly difficult, and asked a few questions about Newfoundland, and Social Credit theory. Marsh questioned me on monetary policy and trade theory. Suddenly, he asked me if the newly minted creation of the Bank of Canada, the Industrial Development Bank (IDB), would be a useful tool. I said no; despite all the trumpeting and fanfare with which it had been announced, it would have only a minor impact.

My argument was that if you became involved with the IDB, you would lose all freedom to deal with other financial institutions. I had reason to know this from my own experience. S.R. Noble, the president, and Lucien Viau, Quebec manager of the IDB, had approached me about taking over a lumber mill in l'Épiphanie, a town outside Montreal, with the IDB's help. For six weeks, we discussed this on visits to the mill and in communications with the mayor and officials of the town. Finally, I asked the bank officers to give me a copy of the prospective agreement, and soon I received a forty-page document outlining the terms on which money would be advanced. As far as I could judge, if I went along with it, I would no longer be my own boss; furthermore, it looked as if my credit with my own bank, the Royal, would sink to zero. As I recall, everything that the family owned was in play if this deal went through.

I gave Earle McLaughlin, manager of the Royal's Montreal branch, a copy of the document and asked him to have it vetted for me by the bank's lawyers. The answer came back that if I signed the agreement, the Royal would put me on a cash basis; in other words, I would have no credit. In addition, I would be managing the operation at the pace of bureaucratic decisions, and at the mercy of second-guessing in Ottawa. It was not hard to decide to turn this down, and in fact it was a relief to do so, because the sums involved, approximately 4 million dollars, were too big for me to handle. The ensuing meeting with Messrs. Noble and Viau was not pleasant.

I explained this background to Marsh, who grunted thoughtfully. Then Professor Higgins weighed in with a series of questions, mainly on Keynesian definitions, the propensity to consume, the marginal efficiency of capital, etc. He wanted brief answers, on the grounds that I had a "tendency to verbalize." He wanted fewer words, and more content. At any rate, I passed at the doctoral level, and Keirstead was very pleased.

In 1950, I was scheduled to do my M.A. thesis on co-operative enterprise. Harvey Perry, a former official in the federal Department of Finance, and now managing director of the Canadian Tax Foundation, had approached me to do a study examining the breaks that co-ops received in the tax system, especially those resulting from the report of the Royal Commission on the Taxation of Co-operatives. I was happy to take on the subject, which led, incidentally, to a delightful meeting with George Nowlan, the Nova Scotia member of Parliament for Digby-Annapolis-Kings and later a member of the Diefenbaker cabinet. He was a director of a fruit co-op in Wolfville. I travelled from coast to coast, visiting the authorities in every province.

What I discovered, in the end, was that two groups in Canada, so far as I could tell, thought that co-ops were gaining an unfair tax advantage. Imperial Oil, which had a refinery in Regina — a very co-op–minded town — thought it was being hard done by; the other complainant, also in Regina, was a lobbyist for the Canadian millers and their Northern Elevator's Association. Nobody else seemed to care. I did a lot of work on the pricing of co-op and private products, complete with charts of price curves, that didn't prove anything much, and I had to report that I saw no point in writing a report on it and keeping the controversy alive. At the same time, I decided to drop the taxation of co-operatives as a doctoral thesis.

That was when I turned my attention to a much more important subject: the corporation itself.

Trying to sort out my own thoughts, I ran across one of the most important books of the 1930s, *The Modern Corporation and Private Property* by Gardiner Means and Adolf Berle. Berle was a law professor at Columbia, and Means an economist; together, they brought a good deal of practical experience as well as theoretical authority to this vexed subject, and their conclusions ran squarely counter to much of what was being taught at that time about corporate enterprise. They traced the growth of the corporation from a convenient means of organizing competitive economic enterprise to a collection of huge industrial oligarchies. In the theory propounded by conventional wisdom, vigorous competition would always impede attempts to control the market by a single firm or group of firms, but in the business world I saw, and still see, much of the energy of "free enterprise" was going into the ruthless extinction of competition, usually by the buying up of rivals. Means and Berle put it this way:

> The corporate system has done more than evolve a norm by which business is carried on. Within it there exists a centripetal attraction which draws wealth together into aggregations of constantly increasing size, at the same time throwing control into the hands of fewer and fewer men. The trend is apparent; and no limit is in sight.*

The corporation spelled the end of Adam Smith's "invisible hand" and the demise of the passing of control of the firm from father to son. Family enterprises were mortal; the corporation was immortal. This was heresy; it was also, in my experience, observable fact. Humans are mortal; the enterprises they build may grow and swell, but within a generation — two or three generations at the most — the drive and inspiration are gone, and others step in. The first generation makes the money, the second expands, the third spends. But a corporation has no such mortal span; the shares control the enterprise, and they can be expanded forever; more and more wealth can be churned back in to keep the firm growing, while — and it is no small point — responsibility for what it does, concern for the harm it may cause, is shuffled off. This change, and the rise of the new kind of corporation, had taken place with the passage of the series of laws that created the commercial corporation and limited its liability, ninety years before I entered McGill; but economic theory had not yet caught up with the changes.

It did not take much vision to notice that most modern corporations were run by and for management, not the shareholder, but that basic truth never seemed to filter through the texts on the corporate system. One obvious inference to be drawn from the argument of Means and Berle, though never put in words by them, has to do with the distribution of profits within the corporation. Current practice, and it was true even when Means and Berle were writing, is to distribute somewhere between

---

* Gardiner Means and Adolf Berle, *The Modern Corporation and Private Property* (New York: Columbia University Press, 1932), 18.

one-tenth and one-third of the profits to the shareholders. The rest is ploughed back into the firm, for expansion, or accumulated to buy out rivals. On the other hand, if all the profits were dispersed every year, the shareholders could choose whether to reinvest their share or to put it into another firm, one which offered a greater return. Capital markets would have ensured a much better allocation of investable funds than would be provided by their being retained in the existing managerial control.

Prior to entering McGill, I had carefully reread *Principles of Social Economy* by Valerie Fallon, S.J.; *Beyond Supply and Demand* by John S. Combs; and *The Managerial Revolution* by James Burnham. The first two deal with the institutional relationships in a capitalist economy, and the last with the particular institution of control, which the author finds resides in management, rather than ownership. Burnham is critical of *The Modern Corporation and Private Property*, but he owes much to that book.

I did not have much trouble in keeping level with what might be called the sociology of economics, that is, the study of the structure, development, and functioning of the economy and the public policies necessary to the achievement of society's goals. What did trouble me was the unexpected emphasis on the theory of the firm and its pricing under conditions of pure competition. While I came to realize that a pure competition model might be useful for analytical purposes, the fact that such conditions were an anomaly in the business world was, to say the least, confusing. I treated this whole series of courses as similar to doing scales endlessly in learning to play the piano.

In business, one analyzes price and output decisions, but the emphasis and the analytical techniques employed are based on total-revenue–total-cost information. These are not abstractions, but data based on actual price and output decisions, and they tell managers the break-even point (the price at which costs and sales are equal, and beyond which profit begins). Break-even-point analysis graphs fixed costs (rent, for example) as invariant over volumes, and variant costs (such as direct labour, marketing, and administration) as changing with volume of sales. The diagram yields information on the point at which costs equal revenue (thus, break even) and the increasing volume needed to obtain the desired profit. The price decisions include the nature of market decisions, and the nature of competition.

Adam Smith said that economic matters resolve themselves as if an invisible hand were at work to determine the outcome, and economists have been trying to prove it ever since. Commerce is not, in fact, settled by an invisible hand. It is settled by monopoly, oligopoly, imperfect competition — the decisions of thousands of entrepreneurs and millions of consumers all seeking their own private advantage.

My second year as Professor Keirstead's assistant in the fourth-year course on economic analysis gave me ample opportunity to compare what might be called the economics of business enterprise with the uses of marginal analysis. The real world versus the academic one.

By this time, I was just beginning to become familiar with the works of John Maynard Keynes, whose master work, *The General Theory of Employment, Interest and Money,* argued that when massive unemployment struck the economy, contrary to the almost universal views of other economists, it was not necessary for government to withdraw and wait for the market to solve the problem. Governments could and should intervene to create demand; today, we could call it "kick-starting the economy." Keynes was a thorough and unregenerate capitalist, who made a personal fortune in investments (and also did well for his college, in Cambridge), but of course he was attacked as a socialist radical. I found him easier to understand than other theorists, though even he seemed to take a delight in making the simple arcane. However, I could easily grasp that the crucial point in Keynes's theory was the substitution of human will for so-called automatic market processes. We were being told that any intervention by clumsy politicians would simply sabotage economic recovery; best to huddle in our lounges and wait it out.

Needless to say, the Canadian business community was anti-Keynes, even when his theories, put into practice by President Franklin Roosevelt, had set the United States well on the road to recovery far ahead of Canada. At the same time, our businessmen were lined up at the Department of Supply and Services in Ottawa, looking for the contracts offered by an increasingly interventionist government. I was rather pro-Keynes, at least in some of his arguments, and this resulted in some very sharp, and interesting, discussions in and out of class. In point of fact, the depression gave greater validity to Keynesian theory than did the relatively prosperous late 1940s and early 1950s.

In the real world, the value of much of Keynes's argument had been made manifest, but in the business world, and in much of the academic community, it was still being dismissed out of hand, and for different reasons.

Business loved the shelf of projects that C.D. Howe, Prime Minister Mackenzie King's most powerful cabinet minister, had in place to thwart the first signs of a slowdown; but at the same time they feared the growing intervention of government. So there was an ambivalence at work in the clash between theory and reality. Yet it was the tendency of at least some of my colleagues to ignore any such clashes and go on teaching the old lessons about a world of perfect competition, which never had existed and never would. Theories are fine, and I admire them, but economics, it seemed to me, had been taken over by analysis that tried to show what the market *could do* — economists seldom get that right — rather than showing what in fact the market *did* — the only thing they can get right.

The real world turned upside down when the Joint Stock Companies Act of 1856, passed by the British Parliament, created the modern corporation; but the economists scarcely even looked up. In 1890, Alfred Marshall, dean of the profession, still did not see the corporation as a valid replacement for the individual, closely held firm as the model instrument of economic analysis. It was not until 1932 that Berle and Means wrote the first academic account of the corporation, and they were totally ignored.

University circles have responded slowly to the new reality in the economy, to say the least. Even now, one sees a specified Nobel Memorial Prize (judged and awarded by the economic profession) given for a paper on "The Kinky Oligopoly Demand Curve and Rigid Prices." It is as if our physicists were still studying the transmutation of matter, or still searching for a perpetual-motion machine.

Despite its dubious claim to the honour, economics continued to be treated as a science — this is still the case — in the classroom, which meant that students bent over elaborate systems of simultaneous equations that had about as much practical application as the labour of theologians in an earlier era who liked to debate how many angels could balance on the head of a pin. You did not need to believe in the value of the mechanism, and you could not use it in the industrial sphere, but you had to go through the drill in order to teach economics.

During this period of learning and teaching, I was refining my own approach to economics. At least I knew, by now, what I did not accept: namely, the standard approach to economics as a science devoted to explaining the perfections of capitalism; and what I did not want to do: namely, waste my time studying the tax benefits accorded to co-operatives. I felt that I was ready to tackle something more challenging. Accordingly, when I set out a new topic for my thesis, it was, rather grandly, "Theory of the Business Enterprise," and so listed in the *American Economic Review*. I proposed to fit modern observation into the notion of competitive enterprise, ranging back in fact to Adam Smith's *The Wealth of Nations* and its argument that full and free competition, unfettered by state interference, would provide the greatest welfare for the greatest number of people. Even in Smith's time, the problem with the argument was that full and free competition was more fable than fact, and in our own day, increasing corporate concentration and monopoly were making the theory nonsense, although it continued to dominate the speeches of business leaders, in between bouts of taking over each other to reduce competition.

I was called to a meeting with Keirstead, my thesis director; Ben Higgins; and Donald Marsh. They had read my work to date, and suggested to me that I should skip my M.A. thesis and develop my new proposal instead into a full-blown Ph.D. study, under Keirstead's supervision. I was ecstatic, but alas, it was not to be. Instead, I was plunged into a new business entirely.

## A BATTLE ROYAL

In late 1952, I got a call from Royal Bank manager Earle McLaughlin, who asked me to come in to see him about a business proposition. This turned out to be a company called Hygiene Products Limited, a firm with sales of $4 million a year of paper towels, cleaning materials, and other household products right across Canada. It was in debt and sinking fast, and the Royal Bank had a very bad $400,000 loan on its hands. After my success with Bulldog Grip, now Canadian Adhesives, the bank had the happy thought that I might take this loser off its hands. I had a look at it and decided that, as a going proposition, Hygiene Products made little financial sense. Its main assets were in three buildings, one in Montreal, one in Toronto, and one on Hornby Street in Vancouver. The company was rich in fixed assets but had no money to pay for operating expenses. I said no thanks.

Soon after our talk, Hygiene Products was pushed into bankruptcy by its creditors, and a settlement offer was made to them that amounted to about thirty-five cents on the dollar. Some months after that, I read an item in the local paper suggesting that the first payment, of five cents on this thirty-five cents, was in doubt. And within a few days, there was another call from Earle McLaughlin, wanting to have another little chat. There is a vast difference, from the point of view of an entrepreneur, between taking on a troubled business for the value of fixed assets, such as buildings, and taking it over at thirty-five cents on the dollar; so this time our talk went much better, and I agreed to take on Hygiene Products, with the help of another loan from the Royal.

Within ten days of arriving at this agreement, McLaughlin called back to say it was all off; he was sorry, but he couldn't keep our bargain.

I said, "Well, you agree that we have an agreement."

He replied, "Yes, but I am telling you we can't go through with it."

I went charging down to 360 St. James Street, where he explained to me as nicely as he could that he had lined up Kruger Inc. to take on the project and that this firm had far more assets than I did, and therefore more security to back the necessary loan.

I told him I was going upstairs and would be back to see him in a few minutes.

"Why?" he asked.

"I am going to tell your head office that they have a manager down here who makes agreements, and then breaks them."

McLaughlin knew that his actions would not be seen in a kindly light.

Just as I got to the door, he said, "Wait a minute, maybe we could look at this again."

Within a very short time, I had the original agreement back in place and bought Hygiene Products for a little less than $25,000, while assuming debts of close to $400,000, including the money owed to the Royal.

I also had an agreement that I would not be charged more than the prime rate of interest, an agreement that has lasted to this day, with consequences we will meet in chapter 11. Somehow, McLaughlin and I never became fast friends after that.

These frantic business activities put an end to my Ph.D., and the result was that I never did get a postgraduate degree. I continued to attend McGill, as an invited guest of the Department of Philosophy's faculty seminar. Keirstead was disappointed and let me know it, but I really felt that I had no choice. Little did I know that my actions would in fact soon lead me back to academe with — if I may put it this way — a vengeance.

One of my first acts at Hygiene Products was to first curb, and then oust, the accountant the Royal Bank had put in there to ride herd on the debt; this one move tremendously boosted morale at the Montreal plant, where a dismaying sense of helplessness had taken over as the company drained away $15,000 to $18,000 a month in expenses over income. The three buildings had been sold by the creditors' committee, and the company was now operating out of rented premises in east Montreal and Toronto. Six years later, in 1960, I sold I sold Hygiene Products for $350,000. I put the money into Canadian Adhesives. This transaction put me on the way to becoming more secure than I had ever expected, and it opened up new opportunities.

## A CALL FROM CYRIL JAMES

I confess that I did not anticipate that one such opportunity would be at McGill, where I had done a lot of work but had not, so far, accomplished anything in the way of a degree. McGill at this time was being run, essentially, by two men — Cyril James, an economist (I did well in his seminar), and J.W. McConnell. James had come from his native London to teach at the Wharton School in Philadelphia. In 1937, he agreed to come to McGill to direct the School of Commerce for two years, on leave. He had been recruited by Lewis Douglas, then McGill's principal, with the strong backing of Chancellor Beatty. Within two months, Douglas had quit, and James was catapulted into his place by the offer of an unheard-of salary of $10,000 a year — a great deal of money then. James was a brilliant man, a diligent scholar, and a hard worker; he seized the reins at McGill and ran it for two decades with crisp authority and, as we shall see, occasional outbreaks of rebellion from the ranks.

Among his other hidden talents, he was thoroughly bilingual, but his facility in French was never on display. McGill was sternly, starchly anglophone and anglophile, so much so that one professor not long before my time insisted on being paid in pounds, shillings, and pence. James did nothing to disturb this rigid and narrow view. When he spoke to his counterparts at the Université de Montréal, it was always in English, and it wasn't until he was overheard speaking in flawless French to the French ambassador at a reception that this talent was revealed.

McConnell was one of Quebec's — and Canada's — foremost businessmen, owner and publisher of the *Montreal Star,* a major shareholder in a number of large companies (including Ogilvie Flour), and a noted philanthropist who took personal charge of the university's fundraising on the corporate side and also made large donations in his own name. He was not a man of broad intellectual tolerance, and ordered that the CCF party never be mentioned in the pages of his newspaper. This policy remained in force until the CCF won control of Saskatchewan in 1944, when it then burst forth, fully formed, like Venus rising from the sea, in the reluctant pages of the *Star.* McConnell was also a friend, ally, and campaign backer of Maurice Duplessis, and the *Star* supported the right-wing premier not only in his virulent anti-union crusade, but in the enactment and enforcement of the notorious Padlock Act of 1937. This legislation, which was finally overturned in 1957, authorized the closing of any premises suspected of producing or distributing communist propaganda. Communist propaganda was nowhere defined; it was whatever Duplessis said it was. (One of the most effective and vocal opponents of the act was Frank Scott of McGill.) Between them, James and McConnell ran pretty well everything that had to do with McGill.*

Keirstead didn't get along with James; thought he was too arrogant, too illiberal, too inclined to make up policy on the run without consulting

---

* So much so that when McGill, on the advice of the Duplessis regime, turned down an offer of financial support from Ottawa, and Quebec decided to make up the lost money, the cheque was addressed and sent directly to McConnell, who deposited it in the university account.

the academics who would have to carry it out.* That undoubtedly had something to do with a suggestion that I take over as director of the School of Commerce; I would be seen as Keirstead's ally. The first approach came from H.D. "Bus" Woods, who was retiring as director in mid-1953. He wanted to offload the Commerce job and concentrate on an industrial relations centre he had established. He told me there was a candidate for his replacement, a senior official with Alcan, but he wanted to put my name forward. I said I would think about it.

The School of Commerce had been established in the mid-1930s in co-operation with the chartered accountants of the province. It was developed, essentially, as a school for accountancy, and at that time there were five courses in accountancy out of the twelve needed for a degree. Students who couldn't get into other Arts courses were nearly always allowed into Commerce, even if their marks were dubious. It was a standing joke at McGill that the football players went into Commerce. Students were allowed to make up their course list from just about anywhere, so you would have students who took, as a credit, first-year Psychology in their first year, and then first-year Sociology in their second. A major commitment of the school was to offer a three-year accounting program under the aegis of the Institute of Chartered Accountants, which made this much more of a trade school than anything the rest of the faculty would recognize.

If I was going to take the job on, it would be, to put it mildly, something of a challenge. Naturally, I said yes. Actually, I was thrilled by the idea, although not thrilled by the fact that I was still struggling with Canadian Adhesives and Hygiene Products. I had purchased three wartime buildings, put Hygiene into one of them, and was still working to bring down its debt load to manageable proportions. (The Royal Bank was still owed slightly more than $300,000.)

The result of my indicating an interest was a phone call from James inviting me to apply for the post. Actually, given it was James, it was a virtual invitation to take the job, presuming I could survive the scrutiny of a committee made up of two members of the Faculty of Arts, two

---

* I found it fascinating that the major biography of him, *James: The Man in the Ivory Tower*, does not contain a single reference to Keirstead, although Stephen Leacock gets in twice.

members of the Department of Political Science and Economics, two members of the board of governors, and Cyril James as chairman. I later learned from a member of this committee that my appointment, even with James's backing, was no pushover. The Arts members were not at all sure that a man with a single B.A., and not much university experience, was the right person for the job. Apparently, what turned the tide was the immediate and vociferous statement by one of the members of the board of governors — Sidney Dobson, the chairman of the Royal Bank — that he vigorously opposed my appointment.

"Why?"

"We need him for the Royal Bank. He keeps rescuing sinking companies for us."

This persuaded the other members that my credentials might be good, after all, and I soon received a call from Cyril James offering me the post for five years, at $8,000 a year. I was delighted, but had to explain that I was in the middle of a business rescue that would take up all my time. Would it be possible to put off my appointment until September?

Exactly what he had in mind, James replied, and that was that.

## REVAMPING THE SCHOOL OF COMMERCE

When I took over, the school had a very small faculty, and some accountancy classes in the evening program were taught by accountants from the professional firms downtown, part-time teachers. It was run alongside the Department of Political Science and Economics in Purvis Hall. I was able to make two full-time appointments immediately, in Marketing and in Management. To meet the problem of our low entrance standards, a colleague came up with the commonsense suggestion that students not be admitted to Commerce unless they had the qualifications for a regular Arts or Science program. I put this through the admissions committee, and it went through like a breeze, leaving open the question as to why it had not been done before. Gone forever was the second-class aura of a Commerce degree. We were on a par with Arts and Science, at least to start.

I was determined to expose my students to business economics, as well as theory, and this meant a gradual revamping of all the courses, over a period of five years. I moved cautiously, with the support of an advisory council, made up of twenty-two of the city's best-connected business elite (all male, needless to say, in those days). Among them were the presidents of the Royal Bank, the Bank of Montreal, and Canadian International Paper. Another member was Sam Bronfman, head of the Seagram empire. Sam and I became good friends, but he did not attend many meetings of the advisory committee. "Call me when you really need me," he said; and I did.

I taught investment analysis and corporate finance as well as money and banking to the economics students in Arts, as well as to those in Commerce. I would sit on the edge of my desk, and we would go at everything from technical theory to ethical issues. There was only one class I can remember that got completely out of control, and it was my fault.

I had received an invitation to go to the bar mitzvah of the son of Philip Vineberg, one of my treasured colleagues, and one of Sam Bronfman's lawyers. The invitation read "9 a.m.," so at 9 a.m. I turned up at the synagogue, to find only a few people there. Phil showed up at about 10:15, for what turned out to be an all-day affair. While I was waiting, a distinguished-looking man appeared, saw me, and crossed over to greet me.

"Shalom," he said.

"Kierans," I replied, and stuck out my hand.

He was so tickled by my faux pas that I told the story to my financial analysis class the following Monday. They all broke up. Every time I would get them back to work, somebody would call out "Shalom" and they would all fall about. About twenty minutes into the class, I had to cancel it.

At the evening celebration of the bar mitzvah, I ran into "Mr. Sam" (as Sam Bronfman was known) and said, "I didn't see you at the synagogue." He replied, "Kierans, when we get these ceremonies down to forty minutes like you Micks, then I'll go to synagogue."

Sam very much wanted to be accepted by the Anglo community, and was a generous supporter of the university, which was ready to accept his money but not to recognize him. There remained a certain amount of anti-Semitism in some quarters of the university, and among some members of the board of governors. James was certainly not one of them.

I gained an insight into the fundraising business one day through Arnold Steinberg, a nephew of emerging supermarket magnet Sam

Steinberg. Arnold was in the School of Commerce and had become quite a fixture around the office; he was a bright and curious young man. He recounted the following illuminating tale to me.

McConnell, as part of a fundraising campaign that was shortly to get me into trouble, called Sam Bronfman and told him that he wanted to put down Sam's "community" for one million dollars; Bronfman said that would be fine. Sam called together twenty businessmen to a dinner and explained that the university was expanding and needed more funds, and that Mr. McConnell didn't want a big public campaign. If the twenty men at the meeting would meet their responsibilities, one million dollars could be raised there and then. Forms were provided. Sam Steinberg, then just beginning to make a real mark in the grocery business, filled out his cheque for $5,000; Bronfman looked at it, handed it back, and said, "Sam, you've dropped a zero."

So Steinberg made the amendment and then, that night, he and his brothers scrabbled together every dime they could raise to make sure the cheque didn't bounce.

To give you some idea of the atmosphere at McGill at this time, consider the story of Neville Linton, a fourth-year student from Jamaica who had succeeded, in his final year, in becoming the editor of the *McGill Daily*. He turned up in my office with his final editorial of the year, which was, essentially, an attack on the makeup of the board of governors. It said the members were "basically Protestant and Anglo-Saxon in character…One would expect that steps would be taken to ensure the support of the Jewish community since the benefit to the latter is clear. Yet there are no Jews or French Canadians on the Board of Governors even though we understand that prominent men have shown an interest in serving." (This last bit was a far-from-subtle reference to Sam Bronfman.)

"Why are you showing me this?" I asked Linton.

"What do you think of it?" he said.

"Well, it's all factual."

"But do I still get my degree?"

I was astounded, and assured him somewhat testily that his editorial had nothing to do with his graduation; his piece ran in due course, to considerable offstage grumbling from offended board members.

However, the narrow-mindedness in the McGill establishment that it portrayed slowly began to disappear. Linton, incidentally, received a first-class doctoral degree from an American university and became a full-time member of the Economics Department of the University of Alberta.

Things were going along busily, and in the main, well, when a serious battle developed at McGill in 1956 over the principal's insistence on establishing a full-blown postgraduate business school. James was a fine economist and historian; he was also very good at dealing with people. Seeing him in faculty meetings, we always thought he presented to us the face of the board of governors and the business community they represented; but in board meetings, he was very much the academic, fighting for the freedom of his professors to teach as they saw fit.

However, his real problem, from the point of view of those of us who worked with him, was his conviction that he *was* McGill, and that he alone knew what was best for the university. As far as I was concerned, he became filled with what might be called "Western" envy. The University of Western Ontario had a first-class postgraduate business school; so did Harvard. He argued that McGill must follow suit, or fall by the wayside.

As he kept pressuring me for some progress, we agreed to hold a meeting of the advisory council. I thought of the members not only as a counterbalance but also as a source of ideas. With Dr. Cyril James present, the council looked at the proposal and agreed with me that we were in no position to launch such a project at this time, though we might be in another five years. Our more urgent objective was to remake the reputation of the undergraduate school, before undertaking the building of a graduate program. That seemed to be the consensus, or so I thought.

Then, a few days after that meeting, I got a call from Vernon Johnson, president of Canadian International Paper, who said, "Eric, I've thought a lot of things about you, but I never thought you were a liar."

When I asked him indignantly what he was talking about, he asked me, in turn, if I had seen that morning's issue of the Montreal *Gazette*. There it was, the announcement of a fundraising campaign, spearheaded by J.W. McConnell, and aimed at gathering in $6.5 million from corporate sponsors for a new engineering facility, an expanded Department of Otolaryngology (ear, nose, and throat diseases) in the Faculty of Medicine, and the expansion of Purvis Hall to make room for a Graduate School of Business.

I said, "Look, I'm just learning about this; I'm reading the same paper."

He said, "You're kidding." Then he added, "What are you going to do?"

I replied that I was going to write a letter saying that this was never agreed upon and should not go ahead. I admit that it never occurred to me that this might have been just a promotional ploy of the principal's, a handle to hang the fundraising on rather than something he intended to push ahead with right away. In any event, I fired off a five-page letter, ringing with wrath, to James, with copies to the nine deans of the university. My letter stated defiantly that the launch of a graduate school was at least five years away. The result was one of the more interesting meetings I ever attended. James was going to lay down the law to us, but that is not what happened.

The literal-minded dean of engineering turned up with a stack of drawings, charts, and notes for his new facility. He was as pleased as a kitten with a bowl of cream. James was not concerned with him, but went directly after me and, with considerable skill, deplored the intemperate nature of my communication. I replied, with more force than finesse. Then Lyman Duff, the dean of medicine, stood up; and where I had used an axe, he used a scalpel. He and his faculty expected to be consulted about major initiatives affecting his department; there were many priorities that came ahead of otolaryngology, and he was more sad and hurt than angry that our revered principal would announce to the world something that had never been put to the people who would be responsible for carrying it out. Well, this of course hit all the deans where they lived, and the end result was that the campaign went forward and $9 million was raised — from Sam Steinberg et al. — but none of the money went to otolaryngology, nor to an M.B.A. program (the latter was established years later).

Another result was that James vowed to have my head, despite the cautionary advice of J.W. McConnell, who, when James told him in early 1957 that he was looking for a replacement for me, said to him,

"Cyril, it does you good to have a little opposition once in a while. Leave Kierans alone."

Nothing outward happened, and James and I continued to correspond and chat — not merrily, but necessarily. However, I knew that I was roughly in the position of the gentleman whose neck has just been sliced by a scimitar.

"I didn't feel a thing," he says.

"Wait till you nod your head."

*Four*

——— ·◆· ———

# THE STOCK EXCHANGE

*The Lord in silence works*
*Towards mysterious ends;*
*The same omniscience works*
*In dividends.*

— A.M. KLEIN, 1932

ACTUALLY, I DID NOT LEARN about the attempt to replace me as director until much later. Principal James could not fire me, because I certainly had done nothing to breach my contract; he could only bide his time. Unlike most university teachers, I was not dependent on my salary from McGill, although it did serve me well in that throughout those years I was able to get by without drawing any salary out of Canadian Adhesives; instead, every cent went back in to help develop the company.

Soon after my father retired from Canadian Car, it became apparent that he was really a lost soul. Most men of his generation did not know what to do with themselves when they were suddenly retired after forty years of service with the same firm. This was particularly true of retired veterans of the CPR and CN. Their lives had been wrapped up in their work, and with their long hours they had little opportunity for wider horizons or other interests. They were not great readers, and time became a burden. My father lost twenty pounds in three months. I realized that with his cheerful disposition and willingness to tackle almost anything, he would be a great help in the shipping room; before long he was happily rising with the lark once more, and catching the streetcar and then the bus down to the east end to work for me, rather than Canadian Car. He rapidly regained the weight he had lost, and lived for another seventeen years. He became so popular with the drivers that when there was a bus strike one time, a couple of the drivers came to see him in the plant on Marien Avenue in east Montreal to ask if there was any way they could help him get to work; he was that kind of man.

Although matters were thus proceeding busily, but satisfactorily, at Canadian Adhesives, the same could not be said for my job at McGill. It probably didn't help when I suddenly made a run for the Liberal nomination in the federal riding of Notre-Dame-de-Grâce (NDG) in February 1957. This was the result of a call from my cousin Emmet, a lawyer and stalwart Liberal, who was part of a group of Young Turks in the party. NDG was a safe Liberal riding (still is, for that matter), which George Marler, the federal Liberal lieutenant for Quebec at this time, had picked out as a suitable launching pad for one of his proteges, Eddie Asselin. There was to be no nomination meeting, just a laying on of hands.

Emmet and his friends wanted to contest this coronation, and determined that I might be the suitable candidate through which to raise a rumpus. I thought about it for a while and decided, Why not? I had checked at McGill, and found that a previous dean of arts had run in the past, so there could be no objection raised there. In fact, many of my colleagues thought Principal James would probably have donated to the cause.

I confess that the devil got into me when I decided to run. I hadn't a chance. For one thing, I had no constituency in the party and had done none of the spadework that justifies a candidacy; for another, I spoke little French, and the riding had a considerable French population. And, of course, I was going up against the party machine. I had a bit of fun; we put out a pamphlet extolling my virtues as a dynamic businessman and academic, and I made a few speeches. We did force a nominating convention, on February 27, 1957, at the YMCA on Hampton Avenue, and it came out just about as anyone might have expected. I was defeated by 240 to 160 votes. I took comfort in the fact that we had at least forced what was for then a large and enthusiastic nomination meeting.

I learned a little something about party politics in the aftermath; Marler blocked my attempt to become a delegate from NDG for the Liberal leadership convention held in Ottawa the next January to pick a successor to Louis St. Laurent. This was to teach me not to buck the party brass — a lesson that, I'm afraid, never sank in. So, I boarded the train to

Ottawa as the representative of Esquimalt-Saanich from Vancouver Island, courtesy of Jimmy Sinclair, and voted for Paul Martin, Sr., as the new Liberal leader, and leader of the Official Opposition. However, Lester Pearson won the leadership and subsequently lost the election on March 31, 1958, to John Diefenbaker's Progressive Conservatives.

## I DRIFT ON AS DIRECTOR

When time came for my McGill contract to be renewed, in September 1958, nothing happened. I continued to lead the School of Commerce, deliver lectures, discuss issues of great moment — and some of less or little moment — with my colleagues, and enjoy the exchange of ideas with my students. However, I was not sanguine about my future at McGill, and I was not planning to buy anything on time based on my salary there, which had by now been raised to $10,000.

Then, in September 1959, I was on the way back from a trip to Toronto, where I had been addressing McGill grads, and I ran into Herb Crabtree, a staunch supporter of McGill as well as a prominent member of the Montreal Stock Exchange. He asked me how things were going in my adventures with James, and added that I must find my position difficult. He then told me that the exchange was looking for a new president, which surprised me because the current president, Harry Norman, former managing partner of Price Waterhouse, had been in the job only a couple of years. Herb said that there was quite a lot of dissatisfaction with Norman, who was seen by the members as too rigid and unwilling to listen to their views. Apparently, there was dissatisfaction on both sides, because Harry had indicated that he wanted out, so it wasn't a question of unseating him.

Herb wanted to know if he could mention my name to Ernie McAteer, the chairman of the exchange. There were two exchanges, the Montreal (MSE) and the more junior Canadian Stock Exchange — the latter essentially an exchange of smaller firms, both industrial and mining. The job, if I took it, would encompass both exchanges, but Montreal was the key one. I said yes, and the more I thought about it, the more the idea appealed to me. I was clearly not going anywhere at McGill, and while I had no experience whatsoever as a stockbroker, I had a deep interest in exchanges, investment, and finance, and what they mean to an economy. I saw the exchange as not merely the stock casino it had become in recent decades, but as a social and economic instrument, very much a part of the community.

The exchange was where budding entrepreneurs could go to raise money to launch their bright ideas — and escape dependence on the big banks. This has been rather foreshortened by the big banks today, since every major brokerage in Canada is now controlled by a bank; but at this time, it was illegal for banks to be in the investment business directly. The exchange was where ideas and opportunities became clothed in the elements of finance, and it had a direct connection to the community from which it sprang, enlisting the energies and capital of that community to build long-term growth, jobs, and opportunity. While it is true that more and more this necessary instrument of growth was being used merely as a place where people could place bets, hoping to make a quick return, even this function had some utility; the market, as it was supposed to do, would tend to make choices towards greater efficiency.

Within a week of that first conversation, I was invited to lunch with McAteer and Jimmy Langille, chairman of the Canadian Stock Exchange. We got along well and seemed to be in agreement that, among other things, the exchanges were both in deep trouble and in need of new leadership. One evening shortly after that, Terry and I were out driving and I took her past the ornate, old exchange building on Saint-François-Xavier Street, not far from the Place d'Armes.

"That's where I may be working pretty soon," I said.

"If that's what you want, dear," was all she said.

There were a couple of follow-up conversations with McAteer, during one of which Ernie said, "We haven't talked about salary. We were thinking of starting you at $20,000 a year. Would that be all right?"

Since it was double what I was getting from McGill, I allowed that it would do for the present, and in very short order, the matter had been put to the boards of both exchanges. That was in November 1959, but we agreed that since I had a number of things still to clear up at the university, no announcement would be made until January, and I would take over the job after the end of the academic year.

The first I knew that the announcement had been made was when Jack Weldon and Thomas Asimakopulos, colleagues in the Economics

Department, came bursting into my office at Purvis Hall to offer their congratulations. Jack said they nearly fell down the two storeys from their offices to mine in their hurry, but they did wonder what would happen to the school when I left. They also wondered how James would take it — possibly by sacrificing a lamb in gratitude to the gods of fortune. Actually, he took it very civilly, called to congratulate me, and invited me to lunch at the University Club. I had two lunches with James, one when he hired me and one when he bade me farewell; both were at the University Club, and both were accompanied by many stares and much whispering by other diners.

## I TAKE OVER AT THE EXCHANGE

I moved into a comfortable office on the ground floor of the Exchange Building in the heart of the financial district, on Saint-François-Xavier Street, and set about learning something of the background of the exchange. An unincorporated group of traders called the "Board of Brokers" met in 1862 in a private office, then a rented room in the Board of Trade building, according to a book by Stephen Leacock, to buy and sell the shares of Canadian and some foreign corporations. A provincial statute was passed in 1874 to incorporate the Montreal Stock Exchange, which dealt in sixty-three issues, including the stocks of twenty-one banks and railway companies, as well as government issues and some industrial stocks. In 1904 the building on Saint-François-Xavier went up, and the number and volume of issues traded began to expand.

As the nation grew, so did the exchange, with Montreal as the effective financial centre of Canada, as well as its commercial centre. One-sixth of everything made in Canada came out of Montreal in the first decade of that century. The city held a dominant position until the huge expansion during the years after the Second World War, when Toronto began to compete with, and then pass, and then crowd Montreal into the shade. This sea change seemed to take place without much response here. Right through the 1930s, the MSE was prominent in industrial and financial stocks, and if a Toronto firm wanted to push through a big deal, float a new bond issue, or launch a new industrial stock, it would have to come down to Montreal. The great Montreal families — such as the Holts, Nesbitts, and Pitfields — dominated, and Sir Herbert Holt, chairman of the Royal Bank, made damn sure things were done through Montreal, not Toronto.

However, in the end, an exchange is a reflection of the community, and as Toronto became a wealthier community than Montreal the balance of power, influence, and stock sales began to tilt. By 1943, slightly more industrial stocks were moving through the Toronto Stock Exchange (TSE) than through the MSE, although we continued to be better known than Toronto in Europe, especially in London and Zurich. When the huge oil boom began in 1947, followed by a massive expansion in mining, those stocks began to swirl, more and more, through the TSE. This was not surprising, considering the condescension with which outsiders were treated at the MSE. As a matter of fact, they were also treated with yawns in Toronto, and a great many made permanent arrangements in New York as a consequence.

I spoke to entrepreneurs in Calgary who told me that they would go down to Montreal, caps in hand — or, Stetsons in hand — and come away with little more than the memory of a derisive laugh. Montreal was not interested in taking risks, and the oil business, God knows, was full of risks, at that time. Toronto was somewhat smarter, but New York was avid to get the financing of these new ventures, with the result that the MSE and the Canadian were left at the post. When I took over, we were handling roughly 17 per cent of the action in industrial shares, and the TSE had 76 per cent. There was talk of closing down the exchange, giving up, and letting Toronto take over entirely. In effect, this is what happened in 1999 when Montreal accepted a new arrangement under which only derivatives move through the MSE, as part of a national rearrangement of the stock markets. This rearrangement will do what I always feared; it will disconnect the exchanges from the community to which they belong, in the name of a global market, and weaken their utility as social and economic instruments for the society around them.

But at that time, this was still a long way in the future; yet it was clear that, in Montreal at least, we were in serious trouble. One of the things that struck me forcibly the first time I visited the Exchange Building was that there was a full bar just a few feet off the exchange floor. This did not strike me as a happy omen, and I closed it. The presidents of the companies listed on the exchange would certainly not approve of a bar virtually on the trading floor. Incidentally, there was a bar in the boardroom, which I also closed in the name of fairness and to set an example.

But drink was not the central problem of the exchange; what was, was its air of superiority and exclusiveness. There was not a single Jewish stockbroker among the eighty members who made up the two exchanges (in these matters, the exchanges were virtually the same), and the French community was represented by a score of tiny firms, with the exception of the large investment company Lévesque-Beaubien. Moreover, nearly all the French firms were hived off into mainly the mining sector in the Canadian.

When I gave my inaugural lecture as president, the speech was based on why capital markets are a better means of raising investment money than either by bank loans — so often accompanied by huge costs and massive interference — or by the owners and managers of firms ploughing back profits, which was basically the way I was building Canadian Adhesives. Money markets offered a whole range of possibilities; profits could be switched into mining, resources, finance, manufacturing — wherever the opportunities and challenges lay. Clearly, entrepreneurs in, say, the buggy-whip business were more likely to put their earnings back into buggy-whips than in any new-fangled thing like a horseless carriage. The role of the stock exchange, then, was to help allocate scarce resources efficiently for the betterment of the community as a whole. Not a word of what I said then has changed, but anyone who follows the markets today can see that they are less about allocating resources than about whisking derivatives around the world. As for myself, I could not think of anything better than investing profits in myself; but if I had shareholders it would be up to them to scan the listings on the exchanges to look for better growth rates and dividends. The adhesives industry at that time was not noted for either rapid growth or security of return.

The functions of an exchange president are really mainly a matter of public relations. The president is responsible for the good name of the exchange, so one takes such steps as one can to make sure that the exchange itself, and the brokerage fraternity, act with integrity. When you boil it all down, the name of the exchange is 90 per cent of what foreign investors look for. Here, we had a small advantage, because the mining scandals that beleaguered the TSE at this time, and the whole climate of distrust that still clung on from the frauds and failures of the 1930s, not only hurt the mining sector, but coloured the views of outsiders towards the TSE. That exchange brought in a retired major general, Howard Graham, to clean things up; this was after a series of scandals caused Mr. Justice Arthur Kelly to call the place "a private gaming club," and Viola MacMillan of Windfall Oil and Mines, Ltd., was sent to jail in 1964 — as a sacrificial ewe — for stock price manipulation.

However, to begin to retake our old place in the sun, it was necessary to convince Quebecers, and the French Canadian population in particular, that investing in equities, instead of merely sticking the money in municipal bonds, was not always hazardous. We had to be able to show that stock investments offered enormous advantages not only in income, but in security for their retirement years, at a time when Canada had no decent pension plan. The French press had little more in the way of financial reporting than the stock prices that were furnished by the exchanges. They had scant commentary, and no analysis.

## I NEED FRENCH

To make these arguments where they would do the most good, I needed French, so I began to take French lessons every day. The exchange hired Charles Denis, an ebullient, intelligent, and energetic man who came from France, as director of public relations. In addition to his regular duties, he was helpful in improving my vocabulary, but despaired of ever improving my accent. I once ran into Hugh MacLennan, author of *Two Solitudes,* on the steps of one of the McGill campus buildings, and he said that what hampered us most in this pursuit was that we were no longer kids. We hesitated to appear ignorant, where children would plunge right in and bang away until they got it right. This was illuminating, although not comforting, but I kept at it. Eventually, I could work in French, though I was not bilingual (a much abused term that ought by rights to refer to those who switch so easily from language to language that they are scarcely aware of which one they are speaking).

It seems incredible to think of now, but one of the first complaints I heard when I came to the exchange was from an English broker upset because a French-speaking trader had actually spoken in French on the trading floor. I also learned that an exchange employee had been reprimanded for corresponding in French with a francophone broker. I put an end to this sort of nonsense and my efforts were very much appreciated by the French members of the exchange. They became one of my strongest assets. They controlled twenty-two of the eighty votes on the exchange, and soon came to see themselves as a power, for the first time. I needed and used that block of votes to break down the prejudice against Jews.

The constitution required an 80 per cent approval to admit new members, and this meant that sixteen brokers could effectively blackball any nomination. I proposed that in the future, 50 per cent plus one be enough to approve new members, and when that produced the expected uproar, I backed off to a 60 per cent vote as the new standard. This was passed at a noisy meeting, held on the floor of the exchange, of all the members; the francophone members voted en bloc. Under the new rules, a Jewish candidate was finally accepted. The change quickly became one of those things that had people saying, "You mean, you had to fight for this?" and the MSE was incomparably the gainer.

In the three and a half years I was there, aside from engaging in public relations and making tours of Europe and promoting the Montreal and Canadian Stock Exchanges, I spent a good deal of time speaking in Sherbrooke, Chicoutimi, Thetford Mines, and anywhere else I could round up an audience to hear me talk about the need for Quebecers to invest in their own economy and the advantages. Charles Denis, who had come to me with a solid background in journalism as a financial writer with Canadian Press before taking a graduate course at the Université de Montréal, was of enormous help in this.

He was charming, cheerful, and connected, knowing just about everybody in the news business in Quebec. He quickly established contacts with more than fifty weekly newspapers across the province, the majority of them being French, and would see to it that they were constantly furnished with stories about investors and investments moving through the exchange. This proved to be a powerful platform; most weeklies are faced with vast acres of blank space to fill, and Charles would swoop in with well-written articles about exciting things happening on the markets. They ate up not only the stories, but the underlying argument that despite years of being told that they were a backward society, they were not.

My presidency coincided with the onset of the Quiet Revolution; Jean Lesage and his Liberal party won a narrow victory on June 22, 1960, shortly after I moved into Saint-François-Xavier. Quebec was changing, anything was possible.

Well, not anything. According to many members of the MSE, it was not possible to move into a new building, even though the old one was incapable of handling the new business, new methods, and new communications we would need to serve the needs of the financial community for the rest of the century. Many of the older members just didn't want to move, and for some of the larger firms, like A.E. Ames and Dominion Securities, it was pointless — their headquarters were in Toronto, and Montreal was just a fragrant backwater on the financial scene. However, the Società Generale Immobiliare of Rome, which was interested in coming to Montreal, approached me with a plan that would change all that. The Italians had a theory that Rome, Montreal, and Buenos Aires were to become heavyweight financial centres of the world. They never explained what was to happen to New York or London. Their purpose in coming to see me was their desire to find a prestige occupant and name for their proposed new building. "Exchange Tower" was suggested as a name for this structure and would have suited them fine. I thought that this was the opportunity of a lifetime.

They were fixed on a block on Place Victoria, about halfway between the spanking new Place Ville Marie complex and the old financial district, but my first attempt to get the proposal for a new building was shot down at the board of governors. Then we featured the Italian group's proposal in the exchange's *Monthly Review.* This article emphasized the advantages that would accrue to the entire city, not just the financial sector, from the jobs this new investment would bring. I was always available to the journalists Charles brought in to see me, and the ensuing campaign of favourable publicity, along with the support I had, not only from my allies among the brokers, but also from the outside — Mayor Jean Drapeau was very much in favour — caused the board to reverse itself and approve the plan. The other factor was that the Italian consortium, by this time, had made us an offer that we couldn't refuse; it amounted to virtually rent-free accommodation.

Then an alternative project was advanced, by William Zeckendorf, the colourful gentleman who had built the Place Ville Marie tower in downtown Montreal. His idea was to take over the old Royal Bank building — since he had moved the Royal into the Place Ville Marie — expand it, and offer us space on the ground floor. Our presence would ensure that other tenants, especially brokers, would move in, so he offered to rent the MSE forty thousand square feet of space for a nominal rate. The price was right, but not the place; we needed to move into a new building, with purpose-built facilities, not retrofitted ones.

There was another, similar proposal from the Canadian Imperial Bank of Commerce (CIBC), which had built a new tower uptown and had their former Quebec headquarters on St. James Street as surplus. At another noisy meeting on the exchange floor, I derailed the argument that we ought to accept second-class arrangements simply because a bank wanted us to, and the CIBC proposal was rejected.

Among other things, I said, "The exchange has several million dollars to finance its future, but not a damn nickel to bail out the CIBC." Thunderous applause, particularly from my twenty-two French members.

We were not able to put up the three-tower complex I had first wanted, but we did get a splendid new building at Place Victoria, financed by the Italian consortium, and eventually a second tower. The old building became the home of the Centaur Theatre Company. Well, why not? The place had seen enough drama in its day. The MSE rented the bottom floors of Place Victoria, and when it was officially opened in 1964, I was at the head table presided over by the Hon. George Hees, who had succeeded me as president of the MSE. It was a little galling. George was masterful at giving the impression that when it came to getting these splendid new quarters, he had done it.

## JOHN DOYLE COMES TO CALL

One of the more interesting characters who called on me at the exchange was John C. Doyle, whom I had never before met. He was, I later learned, a close friend, confidant, and adviser to Joseph R. Smallwood, the premier of Newfoundland. Joey had given Doyle's company Canadian Javelin, which was listed on the American Stock Exchange, huge forest concessions in Newfoundland, and I was to have more dealings with Doyle later. Our first brush was merely a sort of opening shot.

The first I knew of him was when a large, loud, brash, blond-haired man turned up in my office dressed in a very fine suit, and aglow with rings. He wanted his company listed on the MSE, and he wanted it done now. I told him to give me all the information he had about the corporation, and I would get back to him. He seemed to think I could wave a wand and dispense with the formalities of ascertaining whether we wanted his firm listed on our exchange; I got the impression that he was in a panic to get the listing. I soon learned why. While an exchange does want listings, it has the responsibility of investigating the newcomers thoroughly. During the course of going through this application, Doyle was housed in one of Montreal's best hotels, wining and dining different members of the board of governors. Promises of large commissions and heavy trading whetted the appetite of the brokers. Doyle's tactics made me suspicious.

I called a contact at the U.S. Securities and Exchange Commission in New York, whom I had helped on an earlier occasion, and who now said, "I can't tell you some of the things I think you ought to know, but I will contact someone from the Department of Justice, who can." He suggested that I was right to have some concerns.

Very soon there was a call from a man in the U.S. Justice Department in Washington, who asked the receptionist, "Who is your top lawyer? Put me through to him." So she did. What he had to say to our legal department was that if we would just wait a couple of days, there would be a story in the Hartford, Connecticut, newspapers about Doyle. And so there was. He had been convicted of eleven counts of mail fraud for the purposes of stock transactions, and had skipped out of the country — one step ahead of the sheriff. Joey's pal was a fugitive from justice in the United States, where a three-year jail term awaited him. Chicago-born Doyle could not go home again. Clearly, he expected to be delisted in the United States; thus, his anxiety to get a quick listing in Canada.

This apparently did not dim Premier Smallwood's enthusiasm for him, but it did mine, and he did not get his listing. (One of Doyle's companies was listed on the Toronto Stock Exchange, but was removed for failure to supply requested information about its activities.) I assumed I had heard the last of Doyle, but I was to have two more encounters with him before long. Incidentally, the members of the board of governors were usually quiet after this.

## BACKING INTO POLITICS

I came back into the political arena without really meaning to do so, while I was still president of the exchanges. There were three more-or-less interlinked events that propelled me into that turmoil. The first was a speech I made at the Mount Stephen Club in Montreal in the middle of the 1962 federal election, which was very much a cliff-hanger and resulted in a minority Tory government. I said during that speech that I had examined the economic content of the various party platforms, and the only one that made sense to me was that of the New Democratic Party (NDP).

The NDP platform, I argued, was at least consistent, whereas those of the two old-line parties were self-contradictory. The ruling Conservatives, who were forced to devalue the dollar to 92.5¢ U.S. in the middle of the campaign (because of a speculative run on the currency), had concocted a theory proposed by Prime Minister John Diefenbaker that we had somehow achieved two separate dollars. One was a domestic dollar, which "you use to support yourself and your family." This retained its old value. The other was the 92.5¢ dollar, which was "marvellous for the tourist trade." It was, in a word, nonsense.

The Liberals attacked the sudden devaluation of the dollar, but said nothing about allowing it to seek its own level, which was the advice that I, and almost every trained economist, would have proffered in the situation. The Liberals ran under the inspiring but somewhat foggy slogan "Take a stand for tomorrow" — without ever spelling out what that stand meant. The NDP were pushing for a liberalization of trade policy ("free trade," or at least freer trade, but not in the way the phrase is used today). More important, from my point of view, they were in favour of a flexible exchange rate, which was consistent with, and essential to, a freer trade policy.*

I said so. I said that "neither the Liberals or the Tories have any economic policy at all. The only people who seem to have a coherent

---

* This is not a complex point. If you open up trade policy and do not allow the value of currency to fluctuate with the changes of cash flow, the result will be pressure on the currency to move either up or down. Speculators, seeing this pressure, will quickly begin to gamble on the shift, and the pressure will become unbearable as they buy or sell according to their bet. This is precisely what pushed the panic devaluation we had just seen. It was not a mystery.

economic policy are the NDP." I didn't see any reporters in the hall, but there turned out to be one man from the *Montreal Star* at the back of the auditorium, with his ears out on stalks and his pencil flying all through my speech. He reported it in full, and with regrettable accuracy, so I couldn't even claim that I had been misquoted.

Well, you would think I had come out for Karl Marx, cut-rate brokerage commissions, and free love. For the president of a stock exchange to admit that the devotees of the Red Dawn might have something practical to add to an election campaign was not to be considered for a moment. It was not long before my telephone was vibrating with the rage of the calls aimed at me.

Ernie McAteer, the chairman of the MSE, was the first to get through.

"For God's sake, what am I going to do?" he asked.

I said, "Look, Ernie, do flexible rates and free trade go together or not?"

"Of course they do," he said.

"Well, then, what's wrong with saying so?"

He didn't reply to that, for the obvious reason was that it wasn't my talking sense that created the difficulty; it was my saying that the NDP was talking sense.

"The board of governors are demanding a meeting tomorrow morning at ten" is what he said.

"Am I invited?"

"I've just been talking to Jimmy [James Langille, chairman of the Canadian Stock Exchange at this time] and he said, 'I don't think we should have Eric there at the beginning.'"

I said, "I agree." And the next day, I wandered around St. James Street for about three-quarters of an hour, and then went in to the exchange. There was no fatted calf on the table, but the members had had a little time to cool down, to reflect that the president of an exchange is bound to have some opinions, and may even — curse the luck — voice them. They forgave me, grudgingly.

## I EMERGE AS THE "SHARK OF ST. JAMES STREET"

My next foray went over rather better. During that 1962 election, the public, not for the first or the last time, ignored my suggestions and returned the Conservatives to power, but in a minority position, with

116 seats in a House of Commons of 265. At the same time, the voters returned 100 Liberals, 19 NDP, and 30 members under the banner of the Social Credit Party, which had been wiped out in the previous election, in 1958. The wipeout had occurred because the Socreds, inheritors of the banner and notions of "Bible Bill" Aberhart of Alberta, had become simply, as its own literature proclaimed, "the real conservative party of Canada." Yet voters who wanted conservatism felt they could get the real article in John Diefenbaker, so why would they vote for a substitute? However, in 1961, there occurred a union of Social Credit with a new outfit, the Ralliement des Créditistes, ruled by the dominating personality of a single man, Réal Caouette, a successful automobile dealer in Rouyn-Noranda, Quebec.

Caouette was a wonderful rabble-rouser, a man who spoke without notes and told his impoverished fellow Quebecers many things they wanted to hear. He told them they came into the world on a finance plan but died on a budgetary plan. The first, Caouette explained, bought the layette, the second paid the undertaker.

He had come across the works of Major Clifford Douglas, who first propounded the Social Credit theory, and unlike his western confreres, Caouette still believed. The upshot was a Social Credit party with two chairmen, two campaigns, and two philosophies. Robert Thompson, the homespun western leader, who suffered greatly from foot-in-the-mouth disease (he was worried that the House of Commons was turning into "a political arena," and noted, "You have buttered your bread; now you have to lie in it"), stood for old Toryism and all the old grievances, many of them legitimate, of Albertan estrangement from central Canada.

Caouette, the party's deputy leader, stood for the weird policies of Social Credit, and the notion that by creating new shoals of money, a government of its adherents would waft us all to wealth. The Socreds won thirty seats in 1962, which was an impressive total, especially when you consider that they had lost every seat in 1958. But twenty-six of those seats were in Quebec, and the other four were evenly split between Alberta and British Columbia. Caouette was the practical, if not the official, power in the party, and guardian of the sacred flame.

What made the situation tricky was that the Socreds held the effective balance of power; while they couldn't, by themselves, keep Prime

Minister Diefenbaker in office, they could, any time they joined the Liberals and NDP, boot him out. Their price for refraining from doing this was quite modest; they demanded an easing of monetary policy, but not social credit — in the sense of a monthly government payment to all Canadians.

However, the self-destructive skills of John Diefenbaker soon threw us into another election. The government lost a vote of confidence on February 5, 1963, and as luck would have it, I was scheduled to speak to members of the Richelieu Club in Chicoutimi three weeks later, on February 27. I made up my mind to enter the fray, because it seemed to me there was a strong likelihood that Caouette might do even better in this election than he had in the last. He was publicly boasting that he would get at least fifty seats in Quebec.

While at McGill, I had made a thorough study of the Social Credit position and had written a paper on it. Charles Denis had read my paper, translated it, and made the arrangements for the speech in Chicoutimi, in the heart of Caouette country. Up to that time, the only serious attacks mounted on Caouette had come from Jean Marchand, then a prominent figure in the Quebec union movement and a supporter of the NDP. His views were not likely to be taken seriously by the mainstream, even though they made good sense. I decided to use the Chicoutimi occasion to attack the Créditistes head-on, not to challenge the populist Caouette but the brand of snake oil he was selling. This was not hard to do; their theory was based on the notion that there is a vast gap between what is produced in the economy and what is spent. (Formally, this is the "A plus B theorem"; informally, it is nonsense.)

I noted that "Mr. Caouette tells us that there is a $13 billion gap in purchasing power to fill, that this causes unemployment," and that Social Credit reforms would balance the books by creating a "social credit" of $100 a month, which would be distributed to every Canadian. There would be no such credit, I said, because to create money out of thin air would produce instant inflation and destroy the economy for all Canadians.

It is an axiom of economics, which occasionally stumbles into common sense, that you cannot create new value based on airy nothing, because it will destroy the current price system. Moreover, the whole notion was based on a complete fallacy, the "fact" that there is a huge gap between national production and national income. The only way this shortfall could be achieved, and the way Caouette achieved it in his speeches, was to ignore payments to governments for the services they provide — through sales and other taxes. To put it another way, the underlying "truth" of Social Credit was that the economy produced much more than it consumed, and because of this gap, unemployment and poverty occurred. If you closed the gap by putting more money into the hands of consumers, all would be well. The gap did not exist; Canadians were consuming, in fact, almost all that they produced, but the Socreds missed this by the simple blunder of not counting two of the major components of the equation: government spending and depreciation. I said:

> The basic error in Social Credit thinking is simply that the individual consumer should buy up the whole output of the country. In fact, he will buy only about two-thirds of Canadian output on the average, but the balance will be consumed by business and government.

In short, there was no purchasing gap, and if there was such a thing, it could not be closed by printing funny money and giving it away.

The speech was well received by everybody, including Caouette, because it gave him the opportunity to attack me as the "Shark of St. James Street" (le Requin de la rue Saint-Jacques) — the bloodsucking, bloated capitalist who wanted to deprive his voters of their lovely payouts. He also speculated that the stock exchange job paid me $150,000 a year, which not unnaturally led Terry to wonder what I did with all the money. Incidentally, Charles Taylor, my old philosopher colleague from McGill, who was running for the New Democratic Party, asked for, and received, on behalf of his party, permission to duplicate the Chicoutimi speech in the election.

**"THERE IS NO INTELLIGENT ENGLISH OPINION," I SAY**
However, even before that I was moving deeper and deeper into the political swamp. I made a number of speeches attacking the complacency and indifference manifest throughout English Canada in the teeth of the challenges facing Confederation. Installed in Quebec City was a new

provincial government that was moving forward with energy, intelligence, and pride to recreate the federalism of the British North America
Act of 1867 and to remove the centralist measures imposed by Ottawa
during the Second World War (we will meet this subject in more detail
in chapter 12). The government was led by Jean Lesage's *équipe de tonnerre* (team of thunder), a cabinet crammed with bright, and restless,
francophones. And the reaction on the English side was either ennui or
fear. I told a meeting of the Canadian Citizenship Council at the Queen
Elizabeth Hotel — in French — that while the separatists were "dashing
forward in a dangerous display" and the Lesage government was showing dynamic leadership, "there is no intelligent English opinion." Right,
I sometimes push too far.

The media, mostly, loved it; and it was not entirely surprising that
both *La Presse* and *Le Devoir* began to suggest that it was time the Liberal provincial party made room for me at the cabinet table. In early May
of 1962, I was approached by the Economic Affairs Committee of the
newly founded Quebec Liberal Federation (one of the reforms Lesage
had pushed through was to set up a separate provincial organization, to
take the place of one dominated entirely from Ottawa — it would be
formally established in 1964); the committee asked me to join it in its
deliberations, and I did. I was not so blind that I missed where all this
was heading, but I had no constituency in the party, and when I was
asked by a reporter if I was interested in politics, I replied, "Right now, I
don't think so. But if a challenge presented itself, I don't know what I'd
do. I'm forty-nine and I don't want to spend the next fifteen years just
making money."

I had already begun to take a direct, if secret, role in provincial
affairs, through my friendship with Douglas Fullerton, then a financial
adviser to the Lesage government. In the fall of 1962, René Lévesque,
whom I had never met but much admired, persuaded Jean Lesage to take
over the province's private hydro companies and integrate them with the
provincially owned Hydro-Québec, and to make such a takeover the
centrepiece of a snap election.

Lesage took the advice; the Liberals won the election handily, under
the *maîtres chez nous* banner, and now had the clout to carry out the program. However, the dilemma remained that if you wanted to nationalize

hydro, you had to take over the existing companies. But what was a proper price to pay for the shares of the target companies? You did not want to pay too much, because that would cheat the taxpayer, nor too little, because that would cheat the shareholders of the nationalized firms, and outrage the financial sector, which was against the whole project in the first place. The dominant firm at this time was Shawinigan Water and Power, and the government had only the vaguest notion of what it was really worth. (In common with many publicly traded companies, what the books showed and the true value of the shares were not always the same thing.)

Douglas Fullerton, with whom I had had prior dealings at McGill, called me one day to tell me that in view of a possible merger, he found it necessary to investigate the early exchange dealings and valuations of a client; it was very hush-hush.

Could he and some colleagues, in brief, have a look at the numbers? I replied that the stock exchange archives could be made available on Saturday mornings, and I saw no reason why the necessary research couldn't be done then. Clearly, to do this during regular hours would set off a storm of speculation, to say nothing of protest, so that was what was done. The Fullerton team were able to make an evaluation of the shares of Shawinigan that was fair and based on the accurate figures, and the takeover went through. Key figures in the Lesage government were duly grateful, although none of this was ever allowed to become public, of course.*

Then came the Gordon affair.

## MY "INTEMPERATE" ATTACK ON WALTER GORDON

Lester Pearson's new government, sworn into office on April 22, 1963, with Walter Gordon as finance minister, set out to transform the nation in "Sixty Days of Decision." The centrepiece was the first Gordon budget, brought down on June 13, which contained, among its other proposed changes, two provisions to confront increasing foreign control of the economy (for which read, in large measure, American control). The first provision was a change in the withholding tax on dividends that

---

* Lesage referred to it only once, when we were discussing something that had to be done in secrecy and silence. "This has to go off," he said, "as silently as the Shawinigan affair."

are paid to non-residents. The tax then stood at 15 per cent; Gordon proposed to reduce it to 10 per cent in the case of companies with 25 per cent or more Canadian ownership, and increase it to 20 per cent for all other foreign firms. The second was a new levy of 30 per cent on the sale of shares of Canadian companies to non-residents.

I thought Gordon was right to be concerned about the domination of the Canadian economy by Americans, and I had, in fact, spoken often on the subject. However, I did not consider the danger to be so strong as to call for a levy. I was later to conclude that Walter had been more far-sighted on the issue of urgency — although I never agreed with the idea of a levy — and I later dedicated my Massey Lectures: "To Walter Gordon who foresaw most of this long before the rest of us."

However, at this time, in my position as president of the MSE, I saw at once that these measures would result in a drastic decline in market values, and I reacted vigorously.

I wrote to Gordon attacking his budget in a letter, which he called, in his memoirs, "intemperate and irresponsible in tone and content." I plead guilty to "intemperate," while rejecting "irresponsible"; if I had any responsibility, it was to react to what I thought was a misguided attack on the very business I was engaged to defend. I was quite wrong, I think, to maintain in that missive that "a non-resident takeover confers great benefits on the Canadian economy," without also adding that it weakens Canadians' control of their own economy.*

However, I think I was right to argue that the 25 per cent rule made little sense as a criterion to impose a higher tax on dividends; control of great corporations can be exercised through miniscule percentages in a world where companies are run by managers, not owners. I was certainly right to argue that the new budget represented a substantial government interference with the free operation of the markets. Although I am more open to the argument now than I was then that this might be necessary, I was at that time speaking as the representative of the people whose livelihoods were directly affected. And I stick to my view that the

---

* The full text of the letter appears in a number of places, including in the appendix to John N. McDougall's *The Politics and Economics of Eric Kierans* (Montreal and Kingston: McGill-Queen's University Press, 1993).

sudden, drastic imposition of the 30 per cent levy was foolish, and bound to backfire.

It was not a tax, which is an impost on an income flow or the changes in capital values between two points in time; it was a straight levy of 30 per cent on established values. Every share you owned in one of the companies that fit the finance minister's Procrustean bed would suddenly lose nearly one-third of its worth. Gordon seemed to have no comprehension whatsoever of the impact this was bound to have on stock exchange values. It was my job, as president of two exchanges, to protect these values from any pressures other than market ones, and to make sure that he understood the damage that would be created.

In any event, I wrote the letter, then rounded up a group of MSE board members and set off to Ottawa to deliver it. Charles and I drove down together; the others went in their limousines. No member of the board of governors of the Montreal Stock Exchange had seen my submission before we left; I was afraid they might want to water down the wording, in which case it would have lost a good deal of its impact. One of the governors told me later that when they got around to opening the envelopes containing copies of my letter, they started to roll down the limousine windows to get some air. But by this time it was too late.

We had arranged for an appointment with Gordon, and a small representative group of us met with him in his office on the afternoon of June 18. This was on the third floor of the Centre Block in the House of Commons. After greetings and companionable chatter, I began to read to him from my letter, which I had already released to the press. The smile vanished from his face as if wiped away by the back of a hand. He had been visited the day before by Major General Graham of the TSE, and Graham had, reluctantly, been persuaded that overall the budget was something to be borne, if not admired. My abrupt attack was a bit of a facer.

"He then proceeded," Gordon later wrote in his memoirs, "to harangue me in my own office and practically incited the stock brokers present to sell the market short when it opened in the morning."

I think I owe something to Walter for his contributions to Canada — we all do — but the last part of his statement ought not to stand unchallenged, because it turns the matter upside down. What I said to him was that when the markets opened, stockbrokers right across the country would see that stock prices were bound to be affected by these measures, and, of course, they would advise clients to short the market.* This was not a threat, it was a prediction, and an accurate one.† The media pounced on the story and gave it massive coverage, and the next morning the expected short selling began. That afternoon, the fifty-ninth day of the Sixty Days of Decision, Gordon rose in the House to withdraw the takeover tax.

When the news broke over the Dow Jones tape just before the close of afternoon trading, members of the MSE and the Canadian Stock Exchange came pouring into my office, hauled me out bodily, and carried me around the trading floor, singing, "For he's a jolly good fellow." It came to me, before we were halfway around the circuit, that there is no perch more slippery than the shoulders of a gaggle of stockbrokers; not long before, many of them were ready to have my hide because I had said nice things about the NDP election platform. Now they were serenading me because they thought I was an anti-nationalist, for about all they understood about Gordon was that he was a nationalist. The more I knew of Walter, the more I liked him, and I was to take a view much closer to his before long (although I still maintain that the whole gimmick-laden Sixty Days exercise was bound to lead to a fiasco, as it did).

Throughout the budget battle, another dramatic development was

---

* Again, not a mystery. An investor who thinks the price of shares is bound to fall will likely sell stock that he or she does not actually own. In the time period before this stock must be delivered to the buyer, if the price does fall, the seller can buy new stock and deliver it. The difference in the two prices will be his or her gain (or, if instead the price goes up, his or her loss). Short selling is simply selling what you do not have and gambling that you can buy it at a lower price. If there is going to be a 30 per cent levy on a stock, clearly the stock price will go down.

† I call to the box John N. McDougall, the political economist referred to in the note on page 74, who wrote of this battle that "most of [Kierans's] observations would strike many people informed on the issue as well taken, or at least defensible on economic and business grounds...Kierans expressly acknowledged at the close of his letter that 'foreign ownership is a problem in Canada'...The issue for Kierans was how best to counter foreign control. Takeover taxes, indeed any attempts by governments to control the operation of capital markets, was simply the wrong answer, according to him." *Kierans,* 45.

taking place. On May 23, 1963, Paul Earl, the provincial minister of revenue, had died suddenly. He had been the provincial member for Notre-Dame-de-Grâce (NDG) for fifteen years. The next day, I had a telephone call from Carl Goldenberg, a Montreal lawyer and quintessential Liberal counsellor, urging me to run in Earl's place. I was interested, but noncommittal. That same day, *La Presse,* in an editorial by Vincent Prince, urged Lesage to bring me into his cabinet, and *Le Devoir* carried a headline that read, "Kierans in NDG?" The *Montreal Star* also wrote urging Lesage to appoint me to his administration. I was being elected by the press, and soon, I heard, Lesage was asking grumpily, "What's all this talk about Kierans?"

It was at this point that the family held council on the possibility of my going into Quebec politics. There were no impediments. Cathy was on her way to becoming a nurse at the Montreal General Hospital. Tom had added an M.B.A. (dean's honours list) from the University of Chicago to his honours degree in Political Science and Economics from McGill. Both were enthusiastic about my possible entry into the government of Jean Lesage. Terry could sense my delight at the opportunity, and was in full agreement.

In early June, I was scheduled to read a paper at the Université Laval in Quebec City to the Learned Societies, on the subject of flexible exchange rates. My fellow panellist was Robert Mundell of Columbia University. As a result of the paper he presented that morning, Mundell was on the road to a Nobel Memorial Prize in economics, which he received in 1999.

Shortly after this panel, I got a call at Laval from Guy Gagnon, an aide to Jean Lesage, who said that the premier would like to see me while I was in town. Would I call on him tomorrow (Saturday) morning in the legislative building?

I was about to change jobs again.

## Five

—•∵•—

# QUEBEC CALLS

*French Canadians today are the products of these twin*
*historical events: A fallen Empire and a stay of execution.*
*So they walk either in fear or in foolish pride.*

— RENÉ LÉVESQUE, 1977

THE LEGISLATIVE BUILDINGS IN Quebec City are magnificent, but the back door, where I presented myself early on a Saturday morning in June 1963, is not so grand. My visit was to be strictly off the record, to avoid any undue — or even perfectly due — speculation about my possible appointment to the cabinet. An officer of the Sûreté provinciale du Québec (as the Quebec provincial police was then known) led me through the corridors, dominated by portraits of the great names in Quebec history, who all seemed to me to be looking down with disapproval. I asked myself, "What am I doing here?" and we arrived at the premier's suite, a spacious, light-filled set of rooms on the ground floor. Jean Lesage jumped up from behind the desk and came forward to greet me with a broad smile. Lesage was a handsome man, but more than that, he had a charm that was immediately obvious and captivating.

The possessor of a large ego, like many successful politicians, he nevertheless had the ability to convince you that you counted, that nothing in the world mattered to him more than listening to what you had to say. A corporate lawyer, he was well versed in economics, and served as his own finance minister. He managed to make politics fun, or mostly fun, and treated his political adversaries as competitors, but not enemies — an invaluable asset. At this time, not long after his second electoral victory, he was at the peak of his power and reputation, the undisputed leader of the Quiet Revolution.

I had some misgivings about going into politics; I had enough on my plate with the companies, and the stock exchange. Terry enjoyed my stint at the exchange, especially with the European tours, when we stayed in fine hotels, saw the sights, worked in spasms, and got to enjoy each other's company without interruption, for a change. But she said, as always, that I should do what I wanted to do, and she would adjust. Still, I was not at all certain that the vagaries and insecurities of politics came into the category of things I wanted to do. I had met Lesage only once, at a gathering of the Reform Club, the ginger group of the Liberal party; my cousin Emmet had insisted on introducing us during Lesage's run for the party leadership. However, Lesage now greeted me as a long-lost friend; we were "Eric" and "Premier Ministre" just sitting down for a chat. I told him that I still had a problem with French, and he said I would soon get over it. We talked about everything under the sun, and every time we came to a subject that might raise a difficulty, he would switch topics, very skilfully.

Finally, I said, "Mr. Premier, you already have a very good cabinet, with men like René Lévesque [the resources and hydro minister], Paul Gérin-Lajoie [the education minister], Gérard Lévesque [the industry and trade minister], and Pierre Laporte [the municipal affairs minister]."

He said, "Yeah, I do have a good cabinet, but there is one thing wrong. All the names you have mentioned are French Canadian."

I began to choose my words very carefully. "What's wrong with that?"

"Well, you know, they're French Canadian, and they like to be big spenders, and I need a *percepteur:* I need an Englishman." Much jollity. (A *percepteur* is a tax collector.)

He was offering me the revenue portfolio, with no bargaining, hesitations, or evasions. I thought about it for a few minutes. Tax-collector portfolios are for the English. No ifs, ands, or buts. No illusions. Soon we were laughing hard. I said yes.

"What about Eddie Asselin?" I asked. Asselin, now a Liberal MP, and the man who had beaten me in the NDG federal nomination meeting six years earlier, was an obvious candidate for the post. He controlled the NDG riding, and reported to Guy Favreau, who was both Lester Pearson's minister of justice and the Quebec Liberal leader, and although René Lévesque and the reform group within the Liberal party were separating the federal and provincial organizations, that process was not complete (the Quebec Liberal Federation came into formal existence in

September 1964). If he chose to, Asselin could make things rough.

"Why don't you have lunch with him? Just a little chat," said Lesage.

So I did that, and we had a very guarded exchange of views. At this time Asselin was having some problems of his own that had to do with investments in the Caribbean, and it was clear that he would not put any roadblocks in my way. Lesage more or less took over. Within a short time, matters were arranged for a nomination meeting in NDG. On the last night of July 1963, in a packed, steamy YMCA hall on Hampstead Avenue — the same hall where I had been defeated six years earlier — the party faithful turned out to nominate me, unopposed, as the Liberal standard-bearer in a by-election called for September 25. I was described, rather grandly, as "the English René Lévesque," and "a symbol of Liberal resurgence." In my acceptance speech, delivered in English and French, I emphasized the fact that I agreed wholeheartedly with the position of the Quebec Liberals on Confederation. Ottawa had taken too much power, too much money, and too much jurisdiction away from the provinces in defiance of the British North America Act, and it was time to wrest some of it back.

Although the by-election was held late in September, I resigned from the exchanges a few days after the nomination meeting, and was sworn in as minister of revenue on August 8. The election itself was no problem. I went around the riding, made a few speeches, shook a great many hands, and watched while the Lesage machine rolled in the vote. Fewer than one-third of the eligible electors turned up, and I was very soon the legitimate minister of revenue.

Terry and I moved into a tenth-floor apartment in the Montmorency, on the Grand Allée in Quebec City, across from St. Patrick's Church, and within walking distance of the legislature. We went home most weekends, either by plane or by train, to spend time with Cathy, who by this time was in McGill, and launching what would be a very promising career. Tom was now working for the brokerage firm Nesbitt, Thomson. I still owned Canadian Adhesives, and it was being run with such efficiency that I really didn't need to do much. Sales figures and expenses in my break-even charts told me how the company was performing.

Matters were not so well organized on the departmental front. The Department of Revenue was a new division, which had been hived off from the Department of Finance by Lesage and given to Paul Earl to run. It was in appalling shape, as I quickly discovered. The senior bureaucrats had been left to make too many decisions on their own, and they were not, I say gingerly, in step with the times. Obviously, Lesage had not been about to allow any of his best deputies to be seconded to Paul Earl, who wound up more or less with the people other departments were not fighting to keep. The department's deputy minister had been in the civil service at the time of Louis-Alexandre Taschereau; many of the other senior managers dated from early in the Duplessis era and were not exactly up to speed with the new Quebec. But I couldn't move or lose them, since I had just taken over.

## TAXING THE CHURCHES

One of the first issues I had to deal with was the vexed question of the church and taxes. On Mondays, I worked in the Montreal offices of the department; I had Sir Herbert Holt's old office, with its own private elevator. I was toiling amid this splendour one day when the Montreal director came in with a letter from a lady in Joliette, who was complaining bitterly about one of her neighbours. This female neighbour had boasted to her that she had $83,000 in savings, earning interest of 4 per cent, on which she paid not a penny of tax. The trick was that she had it invested in a local religious community, which issued no documentation whatsoever — a practice that had been prevalent throughout the province for decades. It was clear to me that by bringing me this letter, the director was testing me, to see how I would react. He soon knew.

"What is this?" I asked.

"She is referring to what has become accepted practice, to ignore this sort of thing."

"Why?"

"Well, it is possible to proceed in these cases, but since the law has not been used, our officials naturally don't want to proceed unless they have the backing of the minister."

"They have it," I said. "Go ahead."

He suggested we call in a number of the senior officials, and we did that. We discovered that the way the law read, people who invested money with a religious community had to declare the interest earned as income. The community also had to declare how much had been invested and the amount of interest paid. However, if they made no declaration, the people who loaned the money to the community could put it out at comparatively low rates and still be far better off than if they had to declare the interest as income.

I went to Lesage with this, since it had serious political overtones, and he said, "This is what you're here for. Do what you need to do," so I ordered a circular to be drawn up and sent out to the religious communities all across the province informing them of their duties. I went further and demanded an accounting of all the monies that had been paid out this way over the past five years. The law, incidentally, had been passed nine years earlier, but neither the federal nor the provincial government had begun to enforce it.

Within twenty-four hours, the opposition parties had the full details of how we were persecuting the religious communities, and a couple of the cabinet ministers were pretty upset. Fortunately, I was known as a strong and faithful Catholic, which eased the situation considerably, because it was mainly the Catholic communities that were involved. They naturally went to see Émile Cardinal Léger, who told them bluntly that the law was the law and had to be obeyed.

So they next went to Archbishop Maurice Roy, in Quebec City, who received them with more sympathy and called Lesage. Lesage responded that this was a matter for the minister of revenue, and "Your Grace would do better with him." He also added, "C'est un Irlandais qui est plus cléricalisé que nous autres."

I had three meetings with the archbishop, who was well prepared and argued beautifully; he would always leave some points open, which would necessitate another meeting. I even had a call from the provincial of the Jesuit order, who was, by this time, my old friend Bob Mac-Dougall from Loyola, now working in Jesuit headquarters in Toronto. He was not trying to put pressure on me, just trying to find out what I had done to make everybody so excited. I explained that it was a matter of religious orders not issuing reports to governments on interest payments on sums invested with them, and he said, "Oh, well, I guess we'll just have to live with it."

However you approached the problem, there was something you

could not get away from: people were receiving income and, through the aegis of the church, not paying taxes on it, and that could not continue. A group of nuns came to call on me in Montreal and, seated around Sir Herbert's magnificent directors' table, gave me a lot of pious talk about charity and forgiveness. But on the way out, one of the younger nuns came over to me and whispered, "Vous avez raison." (You are right.)

I thought so, too.

We had a lot of fun in the National Assembly with this issue. Danny Johnson would get up and ask if the minister of revenue had been down to genuflect before the archbishop today, and if not, why not? And I would reply in kind.

The only weak point in my argument was in forcing the communities to go back five years and dig through their mostly chaotic records to come up with the amounts of these deposits and the interest paid thereon. The archbishop was onto this, of course, and at our third meeting in his office in Quebec City, he rocked back and forth in a beautifully carved rocking chair — like John Kennedy, I thought at the time — and said, "Are you sure your only motive is to see that people pay their just taxes, or is there something political in this?"

"What do you mean? I don't quite follow."

"If you go back five years, it may or may not yield significant revenue, but it would seem that you mean to spread as wide a net as possible, to catch people who really had no control over these matters." What he meant was that going back five years brought me into the Duplessis years, and information about the sources of the funds.

It was a good point, but historical rather than political. This whole business went back to the turn of the century, when the emerging caisses populaires were just beginning to expand. Families in those days, if they had any extra money, were reluctant to put it into any local financial institution, because if the manager wasn't a blabbermouth, his wife was, and pretty soon everyone in town knew your business. However, if you put the money in the local religious community, it was a somewhat safer and a more discreet way to invest. What the archbishop was suggesting was that during the Duplessis years, a great many things had been built by and around the religious communities in this way, and the sources of funds were not always accounted for.

I was able to assure him that I was not so subtle as that; what concerned me was simply uncollected taxes, so we were able to come to a meeting of minds. We dropped the five-year part of the program, going back one year instead, and the churches accepted their responsibility. From 1965 onwards, the religious communities were required to, and did, file complete financial reports with us. As the archbishop pointed out, the legislation had been passed nine years earlier and had never been enforced by either the federal or the provincial government.

Departmental morale improved considerably when it became clear that I was intent on collecting the money owed to us, and on time.

## THE SALES TAX TANGO

At this time, the provincial sales tax was divided into three equal parts, one each going to the province, the municipalities, and the school commissions. However, sometimes the municipalities collected it, and sometimes they did not, to give themselves an advantage over their neighbours in attracting businesses and families. Between Quebec City and Sainte-Anne-de-Beaupré, a few kilometres away, there were three different sales tax rates in five municipalities, running between 4 and 6 per cent.

Generalizing the sales tax would cut costs and reduce municipal quarrelling. It would also deprive approximately 1,600 mayors and councils of authority and responsibility. Philippe Gimael, director of the sales tax, and an expert in the field, convinced me that we could raise revenues by $54 million annually by changing the rate to a uniform 6 per cent. We went ahead.

Montreal mayor Jean Drapeau and his powerful ally Lucien Saulnier demanded to see Lesage. Lesage told them to see me. When they thundered down on Quebec City, Lesage told René Lévesque, who was a close friend of Saulnier's, and Pierre Laporte, in his capacity as minister of municipal affairs, to sit in on our meeting. The problem was, of course, the increased control the new system would give the province over municipal revenues. The debate was held over lunch in the old Cercle universitaire (university club) building until well after three o'clock in the afternoon, but no opinions were changed on either side.

After the meeting, when I went downstairs with the manager of the university club, I noticed that the private dining rooms on the second floor and the main dining room on the ground floor were still packed.

"Do your members always take this long for lunch?" I asked.

"Only when they have first-class entertainment, as they did today," he replied. The old building, with its ill-fitting doors, had enabled the lunchers to hear every word of our debate. Loud voices had helped.

When Lesage introduced his 1965 budget, he noted that the minister of revenue's forecast had turned out to be wrong. Long pause and groans. "He forecast a $54 million increase in revenues; in fact, it was $57 million."

### "THE MOST EFFICIENT LEMON-SQUEEZER IN HISTORY"

Daniel Johnson made much of this sort of thing, and his colleague Maurice Bellemare, who was charged with keeping track of what I was doing, once accused me of being "le presse-citron le plus efficace dans l'histoire de la belle province" (the most efficient lemon-squeezer in the history of Quebec). It brought down the assembly in convulsions, but I regarded that as a compliment, not an insult.

When I thought we were being unfair, I went the other way. In one case, the subsidiary of an English manufacturing giant had built a large facility near Sept-Îles, and their claim for accelerated depreciation on it had been denied. They felt they were entitled to a refund of $5 million. The file was brought to me by an assistant deputy minister who had done a lot of work on it, and who felt they had a legitimate claim. I went over it with him, and agreed; they got the money back. This went right through the business community at approximately the speed of light. Not long afterwards, a chartered accountant told me that "this has given us all a good deal of hope."

### TILTING AT THE AMES WINDMILL

One of the battles I fought at Revenue actually began while I was still president of the MSE. When Quebec wanted to borrow money, it did so through the A.E. Ames Company, a Toronto firm. Ames and the Bank of Montreal had sole responsibility for underwriting bond issues of the government of Quebec on the Canadian market. Moreover, the brokers through whom the bonds were sold had to agree in writing at the beginning of each year to work through only the underwriting group to distribute new bond issues.

It was not that Ames was a special ally of Quebec; on the contrary, the cartel had done its level best to block the nationalization of hydro in the province. In the circumstances, it was not unreasonable to introduce an element of competition into the game, to try to reduce the very expensive fees and commissions that were part of all these transactions. This was heresy of the blackest sort, an attempt to change the time-honoured and profitable old ways of doing things — a breach in the wall. Jean Lesage had urged the syndicate in January 1963 to consider making these changes, but with little practical effect.

In December of that same year, after I had been revenue minister for four months, our insistence resulted in the creation of a group of bond dealers prepared to proffer an alternative bid on future bond issues. This group was made up of two banks — the Royal and the Banque Nationale; one large brokerage house — Greenshields, Inc.; and some of the smaller brokers who had been connected with former cartel bids. What we had in mind was that there would be at least two different syndicates, who would compete on the handling of all Quebec issues, including Hydro-Québec and other government agencies. I also encouraged Wood Gundy, through Bill Wilder, the new president, to be part of the new group. With the participation of some of the smaller brokers, we hoped that in the end there would actually be competition in the market and lower costs for Quebec taxpayers. The original syndicate had had its way for so many years that it expected nothing to be disturbed. This had been Duplessis's way of doing things, and it did not expect any interference from the new minister.

Ames responded almost instantly with a letter to all interested brokers, inviting them to participate in a new syndicate which would deal with all borrowing, not only by the province but also by Hydro-Québec and Québec Autoroute (the toll-highway company), for the following year. The kicker was that no member of the syndicate was allowed to participate in any other syndicate on Quebec issues that ran for more than one year.

I was outraged, and said so publicly. This brought the head of A.E. Ames, Douglas Chapman, roaring down on us. Chapman was a big, rough, cigar-smoking bond dealer. He once was approached by Daniel Johnson in the club car of a train on the way to Quebec City. "How is it," Danny asked him in his impeccable English, "that governments change, but you never do?" Chapman was arguably the most powerful member of the Canadian investment community at that time.

Chapman claimed that I was trying to put things over behind Lesage's back, and I replied that the premier was fully informed of everything I did. (Not the same thing as approving of everything I did, but that was a nice distinction I saw no need to raise.) Chapman said, "We'll see about that," and made an appointment with Lesage. He ran right up against Jacques Parizeau, the bright young economist then working on contract for the government, and they got into such an argument that Chapman, who was losing, took a kick at Parizeau. Not a thing I'd have cared to do.

Lesage told Chapman that if he had a problem with the new proposals, he should take it up with the appropriate minister. We had a large meeting in Montreal, with representatives of the major brokerage houses gathered together in my office. Many of them had been there before. When Chapman kept shouting and banging the table, I remarked that this approach would not get us anywhere and proposed to withdraw to another room while Chapman and his group cooled down. He sneered, "Yeah, and how many bugs are you leaving behind?"

I said, "I'll give you one hundred dollars for every bug you find."

I later learned that one of the other brokers told Chapman that he was way out of line with that kind of remark, but Chapman didn't care. The ruckus was finally sorted out by Lesage, whose immediate instinct in any of these matters was to find a compromise. He agreed to two separate groups that would bid alternately on each issue; but the groups were composed almost exclusively of the same companies that had been involved all along. Moreover, they produced bids that were so faithful to the ancient formula that all this thrashing around did not save the taxpayer a dime. It did, however, break the absolute control of Ames and lead to a strengthening of the view that Quebecers could and should manage their own financial affairs. That seems evident now; it was apostasy then. The end result was not a gain for Quebec in its bottom line at the time, but it was a sign of change in the offing.

## MISSING CAUCUS

Lesage was very adept at using his personnel; I often felt that he aimed me like a spear at some of the targets he had selected, and just let me go. However, he did not like to be crossed, as I discovered on the lamentable occasion when I missed one of his rare caucus meetings. Two of the new Liberal members elected in 1962 had been caught in a situation where it appeared that money had been exchanged for favours, and Lesage could not get reasonable explanations out of them. He came to me and said, "Look, I'm going to deal with this in caucus, and I will need your support." Naturally, I said of course, and then went to work and completely forgot about the caucus meeting. That day at noon I went home for lunch as usual, and Terry said, "What did you do to make Jean so mad?"

"Nothing," I said.

"Well, you must have done something, because he called here in a blind rage, and you're to call him back right away."

I said, "Uh-oh," but I still didn't know how I had transgressed.

The situation was clarified about one minute after I got the premier on the phone and he bellowed, "You knew I was having this caucus and I was counting on you!"

I said I was sorry, and then I got a little mad and said, "Well, when you give me all these things to do and I'm rushed off my feet night and day, it's not surprising that something gets forgotten."

Not the right thing to say.

"Never mind that. Do you know what Mackenzie King said about a caucus?"

"No."

"He said a caucus meeting was more important than a declaration of war...Hello? Are you there?"

I was there, all right, but I thought it best not to respond.

"Eric?"

"Yes."

"Answer me. What do you think?"

I said, "Well, Jean, that wasn't the brightest remark King ever made." *

---

* Incidentally, I can find no evidence to suggest that King, who said some pretty strange things in his time, ever said anything as strange as this.

That's me, far right, standing fiercely on guard in this family portrait taken in 1919. My brother Hugh, Jr., is at left. My father holds Plunkett, who died in 1924, and my mother holds Kathleen.

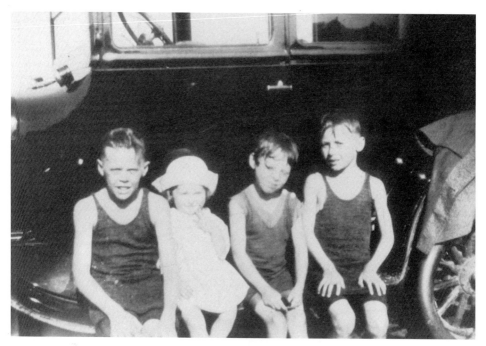

Here we are again, on the running board of our car in the early 1920s. I'm on the left, along with Kathleen, Plunkett, and Hugh. The photo at right shows 737 Convent Street, where we lived for most of my primary and secondary education. The second door from the left led to our flat on the third floor.

Above is the second-year high school class at Loyola, gathered for our formal photo. Below is a recent picture of the college, still a place of peaks and towers, tall windows and happy memories.

The 1935 university debating team at Loyola wore formal clothes and grim expressions. I am in the middle, while the others are L. D'Arcy (left), Ray Shaughnessy, Ray Altimas. The portrait at right is of Terry's father, Edward Patrick Whelan.

Catherine Kierans

Will I or will I not jump into Quebec politics? This portrait was taken by my daughter Cathy in 1963, when I was still president of the Montreal Stock Exchange, but about to take the leap.

Above is one of my favourite pictures, taken in 1961 in our Montreal home. Our son Tom was twenty-one at the time, and Cathy was seventeen. Terry was lovely, as always. Below is more serious business, my swearing in to the Lesage cabinet on August 8, 1963. Premier Lesage, at right, is looking pensive, perhaps wondering what he has done in signing me up.

Two pictures of bliss. In the one at the top, I am acting as Grand Marshal for the 1965 St. Patrick's Day parade in Montreal, with my father beaming his pleasure. John Turner, beside my father, was a Montreal MP at the time. In the picture at bottom, Terry and I are off on a Caribbean cruise in 1966. As you can see, we enjoyed it.

René Lévesque is in two contrasting
moods in these pictures. The one at top
shows us chatting with reporters soon
after we became a team, and he is pleased
with me. He had just become minister
of family welfare, and I minister of
health. At right, however, he is clearly
disgruntled. This one was taken when we
were debating at Trois-Rivières in early
1968, when René was beginning his
long, lonely, and finally successful run
for the premiership. He had been asked
to talk about nationalism to the Quebec
unions, and they had insisted that I be
there, to represent the other side.

There was a gasp on the phone as Lesage digested this unwarranted attack on one of his greatest heroes, and then *bam!* — down went the phone.

I went to the assembly a bit early that afternoon, understandably nervous, and as I walked in, there was Lesage, as usual, striding up and down between the aisles, wisecracking with the opposition before the opening of business. He looked up, saw me, waved, and said, "Eric, comment ça va?" That was Lesage.

I never missed another caucus meeting, because he never called another.

## THE BOTCHED ROYAL VISIT

One of the more interesting politicians I came into contact with in Quebec was Pierre Bourgault, the leader of the Rassemblement pour l'indépendance nationale (RIN), very much a separatist group. At a time when some separatists were saying it with dynamite, Pierre was content to make his points using shrewd, and often very funny, arguments belittling the English overlords. One day when I was going into the legislative building he saw me and called out, "Eric, Eric," as if I were a long-lost friend. He put his arm around me and we marched down the hallway to the assembly, chatting and laughing. I expected to read in the newspaper the next day that I was turning RIN, but he was just being his charming self. We debated often, and he would concede points in the debate, but never, of course, the main one about the future of the province.

His cause was helped, I think, by the reaction of the province during the royal visit of 1964. This turned into something between a farce and a tragedy in Quebec. The separatists made shrewd use of the elitism that is bound up with any royal visit, and the police, apparently determined to prove their loyalty, went whaling into crowds of youngsters with two-foot-long billy clubs; it did not create a good impression.

On the night of the state dinner in Quebec City, Terry and I — dressed to the nines — got into a cab to go to the Château Frontenac, but we very quickly ran into a crowd of demonstrators jamming the Grand Allée. They would range alongside the cab and yell in the window, trying to make one ashamed: "Oh, le pauvre Eric, il doit faire ses hommages à la reine — sa reine!" (Oh, poor Eric, he has to pay his respects to the queen — his queen!) Much of it was in good fun, and they made their point. Regrettably, the police didn't see it that way, and the occasion became known as "the Night of the Nightsticks"; officers wielding their billies — 2,000 of these clubs were ordered especially for the visit — laid about them with vast enthusiasm, and no common sense. Through it all, there was Pierre Bourgault, down in Lower Town, saying, "Look what's going on up there! See how they treat us! Quebecers are just serfs to these people."

One thing did strike me about the Royals, when we were presented to them, and that was their slick professionalism. The afternoon of the state dinner, the entire cabinet was trotted out to be introduced. Lesage would present each of us, first to Prince Philip and then to the queen. When Lesage came to me, he said, "Now, this is the English member of our cabinet, Eric Kierans," and the prince said, "Oh, no, I understand he's an Irishman," and while I was still fumbling for some brilliant rejoinder, the prince was moving me along by the elbow with his left hand, and I was in front of the queen. A smile and a bow, and I was gone. Very few assembly lines work with such smooth precision.

Because I was the English member of cabinet, some members of the anglophone community presumed that I was somehow their Man Friday, although the fact is I had a good deal more sympathy for the emerging and energetic francophone community than for the old-timers who wanted to hang on to privileges that simply could not last. One day I received a delegation from my old alma mater, Loyola, with a request that they seemed to think was perfectly straightforward and that I would naturally support. They wanted full university status for Loyola, so that it could grant its own degrees and not have to go through the Université de Montréal.

I tried to put them off at first, explaining that this was perhaps not the best time to go into this matter, but of course, from their point of view, it was the best time. They had their own English, Catholic member in the cabinet; what could be more natural than that he would want to do right by his old school? Finally, I said, "Look, this province has a population that is roughly 80 per cent French and 20 per cent English.

There are three French universities,* and three English universities.† If you think I'm going to put up a fight for a fourth English university right now, well, I'm sorry, but I won't."

The rector of Loyola, Patrick Malone, was so irate that he wouldn't speak to me for a long time. I was never able to play the role of political fixer, trading in favours for any one group, and in that sense I was never a very good politician.

## A NEW, AND FINE, DEPUTY

On the other hand, one of my accomplishments at Revenue received applause from both sides of the house. In the spring of 1965, we resolved our search for a top-flight deputy minister. Robert Després had been the comptroller of the Quebec Power Company between 1959 and 1963, and regional manager of the Administration and Trust Company from 1963 until I went to see him two years later. We became instant friends.

He told me that he knew a good deal about the Ministry of Revenue. It seems that a large religious community had come to his trust company with a sudden need for some $2 million. Apparently, a donor had invested that amount, at interest, with the community, but he now wanted to get his money out because the Revenue Department was suddenly demanding all sorts of information about where the money came from, what taxes, if any, had been paid, etc. The money, of course, had been put to use, and was now in the fixed assets of the community. Hence the need for the loan to meet the anxious gentleman's request. "C'était la faute de l'Irlandais nommé comme ministre," Després was told.

Reviewing the papers, Després was able to reassure the abbot that there would be no difficulty about granting the loan. That was the good news. The bad news was that the abbot, contrary to his wishes, could not sign for the loan by himself; two other signatures were required. The abbot was horrified. The entire community would learn what had happened and would be convinced that he was a failure, because he had to go outside for a loan. In the end, everything worked out, Robert told me, but he had had to do a lot of handholding before it was all settled in a proper manner.

* At that time, Laval, Montréal, and Sherbrooke.

† McGill, Bishop's, and Concordia.

It took everything I had and all of Jean Lesage's best efforts to convince Robert to come to the department. When he eventually left after five years, he had built the finest revenue department anywhere in Canada. He was the equal of any one of the fine set of civil servants that Lesage put together. I recommended him to Premier Johnson after we were defeated, and three months later Danny thanked me, saying, "Després has been a real asset."

## WE INVENT OPTING OUT

When we went up against Ottawa in the continuing discussions about finance, the Constitution, whatever, Lesage would sit in the front row, and right behind him would be René Lévesque; myself; Pierre Laporte, the minister of municipal affairs; and Paul Gérin-Lajoie, the minister of education. I and others had persuaded Lesage — over the vigorous objections of George Marler — to hire Jacques Parizeau away from the École des Hautes Études Commerciales de Montréal to be his economic adviser; thus Parizeau was usually on hand, too, along with Claude Morin and Michel Bélanger, the latter a brilliant student of finance who went on to become president of the Banque Nationale.

In many of these exchanges, I can say with some conviction, we wiped the floor with our opposite numbers from Ottawa, who seemed to expect that all they had to do was propose something, and that was the end of it. We were often better briefed than they were, and in my mind we had a powerful case to put forward. Ottawa was intruding more and more into areas of provincial jurisdiction, and proposing national programs that would then be thrust down the throats of the provinces. The trick was that once Ottawa put one of these programs in place, any province that didn't accept it would find that its taxpayers were paying, through their federal income taxes, for benefits that flowed to everyone but themselves, a recipe for financial and electoral disaster. With Ottawa, the approach was to accept its plan, or no money would be transferred.

That was why we came up with the notion of "opting out." If Ottawa wanted to launch some new scheme, the province could either accept the scheme or take the money that would have come to it under the scheme, to use in the same area. It had to be in the same area, of course. Health funds could not be transferred to education, and vice versa. (This is no longer the case, by the way.) The great problem was that no other province ever wanted to opt out. (Ontario might have done so when medicare was first introduced — Premier John Robarts was certainly outraged by having to accept a program with which he did not agree, or lose the money — but the process had not been refined at that point.)

We had met in Ottawa to talk about joint programs, and the meeting broke up without any agreement, so another session was scheduled for Quebec. The feds naturally assumed that this would take only a short time, since in their view they always had justice on their side, so to fill in the day, they put a proposal on the agenda that they knew Quebec would have to go for, because it was one of Lesage's ideas. The program already existed in Quebec; it had been a campaign promise and was carried out entirely by the provincial government. It required children to stay in school until the age of sixteen, and because this was a hardship in rural areas, where young people were needed to help on the farm, the government reimbursed the farmers in such cases. At this meeting, Ottawa proposed to take over this idea, and it would pay half the cost, including half the cost of the Quebec plan.

This discussion had not gone on very long when Premier Robert Stanfield of Nova Scotia unlimbered himself from his chair and said, "Well, Mr. Chairman, I can see that my good friend from New Brunswick, the Hon. Louis Robichaud, is going to be in favour of this idea" — Robichaud nodded vigorously — "and so, I suppose, will many others. So far as I know, this is not a problem in Nova Scotia, but I suppose if everyone else is getting something, my people will want it, too. Now, as I understand the proposal, what it means is that for every dollar spent in this way, Ottawa will put up fifty cents. Is that correct?"

It was correct.

"Well, then, Mr. Chairman, my question is this: Where do I get the other fifty cents?"

## THE CRUCIAL BATTLE WITH OTTAWA

Ottawa would not yield tax points to the provinces to do the things that we believed fell within our jurisdiction. In effect, Ottawa said, Well, give up the jurisdiction. Lesage kept arguing that by shrewd bargaining we could back the feds off; Confederation was flexible, and could be made to work to accommodate the new realities. I hoped he was right.

In the pension debate of late March and early April of 1964, we proved we had a winner. Claude Castonguay, a brilliant and imaginative actuary, as well as a Quebec nationalist, drew up a proposal for what became the Quebec Pension Plan (QPP). When we were summoned to Ottawa to accept the federal version, which every other province but Ontario seemed bound to agree to — although Ontario had only a very feeble plan of its own — Lesage gave a rough sketch of ours. (All the final details had not been worked out yet.)

The Ottawa plan was to be unfunded; that is, the costs would be paid, mainly, out of general revenues, and contributions would be made gradually as more of the elderly became eligible, and more money was required. Ottawa could afford to proceed in this fashion because it had swallowed so much of the available tax room that it could meet the requirements out of general revenue. The Quebec plan proceeded from the other end; it was to be a funded plan, with the money set aside from the beginning. This would provide a pool of capital that could be invested, in turn, to make more money, as well as to cover the costs of the plan. It was Lesage's dream.

I did what I could to reassure the financial community that we were not engaged in some sort of socialist adventure, but a sound fiscal program, which would have an enormous beneficial impact on financing both the private and the public sectors, because of the creation of the investment pool.

The difficulty was that in order to make our plan work, Ottawa had to be willing to give up the necessary tax points for us to collect the funding. In theory, it was pledged to do so; this was all part of Lester Pearson's much-touted "co-operative federalism." But when it came down to it, the federal power-brokers simply would not do what they said they would.

Tom Kent, who was Prime Minister Pearson's chief policy adviser at this time, had a good deal of sympathy for our position. With his usual clarity, he noted, "The federal government ought to have less money to spend, in favour of the provincial governments having more."

In his book *A Public Purpose,* Kent described what happened when the Quebec Pension Plan was brought before the federal-provincial meeting:

Jean Lesage produced a risky but brilliant stroke. He told the conference, in confidence, what the Quebec Pension Plan would be. It had been decided in outline, though it was far from ready for presentation to the Legislative Assembly. The brainchild chiefly of Claude Castonguay, it was an excellent plan for its purpose. It would provide appreciably larger pensions than we proposed, and with the supplementary and survivor benefits that we did not have the constitutional power to include. It would generate, for many years, large investment funds. One could almost see the other provincial premiers licking their lips…With such a plan in Quebec, Ontario would never go along with ours. That was dead.

The obvious solution was for Ottawa to give way, allow Quebec to have its own pension plan, and improve its own plan to match, but many of the federal cabinet ministers feared that that would be seen to be "truckling" to Quebec. It took another series of protracted negotiations to produce a final solution. In 1965, Ottawa and Quebec passed similar legislation, based mainly on the Quebec plan (but with some minor improvements imported from the Ottawa plan into ours). The necessary tax points to make it work were surrendered, though grudgingly — as a favour, not as a right. This gave the very impression we most wanted to avoid: that Quebec, rather than striking a blow for all the provinces, was somehow getting special treatment. However, in time, it became clear that our funded plan was superior to Ottawa's, and several premiers admitted as much.

The establishment of the QPP was a great triumph, and should have been welcomed everywhere in Canada. Instead, it was painted by most of the media outside Quebec as another raid on the federal treasury. Just the same, it was this initiative that produced the pool of capital in the Caisse de dépôt et placement du Québec, Canada's single largest pool of investment, which now runs at over $120 billion. In turn, that gave Quebecers a tremendous sense of pride and achievement, as well as a much better pension plan than would otherwise have been the case.

However, the lesson — that the provinces might have something to teach Ottawa about social and economic planning — was either missed or deliberately ignored. That became clear when Ottawa announced its medicare proposal in 1965, delivering it with all the panache of the family cat arriving at the front door with a deceased mouse and laying it proudly on the mat.

Prime Minister Pearson brought this up almost casually towards the tail end of the July 1965 federal-provincial conference. He told us Ottawa was planning to produce a National Medicare Insurance Act, that it would cost about one billion dollars a year, and that the provinces would be required to pay half of this. I quickly worked out that Quebec's share would come to $125 million a year, a very large amount of money that we were to be committed to spending, without a word of consultation.

What really bothered me was the sheer gall of it; health was a matter of provincial, not federal, concern under the Constitution. If we were to have a medicare plan, and Quebec had already indicated that it was in favour, then we ought to be in on it from the beginning.

But this bland statement proved that the federal government was prepared to commit provincial governments to spending huge sums of money out of their own treasuries in areas that were primarily theirs, and do it without even bothering to consult them. The kicker was the usual one; any province that didn't go along would see its taxpayers putting out money through the federal income tax for benefits that would flow else-where. Premier John Robarts of Ontario was even angrier than Lesage, and denounced the program in somewhat tempestuous language:

> Medicare is a glowing example of a Machiavellian scheme that is in my humble opinion one of the greatest political frauds that has been perpetrated on the people of this country. The proposition is this: you are taxing our people in Ontario to the tune of $222 million a year to pay for a plan for which we get nothing.*

But in the end every province, including Ontario, signed on. My objection was — and remains — not to medicare, but to the way it was brought about, and my eternal regret is that the provinces did not rise up in one body to object. Except for Robarts, we were again on our own.

The whole opting-out argument was led by Quebec, but we always thought that we were working, on behalf of all Canadians, in the name of a true federal system, not the centralized monster Canada was becoming.

---

* Quoted in John N. McDougall, *The Politics and Economics of Eric Kierans* (Montreal and Kingston: McGill-Queen's University Press, 1993), 74.

One day in 1965, Lady Barbara Ward Jackson came to see me in Quebec City. The distinguished Cambridge economist was in town for a series of lectures she was giving at Laval. We had met ten years earlier when she gave the Chancellor Beatty Lectures at McGill. On this occasion, we got talking about the opting-out debate that was then going on with more sound than sense, and she said something I have never forgotten:

> You would get rid of half of your difficulties, Eric, if you could get some other province to opt out of something, even if it were only for ten dollars, just to establish the principle. You have a terrific responsibility here.

It always seemed to me that the fact that Quebec stood alone so often in these matters was not a rebuke to Quebec, but to the rest of Canada. This has always been a nation where there is bound to be difficulty in promoting nationwide solutions to economic and political difficulties. But the answer is not to reshape the country into a unitary state for the greater convenience of Ottawa bureaucrats; rather, it is to construct programs on a national basis, which means including the provinces, not brushing them aside. When I said this in Ottawa, as I often did, I was treated as just another provincial bumpkin who lacked the good manners to keep his place.

Despite the disagreements within the Quebec government, and they were many in the boisterous Lesage administration, it was a comfortable place to work. I remember when we were drawing up the budget for 1965; we did it in the Lesage living room in Quebec City. A gaggle of half a dozen cabinet ministers and as many aides sat around and argued and made calculations, while Madame circulated an ever-charged coffee pot. A stranger coming into the room would not have known who were the officials and who the cabinet members — presuming any of us could be seen through the smoke. It was not exactly a formal way to work, but it was effective, and produced a pretty fair budget.

## ANOTHER WINDMILL

My lack of tact and diplomacy came to the fore in what was perhaps my noisiest brawl as a Quebec cabinet minister, when I went over the head of Ottawa to declare war on the United States — or, at least, that is the way Ottawa seemed to see it. In my years as a student, teacher, businessman, and stock exchange president, I had become increasingly concerned with the wide gap between the theories of economics with which I was now familiar and the world in which those theories were played out.

In the real world, there was no perfect competition, no free market, less and less of the free enterprise acclaimed in the texts. Instead, economies were becoming dominated, more and more, by giant corporations whose only aim was to accumulate profits, and do it their way. I had learned that much of what economists say may be valuable, but none of it is gospel. Corporations' domination was nowhere near as far advanced in the 1960s as it is today, but its outlines were clearly visible then. I had given this subject a good deal of thought when I was suddenly blindsided by an almost chance remark to Frank Howard, then a journalist with the *Globe and Mail*.

Howard had asked me for an interview, and we met one snowy evening just before Christmas. I took him to the Winter Club. We had a long dinner full of talk about Quebec politics, and especially about the Department of Health, which I had recently taken over. When we got ready to leave, the snow was up to our knees. I said, "I'll call a cab," but Frank said, "You'll never get one in this — I'll drive you home." He had a beaten-up old Volkswagen and we were chugging down the street in this when he said, "What do you think of this U.S. stuff?" and away I went.

Not long before this, on December 8, 1965, Henry Fowler, the U.S. secretary of the treasury, had made a speech, the tone of which was rather muted, but the thrust of which was bold and unmistakable. It was very much a case of speaking softly and carrying a big stick, a stick that was to be used by the American government on the economies of its trading allies.

The United States had a severe balance-of-payments problem, almost entirely due to its disastrous and costly intervention in Vietnam, where American combat troops had been sent earlier that year. President Lyndon Johnson, who had promised "never to send American boys to fight Asian wars," was determined to wrest a victory there by the use of overwhelming military might, and that meant a huge drain on the U.S. dollar. Even the vast trade surplus the U.S. enjoyed — $6.7 billion in 1964 — was not going to be enough to reach what Fowler called "our goal of equilibrium,"* so Fowler was announcing a "voluntary" program to ensure that U.S. corporations abroad would remit more to the United States, through management fees, dividends, and capital flows. Some 900 chief executives of American companies were required to report their progress in helping the United States to bring home more dollars every quarter, to ensure that the "volunteers" fell into line. They were to cut direct investment abroad, and expand "repatriated earnings."

I had in the past been a strong supporter of open financial markets, and as we saw in the last chapter, a sharp critic of government interference. However, I had been growing ever more aware that the arrival of a new and rapacious corporation, the multinational, posed an increasing danger to the political and national will of the countries in which it operated. These global giants sometimes owned more assets than many of the nations in which they had factories, and were less and less inclined even to consider, much less to encourage, the policies of local governments.

It was a serious problem, and here was Fowler taking it one step further. He was saying, in effect, that American corporations operating abroad were to consider themselves arms of the secretary of state, foot soldiers in the struggle to pay for American adventures abroad. Canada was already running a massive current-account deficit with the United States† (we still are); it ran at $1.6 billion in 1964. But this was not enough; more was to be extracted as Uncle Sam reached across the border to empty our pockets. We were already in danger of losing control over our own economy, more and more of which was now in the hands of foreign firms. And we were financing our own sellout.

For example, Neil McElroy, chairman of Proctor and Gamble,

---

* Remarks of the Honorable Henry J. Fowler, secretary of the treasury, at a White House press conference on December 3, 1965.

† The reader will know that two important international balances have to be considered: trade, which covers the simple matter of cross-border sales; and current account, which covers the movement of fees, dividends, capital investment, and so forth. Canada usually has a positive trade balance with the Americans, but this is more than offset by the huge cross-border flows of the management fees and profits of U.S. firms operating in this country. That is why we can have year after year of trade surpluses accompanied by massive deficits on the current account.

explained to his shareholders at about this time, "It is customary in our development of overseas markets to use a minimum of U.S. capital, a maximum of borrowing overseas, and reinvestment of earnings abroad." * You didn't even have to bring in much capital to take over an industry in a place like Canada; you could borrow the money from a Canadian bank, repay it with profits carved out of the Canadian market, and send home the rest. You could also use your foreign subsidiary to purchase products from the American parent, pay fat management fees, and send home huge profits. Proctor and Gamble, McElroy boasted, had managed to turn an investment abroad of $11 million into a return to the parent company of $290 million — $47 million as profit and $243 million in purchases.

Not enough, Fowler was saying. We want more. He was telling any Canadians who cared to listen that Walter Gordon had been far closer to the truth than I in 1963. He was telling us that the U.S. government meant to use what George Ball was later to call "these corporations, these mighty engines of enlightened capitalism," as a wrecking ball on the economies of trading partners, and especially of the Americans' largest trading partner, Canada. U.S. corporations were not merely economic arms, they were political arms of American policy, and all the pious clap-trap about the non-political nature of foreign investment was revealed for what it was.

And we did nothing. The official response of the federal government at Ottawa was that this was merely a continuation of earlier American efforts to right its balance of trade, and not a matter for Canadian concern.

I had been brooding on these things, but it was not until Frank Howard asked me point-blank for my comments that I voiced my views. I told him, "Ottawa should have told the Americans to get lost. It should have protested in the strongest possible terms." I said the Americans were changing the rules, insisting that where the national interests of the host countries in which its corporations operated were in conflict with Washington's view of the world, the multinationals must serve U.S. national interests. If American companies operating in this country were to be not commercial enterprises but Trojan horses, we needed to

---

* Quoted in Eric Kierans and Walter Stewart, *Wrong End of the Rainbow* (Toronto: Collins, 1978), 72.

change our attitude of welcoming them in; the Trojan-horse experiment does not work out too well for the host country.

The strongest point that could be made against me was, of course, that this was not strictly my business. Foreign affairs were a matter for Ottawa. But when Ottawa stood on the sidelines with its thumb in its mouth while this was going on, it seemed to me that somebody had to say something. (Walter Gordon was no longer minister of finance; he had resigned after the 1965 federal election, and had been replaced by Mitchell Sharp. I like to believe that Walter might have launched a rocket off to Washington; Sharp just smiled.)

When I came back to my office on Boxing Day — after a brief Christmas interlude in Montreal — Charles Denis rushed in to say, "Look, you've got to call Lesage right away. He's very upset."

"What about?"

"Damned if I know."

I phoned Lesage, and he said, "Look, Eric, we don't have many friends in Ottawa, but Lou Rasminsky [governor of the Bank of Canada] is one of them. What did you do to him?"

I said, "I didn't do anything. I haven't seen him for a long time."

"Uh-huh. Well, have you seen the *Globe and Mail*?"

"No." Just then, Charles came back waving a copy of the newspaper, so I told Lesage, "I've just got it. I'll call you back."

Howard had not used a word of our long supper interview about the Department of Health, but the second page of the *Globe* carried an innocent-looking little box containing my advice to Ottawa to tell the Americans to get lost. Prime Minister Pearson was on holidays in the Caribbean, and the men running economic policy in Ottawa were Rasminsky and Sharp, and it was pretty clear that Rasminsky had called Lesage to complain.

When I called the premier back, I told him why I had spoken out. "You realize what this is going to do to our financial sector. Every American-corporation in Canada will have to cash in as much of its profits as it can and send working capital back to the United States."

Lesage was very reasonable; he knew instantly what the guidelines meant, so he told me, "Why don't you give Rasminsky a call and see if you can get him cooled down?"

It didn't work out that way. Lou was waiting by the phone in Ottawa, and as soon as I came on the line he began to lecture me about meddling in foreign affairs, and he went on to defend the guidelines, which, he said, he had explained to Pearson, who found nothing objectionable in them. I said something to the effect that, well, he wouldn't, would he? And away we went. It was what the diplomats refer to as "a free and frank exchange of views," or as others might put it, a shouting match.

I wrote a letter to Fowler, attacking the American approach, root and branch. This, of course, was a breach of protocol, since any dealings with the United States had to go through Ottawa.

When I reported back to Lesage, he told me that I had better write a letter making it clear that I was not speaking on behalf of the government of Quebec. Every report I have read of this series of events notes that Lesage was "furious" with me, but this was simply not the case. He was covering his flank, maintaining his relations with the federal Liberals and his friend Lester Pearson. He may have leaked out the word that he was upset with me, for his own reasons. But in fact, he was rather pleased with me, because the response of the Quebec public was strongly supportive.

I reasoned he was right to suggest that I make it clear that I was speaking for myself only, so I decided to clarify matters by writing a letter to Paul Martin, Sr., secretary of state for external affairs. After covering the fact that I did not speak for the province of Quebec, I went on with the thrust of my letter, pointing out that the American policy was based on a false premise, and that the balance-of-payments problems had nothing to do with corporate investment abroad. The Americans' problems were caused by "the heavy obligations and responsibilities of world leadership, by Vietnam, etc." Sucking back more money from the multi-nationals was never going to close the gap created there. Second, the United States was promoting other policies that brought about excessive investment in other countries, such as tax breaks to American firms with foreign subsidiaries, to help them compete with, and overwhelm, local firms. And, finally, while the economic implications and the political implications of capital flows were separate matters, I was protesting the political aspect now being brought into play. I wrote:

> In sum, I believe, like you, in the international corporation, but I
> do not believe it can be used as an agent of government...We hope

that international companies, unlike armies of occupation, will always have a role to play. To accomplish this, they must conduct themselves as true citizens of the host country.

When I sent my letters to Fowler and Martin, I released copies of them to the press, which created the usual screams of outrage. I did not understand, and still do not understand, this attitude. I have always believed in open decisions arrived at openly, in debate carried on in the full light of day. I was accused of grandstanding, of chasing headlines. If I had sent my letters in code, or through Ottawa (same thing), they would have vanished from the surface of the planet. My aim was to sound an alarm, not gain kudos for restraint.

The day after I sent these letters off, I was playing squash at the Montreal Amateur Athletic Association and a friend came in to say, "Mike [Lester] Pearson's on the television upstairs. He doesn't like you much."

I went back to my squash game.

The notion that I ought to have maintained silence because I was not a member of the federal government persisted, so I called up the head of the Toronto Society of Financial Analysts and asked for a chance to try to clear up the issue by speaking to the investment analysts. He said sure, and on February 1, 1966, I delivered a paper called "The Economic Effects of the Guidelines," which analyzed the American problem, and the danger of their so-called solution. This led to Pearson's telling a *Globe and Mail* correspondent, "Why didn't Eric tell us this at the time we agreed to the guidelines?" which I found disingenuous and silly. It did not lead to any change in Canadian policy.

I later debated the subject with a member of the Federal Reserve Board in Washington, at the Château Champlain in Montreal. We sat side by side at the head table, hardly ate a thing, argued merrily all through dinner, and then delivered our speeches, repeating all the old arguments about America's needs and Canada's. And I reiterated my concern about the way the Americans were going about meeting their needs. About the only point he conceded was that he thought Washington ought to be more careful in the future about springing policy changes on its trading partners without discussion.

The fuss over my intervention in international politics soon died down; before long, even Mitchell Sharp was moved to complain about the guidelines the Americans had imposed, but of course he did so quietly, diplomatically, and with absolutely no effect. Which, come to think of it, was the same result I had obtained.

On this subject, I was pretty well on my own within the Lesage administration; but there were a great many other issues on which I was joined by René Lévesque, the man who brought me into Quebec politics in the first place. The relationship I built up with René was to give us both so much pleasure — and so much grief.

# Six

# RENÉ

*The soul he said, is composed*
*of the external world.*

*There are men of the East, he said,*
*who are the East.*
*There are men of a province*
*who are that province.*
*There are men of a valley*
*who are that valley…*

— WALLACE STEVENS, *ANECDOTE OF*
*MEN BY THE THOUSAND*, 1954

ONE MORNING CLOSE TO the end of my second year at the stock exchange, the phone rang in my office and when I picked it up a very soft voice said, "Who are you?"

I said, "I'm Eric Kierans, who are you?"

"René Lévesque. You seem to know a lot about me, but I know nothing about you."

Now I understood.

I had delivered a paper a few days earlier, at Assumption College in Windsor, Ontario (now part of the University of Windsor). In it, I had spoken about the emergence of an entrepreneurial spirit in Quebec, especially among the francophone population. The English element, I said, seemed content to rest on its laurels and claimed superiority, while the real activity was taking place in a revitalized Quebec. I went on to point to the vigour of the Lesage government, and in particular its minister of natural resources, René Lévesque, who brought to his portfolio some of the energy, industry, and daring that had been lacking for so many years in Quebec politics.

Lévesque at that time was considered a closet socialist and, it goes without saying, a closet separatist, but I told the audience that "if he shakes [Anglo-Saxon] industrialists loose from their complacency and self-satisfaction, he will have done more to sustain private capitalism than destroy it."

I pointed out that in Quebec, a feeling of frustration was undermining the stability of private enterprise, and "it is important to realize that M. Lévesque and others are not creating this dissatisfaction — they are drawing attention to it...I hope M. Lévesque will be around for a long time."

I had no idea that there were any newspaper people in the conference hall when I made that speech; indeed, I was sure there were not, or I might have shaded my words a little more carefully — although shading my words carefully has never been my strong point. In any event, a reporter from *La Presse* was at the back of the room, scribbling furiously. During the question-and-answer period that followed, an angry American member of the audience announced that his company was worried about the statements coming out of Quebec by Lévesque and others, and was considering pulling out of the province. The exchange that ensued furnished the newspaper reporter with strong material for his article. The following Monday, *La Presse* was telling the world that the president of the Montreal and Canadian Stock Exchanges was an unabashed admirer of that radical, René Lévesque.

Even before the takeover of the provincial hydro system (which had not been formalized until December 28, 1962), René had tended to put the wind up most of the Anglo financial community. They heard his name, and dreamed of tumbrels.

René was not calling to thank me, or anything like that; he was genuinely curious as to how I came to make that speech. So I invited him to have lunch with me that day, at the Montreal Club, a bastion of financial respectability just around the corner from the old exchange building. At first, I intended that we would have a quiet chat in one of the private rooms upstairs over lunch, but when René arrived, a small, slender, rumpled man with a quick, engaging smile and easy manner, I thought, Why waste his charm? And I asked him if he would rather eat in the main dining room. He would.

I might have made a more spectacular entrance with Lily Ste-Cyr, the stripper, on my arm, but not much more. When we arrived at the dining-room doorway and the maître d' appeared, I asked for a table for two. The master of the moment, the maître d' said, "This way, gentlemen," and marched us through the middle of a sea of diners to a linen-topped table on the far side. The clank of cutlery stopped, conversation died, heads swivelled, and eyeballs popped like champagne corks. And amidst the dreadful, doomed silence that descended on the room, René asked me, behind his hand, "Is that for you, or for me?"

"For both of us, I think."

### LESAGE'S TERRIBLE TWINS

There are people whom you may take years to know; others whom you never feel you really know; but every now and then you meet someone and instantly feel as if you had known that person for years. It was that way with René and me. From that very first luncheon — and I have absolutely no idea what either of us ate — we talked to each other with absolute candour and mutual enjoyment. And our battles, and there were many of them long before our brief falling out in 1967, were never marked by rancour.

We talked a few times on the phone after that memorable luncheon, but seldom met, not even when I was helping Doug Fullerton get the numbers that would determine the takeover price of the electrical utilities (described in chapter 4); we were both far too busy with our own concerns. However, I was being drawn into politics, day by day.

I was a fascinated onlooker during the provincial election of October 1962, when Lesage swept back into power on the *maîtres chez nous* platform that led to, and justified, the hydro takeover. René was the star of that campaign.

And, as stock exchange president, I sharply criticized the Diefenbaker government's economic policies, and pointed, in particular, to Finance Minister Donald Fleming's refusal to move to a flexible exchange rate, when it was obviously the answer to the increasing pressure on the Canadian dollar. (This led to a summons to Ottawa, where Senator David Walker, one of Diefenbaker's inner circle, brought me before His Presence, and I received a confused, rambling wigging from Diefenbaker himself.)

Then, as I began to edge my way into direct political action, by joining provincial Liberal discussion groups, and then by attacking Réal Caouette, not surprisingly stories began to float around that I was about to enter politics. On the way back from a meeting of the governors of the Montreal Stock Exchange in Quebec City, in the spring of 1962, Charles Denis and I were sitting side by side on an Air Canada flight, when I looked out the window and saw the farms laid out below us, much as they had been in the days when they were part of a seigneury.

"Look down there, Charles," I said. "Look at those small farms. How can they make a living? We aren't using all the assets we have in Quebec. We've been asleep too long."

Charles chuckled. "What do you want to do, go into politics?"

"Why not?" I said.

Not long after this, I was invited, by Rudy Casgrain, well known in the bond trade, and the son of Thérèse Casgrain, to a monthly seminar put on by his firm, and at which René was the guest speaker. René insisted that I be moved up to sit beside him. We spent much of the evening discussing provincial affairs, and the most important thing he said to me was, "Look, if you are going to go around making political speeches, it's time you got serious about it, and ran for office."

So, my entry into Jean Lesage's cabinet, described in the previous chapter, was at least partially paved by René, and my career there was to be so intertwined with his that we quickly became "Lesage's Terrible Twins" in the media.

We had little in common, at first glance. René was born in New Carlisle, on the Gaspé peninsula, in 1922. His father was a lawyer. Prime Minister Louis St. Laurent told me once that Lévesque *père* was undoubtedly one of the most gifted lawyers for miles around — but he probably never made more than $150 a week. He worked in John Hall Kelly's firm, which was probably the most powerful in the Gaspé. The town, and the legal profession, were dominated by Anglos. René grew up in an atmosphere of combativeness, and his perfect bilingualism was not so much voluntary as forced. He went to university at Laval, then moved into journalism, with Radio-Canada. He gained renown with his coverage of the Second World War and the Korean War, before returning to Canada to a role in television.

There, his quick wit, quiet charm, and pointed analysis promptly made him into a celebrity, with his own weekly television show, *Point de Mire*. He did not become active in the CBC producers' union until the sixty-eight-day strike in Quebec for bargaining rights, which began on December 29, 1958. And he was disgusted, disillusioned, and radicalized when he realized that the English producers, who held much more power in the CBC, would not lift a hand to help their French confreres during that bitter battle. It was this experience that led him to identify himself with the province's attempt to move out of its neo-colonial status in the Canadian federation.

The federal government's view was that the nation could live with a strike in Quebec. There were to be no negotiations whatsoever. René was a member of the delegation that journeyed to Ottawa to plead the cause of the producers. They met with the minister of labour, Michael Starr, and discovered — as René later put it in his *Memoirs* — "that the paralysis of the whole French network was for [Starr] like something happening on the planet Mars."

The strike didn't matter. The province of Quebec didn't matter. The government could live with it. Since it was only Quebec, English Canada could react with smugness and indifference. In adopting this attitude, they were throwing down the gauntlet to Quebec. They were, in effect, denying that there was value in Quebec — its history since 1608, the language, the people, and the land were not matters of importance.

It all came together for René; this was as André Laurendeau had foreseen when a few days before the strike ended he asked, "Is this René's Road to Damascus?" It was. The strike was finally over, and the first management union in the CBC was organized, but René's program, *Point de Mire*, although it ran for the few remaining weeks of the spring television season, was not renewed in the fall.

When Premier Antonio Barrette announced the 1960 election, Jean Lesage called for candidates. René sought to persuade three other rising Quebec personalities — Pierre Trudeau, Gérard Pelletier, and Jean Marchand — to go into provincial politics with him. In his *Memoirs,* he wrote, "If men like them, who were so well prepared, refused to put their shoulders to the wheel, would that change ever come?" That night, René went over to the Windsor Hotel to tell Jean Lesage that of the four key men he had hoped to enlist, only one remained — and that one man was René himself. The others had refused.

Lesage saw René as a brilliant new star with a wide appeal to the younger voters, and recruited him into his *équipe de tonnerre* for the 1960 election, and then had a good deal of trouble trying to rein him in.

When I met him, he was not a separatist, nor a socialist, in the conventional sense. As we got to know each other, usually after work, when we would go out, we thrashed over ideas very thoroughly. He would say, "Let's go out for a beer," although in fact he would nurse one beer over about three hours, while I drank ginger ale; what he went out for was to smoke and talk. It seemed to me that he did not have any particular political philosophy in mind. He was, at base, a pragmatist, who was willing to apply whatever solution seemed sensible, without regard to ideology.

He did not quote from the great philosophers, and his grasp of economic theory was accurate and simple common sense. He had a knack of cutting through complex discussions to the heart of the matter, and of course, he was brilliantly eloquent.

As to his beliefs when I met him, he certainly believed in the creative use of government, and in a government that should make policy when it had the power to enact and emplace changes for the good of the people. He did not believe in the standard to which democratic socialism at that time clung, namely, public ownership of the principal means of production. He felt that if a job could be done effectively only through government control — and that was the test in the nationalization of hydro — then that was how it should be done. But he had no illusions that simply switching ownership of a utility from private to public hands would make it work better.

He was very much a Quebec nationalist, but that was not at all the same thing as being a separatist, a position to which he was forced, he believed, by the inability or unwillingness of the rest of Canada to accede to what he saw as Quebec's minimum conditions for survival. I agreed with much that he had to say in this regard, and I have no doubt I provided him with arguments.

I was a federalist, not in the sense that the word now seems to command — one who believes in the domination of Ottawa over the provinces — but in the old sense of one who supports the union of disparate provinces in a wider federation, for the greater good of all. I believed in a federal union, not what amounted to a single government with appendages, and so, at that time, did René.

This is a subject we will come back to. For now, the point to be made is that during the Second World War, Ottawa rightly moved to seize control of almost all the economic levers of the nation, to conduct the war effort. By the end of the war, Ottawa was collecting — and spending — 75 per cent of all government revenues. Despite a solemn undertaking that these extraordinary powers would be relinquished at war's end, they never were, and most of our constitutional wrangling ever since dates back to this flagrant injustice. A centralized Ottawa doling out subsidies and transfer payments to provinces is not the federal system of the British North America Act.

René and I agreed that this was a state of affairs that should be rectified; our difference was that he saw the battle almost entirely in terms of its Quebec and francophone dimensions, while I saw it as a national problem in the wider sense. We reflected, in other words, the backgrounds from which we came.

It was only gradually and reluctantly that René became convinced that Quebec could never get a fair deal from the rest of Canada. I never openly agreed with that, but I could certainly see why he felt the way he did. For my part, I believed, and still do, that the separation of Quebec would mean the complete breakup of Canada. This grand union would no longer exist.

## "ERIC, SPEAK FRENCH"

One of the first problems I faced in cabinet was that the meetings were conducted in French, and while I had come quite a long way in that language, I was certainly not bilingual. When I got excited, I would switch to English. One day, after one of my longer outbursts, René drew me aside and said, "Eric, you have to speak only in French."

I was about to demur, and stand on my rights, when he went on, "When you speak French, you have to translate; when you translate, you slow down. The way you were going just now, nobody could follow you, not even Lesage and I."

I said, "Oh." From then on, I nearly always spoke in French in cabinet.

## THE BRINCO AFFAIR

The first time René called on me for help on the financial side had to do with the much misunderstood Churchill Falls hydroelectric project. It is a subject still in the headlines today, so this is a good time to set the record straight. One Sunday evening in August 1963, Terry and I got on the CPR train in west Montreal to go down to Quebec. Lévesque boarded the same train at a later station, Mile End, and after a few minutes his executive assistant, a good-looking young man, appeared at our seats.

"Mr. Kierans," he said, "Mr. Lévesque would like to speak to you, if you can spare the time, and perhaps I could sit here with your very charming wife."

That went well with Terry, so I went up to the vacated seat beside René. He handed me a big dossier and said, "I'd really appreciate your opinion on this."

It was the proposal, at that time already well advanced, to tap the immense power potential of what was then Hamilton Falls — later Churchill Falls — in Labrador. The resource was entirely within Joey Smallwood's domain, and he had been working for years to develop the falls for Newfoundland. In his memoirs, he wrote, "My ambition to develop Churchill Falls was born one day in 1926." Thirty-seven years later, he was, if anything, more eager than ever. The proposal outlined in the papers that I saw had the project being built under the aegis of the British Newfoundland Corporation (Brinco), a management group which had been formed for the purpose. The power would be transshipped from Labrador through Quebec, since that was the shortest route to market. Or, rather, markets — for at that time, it was contemplated that about half of the power to be produced would be purchased by Quebec, and the rest by Consolidated Edison of New York, the electrical giant that supplied New York City.

The plan had the backing of Winston Churchill himself, who saw it as "a great Imperial project," * and of the House of Rothschild, but the actual money to make it go forward would be raised by an American consortium headed by a New York–based financial services company, Morgan Stanley. William Mulholland, later president and CEO of the

---

* Joseph R. Smallwood, *I Chose Canada* (Toronto: Macmillan, 1973), 446.

Bank of Montreal, was the principal figure there. The project would not work unless Quebec provided not only the route but the guarantees that the power could be transported over the 750 kilometres; these guarantees would allow the financial people to sell the bonds to provide the cash. What struck me as I went through the papers on my lap was that there was an unnecessary and expensive intermediary here. After about an hour of reading, I handed the dossier back to René.

"Well," he said, "what did you think?"

I replied that it was a proposal with problems. Accepting the cost figures that had Hydro's certification, I said, the project was being put in the hands of a management group instead of an underwriting group that would sell the bonds and leave the management and operation to a joint Newfoundland-Quebec corporation. Newfoundland owned the power, but Quebec would have to guarantee its safe delivery over distances that had never before been traversed with so much power. All the risks would be with the provinces; all the profits would go to a private consortium. Moreover, doing it this way was going to cost too much.

"How much too much?"

"Oh, about 25 per cent, less the underwriting costs."

He started to stub out the ever-present cigarette, stopped, fumbled in his pocket for the package, drew out another, lit it, and said, "Tell me."

So I told him. The way the deal was structured, Hydro-Québec, Brinco, and the government of Newfoundland were making an arrangement to develop power that belonged to Newfoundland, and sell it to Quebec and New York. Why did we need Brinco?

The short answer was "Because Joey says we do," and that was the long answer, too. Premier Smallwood had talked this over with his hero, Sir Winston Churchill, and he knew that Churchill had bought shares in Brinco, as had the Royal Family.* He felt indebted to Churchill; Brinco; Edmund de Rothschild; and Robert Winters, the CEO of Rio Algom, which was a member of the operating company. That was fine; but Quebec owed no such loyalty, and I failed to see why Quebec should pay to indulge Joey.

There was another aspect of the argument that became clearer later,

* Ibid., 450.

but which should be understood here if we are to grasp what is going on in the continuing argument about this subject today. Premier Smallwood was an unabashed bigot on the subject of Quebec, and French Canadians.

He told Quebec journalist Solange Chaput-Rolland, "The French Canadian is one of the most lovable human beings in Canada, but collectively he deserves a swift kick."

His own memoirs display an attitude that explains many of the problems that dogged the negotiations, including these two comments:

> It became perfectly obvious to me, and to my colleagues in Cabinet, that Quebec was taking an altogether selfish view...

And:

> I was convinced that Quebec would show neither scruple nor conscience in its treatment of Newfoundland — that we would be victimized at every turn.[*]

Unless Quebec accepted whatever terms Newfoundland proposed, it was being selfish; if it insisted on trying to get the best deal it could for the risks it was taking, it would be "victimizing" Newfoundland. This has now become holy writ in Newfoundland. It was wrong then, and it is just as wrong today.

When Brinco could not get the price it first proposed for its power — four cents a kilowatt, a price that made the project unaffordable from our point of view — Joey proposed to get Prime Minister Pearson to pass federal legislation to designate the transmission route through Quebec as federal property. Happily, he was talked out of this zany notion by his great federal ally, John W. Pickersgill.

Joey was dealing with Jean Lesage, a shrewd bargainer and a man with ego enough to match his own, so it is not surprising that negotiations dragged on, and on, and on. One of the complicating factors was that Hydro-Québec, through one of the companies taken over in the Shawinigan process, owned about 20 per cent of Brinco, and that irritated Joey, as well.

René kept urging Lesage to propose the elimination of Brinco from the deal as the only way to bring costs down to the point that it could be made to work. In February 1964, Douglas Fullerton put this proposal in

[*] Ibid., 460.

memo form to cabinet; he described Brinco as "an expensive anachronism." If Newfoundland nationalized Brinco, Quebec could buy the power at a price it could afford, and the project could go forward.

René put this to Robert Winters, who called Edmund de Rothschild in Europe. He in turn tracked down Premier Smallwood at his hotel in Stockholm, where he was on a trip with John C. Doyle, the flamboyant developer we met in chapter 4, inspecting a laboratory that was processing samples from some of the Canadian Javelin concessions in Labrador. Joey went ballistic. He wrote in his memoirs, "I was convinced that if we nationalized the project and entered into partnership with Quebec, Newfoundland would truly get the rotten end of the stick."

In these dealings, Robert Winters was the point man for the financial group. He invited me to have lunch with him at the Quebec Winter Club shortly after René put his proposal to him. The premier knew about this meeting, and approved. My position was the same as it had been when I first reviewed the deal in 1963. We did not need a control group, but the two provinces would need an underwriting group, and the same three firms could certainly be involved (Hydro-Québec; Brinco; and Pitfield, McKay as the lead underwriter). No dice.

Later, the Canadian Imperial Bank of Commerce decided to hold its annual meeting in Quebec City. Bob Winters, being a senior director of the bank, obviously had much to do with this. Lesage would be attending the cocktail party that is always a part of these affairs, and he suggested that I go with him. (René made it clear that he had no intention of going.) I told Lesage that there was the risk of differences between us surfacing, and it would be better if I went on my own. He decided that the way around this was for him to go to the cocktail party at six o'clock, and for me to go an hour earlier. Philip Smith in his book on Brinco described my encounter with Winters at the party this way: "Kierans said that Brinco was an unnecessary middle-man. Winters bridled, and their conversation became so heated that other guests moved nervously away."

What resulted from our disagreements was a proposal for what came to be called "the Anglo-Saxon route." Newfoundland would cut Quebec out of the deal altogether; instead of building a transmission line from Labrador west through Quebec, it would send the power south across the Strait of Belle Isle to Newfoundland, across the Cabot Strait, and through New Brunswick and Nova Scotia to a line connecting with Consolidated Edison. This route was longer, fraught with much more difficulty — since it crossed deep water — and would be much more expensive. Yet it would have the advantage, Joey told his legislature, that "the project does not have to be controlled by a single authority outside of Newfoundland."

When he realized this would cost $350 million more than the western route, he did a complete about-face and opened talks with a New York firm on how much it would cost to nationalize Brinco, and bring the cost down. He then named John C. Doyle as his selling agent for the power.

I learned about all of this from Doyle himself. Joey had sent him to Quebec to press privately for a conclusion to the negotiations. He was told not to talk to Lesage, Lévesque, or me, because we were hostile to the deal. So, he wound up in the office of Claude Wagner, then the Quebec minister of justice. Wagner told him, "I think you've come to the wrong office," and offered him a choice of René or myself. He chose me as the lesser — I guess — of two evils.

He came rolling into my office exuding smiles and scent, and said, "You guys had better come to an agreement or we'll send the power the other way, down to New England. You won't get a kilowatt."

If the route had been practicable, this would have been a good argument, because it was becoming clear that Quebec would need the power. But I said, "That's the WASP line, it doesn't serve francophone Quebec at all, and it won't work."

Doyle suddenly barked, "Have you ever been to the falls, ever seen the actual site?"

When I admitted that I hadn't, he said, "Well, let's go, right now. I've got my Viscount standing by at the airport, we could fly out there, have a look, and be back here by late afternoon."

I said thanks, but no thanks. I wanted no part of any dealings that went through John Doyle.

No contract could be struck between Joey and Lesage (whom Joey, just to help things along, called "a shameless and scandalous liar from head to toe"). It was only after our election defeat in 1966 that a deal could be considered, under Daniel Johnson, the new premier. It was never understood or accepted by Newfoundland that, with all the power coming on from the Manicouagan and its string of hydro-electric power plants, Quebec had no immediate need for Churchill Falls. It was not until early 1966 that provincial projections indicated that we would require this huge new influx of power. Consolidated Edison had dropped out of the project several years earlier — too much politics! — so eventually, Premier Johnson approved a Hydro-Québec letter of intent to buy all the power from the Churchill Falls (Labrador) Corporation (CFLCO), which was to be the operating arm in the new arrangement.

That arrangement, signed on October 13, 1966, was based on a price structure that was put in place for forty years, with a later extension of another twenty-five years. Much has been made of this long term. Brian Tobin, the Newfoundland premier at the time of the writing of this book, has for instance charged, "The Churchill Falls agreement was arrived at in an unfair way."

He claimed that, by 1969, "CFLCO had spent $150 million, and faced financial ruin without a power contract." This is completely false. At the time of the contract, Hydro-Québec had invested $100 million in general mortgage bonds to back the project. Morgan Stanley, the American financial house, was in the process of issuing U.S. bonds worth $540 million (U.S.) and Canadian bonds worth $50 million. Quebec had also increased its share of CFLCO from the 20 per cent it held in Brinco to 34.2 per cent. The money on the table was not Newfoundland's; before it eventually took over Brinco's share of the operations in 1974, it owned only 8.9 per cent of the deal. So much for Tobin's claim.

Tobin then went on to allege that Hydro-Québec had "immense power," and "used that power mercilessly to gain a forty-year contract." This was Joey's paranoia, transmitted intact, and it is again completely false. The forty-year contract was demanded by Morgan Stanley, not Hydro-Québec. The bonds were a tough sell. There was only $83 million of equity in the project, and the debt load was $650 million, an immense leverage, likely to intimidate most bondholders. However, to amortize this debt over thirty years would have sent the annual payments soaring to the point that the project could not be justified. Since Morgan Stanley had to sell the bonds on a forty-year amortization basis, they demanded that Hydro-Québec be tied to a forty-year contract. Nothing else would have made sense.

In 1999 Premier Tobin went before the Montreal media to wave a "secret document" signed on February 1, 1984, outlining the need to "reach a compromise approach to a more equitable return to Newfoundland." Joey makes it clear in his memoirs that he saw the Churchill project as a deal that would mean that "during the forty-year contract with Hydro-Québec, Newfoundland will receive over $600 million." However, rising oil prices later meant that while Newfoundland was still making money, it might have made much more, because all power prices rose with oil. Quebec recognized this, and offered to sweeten the pot for Newfoundland. This is the document to which Tobin referred.

Premier Tobin wondered aloud, "What happened to this statement of intent?"

I can tell him. On March 30, 1984, then Newfoundland premier Brian Peckford turned down this offer flatly, and said he would be governed by the Supreme Court of Canada, where Newfoundland had taken the contract to test its validity. On May 3, 1984, the Supreme Court upheld the agreement. No more was heard from Newfoundland.

On May 17, 1984, Quebec repeated its willingness to renegotiate. No reply was forthcoming.

Now let us look at what happened when the power began to flow. By the year 2000, Newfoundland had made $2 billion in profits on Churchill Falls — more than three times the amount Joey cited in his memoirs. However, Hydro-Québec, during the same term, had made $14 billion, by reselling in the United States a resource that originally belonged to Newfoundland.* On an investment of $160 million, which is what Newfoundland paid to buy out Brinco in 1974, the province had done very well; its complaint was, and remains, that Quebec did even better.

Quebec, acting in good faith, struck a deal, which turned out to be more profitable than expected because of the huge jump in oil prices — and therefore all energy stocks — that began in the early 1970s. Recognizing this, Quebec has tried, time and again, to bring Newfoundland

* *Toronto Star*, 14 March 2000, D4.

back to the table, not to trade insults, but to strike a new bargain more favourable to Newfoundland. In March 2000, this process was still going on, and Brian Tobin was still stamping up and down the country crying that his province was being treated in a way that was "grossly unfair."

I cannot see how this is helpful to Newfoundland, Quebec, or Confederation.

Of lesser consequence, but of importance to me, is the manner in which Tobin seriously misquoted me. In an interview he had with Peter Gzowski on the CBC radio program *This Morning,* in March 2000, he claimed that when the contract was announced, I said that "I couldn't believe it." Moreover, I did *not* say that "a contract for twenty years would have been adequate to secure the risk and investment that Hydro-Québec was making." This was an outrageous misstatement.

Premier Tobin went on to say, "But, Hydro-Québec demanded and…according to Eric Kierans, to their astonishment, got agreement for a forty-year contract, with a twenty-five year renewal." This is another falsehood. I agreed with Morgan Stanley's assessment of the risk as requiring a forty-year contract. As for the twenty-five-year option, I know nothing of the reasons for it, or the quid pro quos gained from it. The deal was something agreed to after we left office.

Churchill Falls was not an unfair agreement, nor did the New-foundland government think so in 1974, five years after the original deal was signed, when it bought out Brinco's share for $160 million. We have already seen that Premier Smallwood thought he had crafted an enormously advantageous agreement for Newfoundland. When world oil prices surged, buyers of power at a fixed price gained more than sellers, obviously, but that is not a reason for breaking the contract, as the Supreme Court of Canada had already determined.

If Newfoundland's leaders were to accept the validity of the contract, the way would be opened for an expanded agreement covering all of Labrador's immense hydroelectric potential. This would be to the great benefit of two provinces that are compelled by geography to live together.

## SOMETIMES WE GO TOO FAST

Most of this still lay ahead when Lesage decided that Quebec needed a big steel company — not a publicly owned one, but a private firm with government backing. He was very close to Peter Thompson, the financier, and bullied him into agreeing to an arrangement where Thompson's company would put up $25 million — the province would buy $24 million in shares — and borrow another $200 million, backed by provincial bonds, to get the thing off the ground. It was the kind of deal that gets governments into trouble — always has, always will. The government would be putting up nine dollars to every one dollar from the entrepreneur, but would not have control. This was never discussed in cabinet, but the word was out on the street, and neither René nor I thought the proposal made sense.

I knew Peter Thompson well, and called him up to ask him what he was getting into.

He said, "I wish I knew, and if you can get me out, I'd be eternally grateful."

The next evening, I was down in Drummondville, speaking at the city's 150th-anniversary celebrations, and in the question period afterwards, somebody asked about it. I said, "Well, the cabinet has not discussed this yet, but I personally am not in favour. We would be putting up $224 million, and the private sector $25 million, for a project over which we would have no control. It doesn't seem to me the best way to go about it."

*Le Devoir* blossomed with a headline: "Kierans Dead Against Steel Mill" (translation).

I returned to Quebec for the Thursday cabinet meeting, and sitting in the anteroom was René, all by himself. He had two cups of coffee in his hand.

He said, "Jesus, Eric, one cup of coffee isn't going to be enough for what you're up against. Take 'em both."

I went into the cabinet room and took my seat, and Lesage just glowered at me. Discussion proceeded on various matters, but whenever I would start to say something, he would cut me off with a curt "Not you," and then go on to somebody else. After about an hour and a half of this, he suddenly turned to me and said, "Do you know what they did to Taché back in 1904?"

I said, "Yeah, they threw him out of the cabinet for breaking cabinet solidarity."

That took him aback, but he went on to say, "Then what do you mean by attacking the steel proposal?"

I said, "I answered a question at a very celebratory evening; I was just giving my opinion of a matter that had never been discussed in cabinet."

This slowed him down a little, although he was still sore. "You don't know how to protect yourself," he said. "This is going to come up in the assembly this afternoon, and you'd better handle it correctly."

Sure enough, that afternoon, Danny Johnson got up and tried to make a big deal about a cabinet split, but Charles Denis had rounded up enough precedents for me by then, on instances where ministers spoke out personally on matters that had not been passed by cabinet, and I got out of that one. I was forever grateful, though, for those two cups of coffee.

When the Sidérurgie du Québec finally emerged in 1968, under a Union Nationale government, it was as a Crown corporation. Later, René, as premier, appointed me to the board.

### RENÉ HAS HIS OWN EXPLANATION: ERIC'S IRISH

Lesage also got mad at me because I consistently opposed the idea of bringing in lotteries to raise money. I said they used to put people in jail for the numbers racket, and now governments wanted in on it, but it was still a rip-off. Lesage said, "What you don't seem to understand is that we need the money."

Well, I knew we needed the money, but that didn't mean you could do anything to get it, without regard to its moral or practical consequences. The debate in cabinet was getting to the point that Lesage was beginning to swell and turn red, when René piped up.

"It's easy to know why Eric is against provincial lotteries," he said.

"What's that?" asked Lesage.

"He's Irish," said René. "He knows if you bring in provincial lotteries, it will kill the Irish Sweepstakes." Everybody laughed, and the tension seeped out of the room. And the Lesage government did not bring in lotteries.

### THE NORANDA BATTLE

Shortly after I became revenue minister, I learned that René was planning a reform of the nineteenth-century Mining Act. We got onto the subject of Noranda Mines, whose copper mines at Murdochville had been the site of one of the prolonged strikes that helped to usher in the Quiet Revolution. I told René that Quebec was not receiving sufficient economic rent for our resources, particularly from the mining industry. We were spending more in support of the industry than we were getting back in revenues. René, who had no love for the giant firm, flew up to Rouyn, in the heart of the corporate fiefdom, to issue a stern warning that if Noranda did not learn to behave in "a civilized fashion," it might be necessary to find "structures other than the traditional ones used to run the mining industry."

Not easy to miss the implication that if Noranda didn't behave, it would be nationalized, and Noranda responded by claiming that René was nothing but a tool of the Steelworkers union. The upshot was a meeting between Noranda president Jack Bradfield and René, which turned into a shouting match on both sides. At one point René got so mad that he smashed his hand down on a table, and broke the glass top. Bradfield then asked if he could speak instead to René's colleague, Eric Kierans, who, he was sure, would be more reasonable. René, who knew me a lot better than Bradfield did, begged him to do so.

The result of that was another argument, this time with me, although I didn't break any tabletops. Bradfield threatened that if he couldn't get assurances that Quebec would refrain from interfering in the mining sector, Noranda would redirect its investments to Ireland.

"Fine," I told him. "Do they have any copper in Ireland?"

We couldn't move Lesage to take any measures strong enough to make the mines pay a fairer share to the province. In the end, René felt the same way as Lesage. He found it tough enough to put in place a modern act without trying to raise taxes at the same time. I confess that I had to agree with the reasoning. The increase in taxes would come later.

## A CLOSE SHAVE

René, who was very combative himself, seemed to have a built-in alarm system that went off when he thought I was about to go too far. This happened once around the time when Ottawa had started to offer money for higher education — a field, up until then, entirely within provincial jurisdiction — and Quebec, refusing the grants, felt it had to make good on the money itself. Paul Gérin-Lajoie, as education minister, brought a proposal to cabinet for allotting the provincial money to the various universities. With respect to McGill, he had three options to put before us.

Under one, McGill would get about $90,000 a year; another option would give McGill $800,000; and the third, $3 million.* I naturally felt that McGill, which was falling further and further behind the Université de Montréal, should get the middle amount at least; Gérin-Lajoie wanted it to be the lowest. The debate was going on with a good deal of heat when René suddenly jumped up and said we needed to take a break. I went over to him and said, "What was that all about?"

He said, "You were just about to call Paul a racist." René wasn't wrong, but he wasn't right, either. I might have been on the verge of making an injudicious comment, but I knew Paul was not a racist in any way. At most, I might have said that some people would call the decision a racist one, but that's all. Anyway, René called a recess, and the crisis passed, although the issue remained contentious for some time after that.

McGill and the *Montreal Star* claimed that McGill and Laval deserved as much as the Université de Montréal, but the fact was that growth at these two institutions had remained stagnant over the previous year. Laval's growth was stalled by the creation of the Université de Sherbrooke; McGill's, obviously, by the increasing emphasis in the province on higher education in French. In these circumstances, it was reasonable that the Université de Montréal's share should be higher than the other two, but the flak from English Montreal was loud and continuing.

I offered to talk to the McGill authorities, and Lesage agreed enthusiastically. Lorne Gales, head of the McGill alumni association, arranged a Saturday morning meeting with the McGill board of governors, where I had the agreement of Paul Gérin-Lajoie and the cabinet to discuss the division of funds. In this way, peace was restored.

## THE LIQUOR STRIKE

Lesage was in many ways a very old-fashioned man. His hero, as I have already indicated, was Mackenzie King, whom Frank Scott once skewered

---

* Memory is not as exact as it should be, but the proportions are about right.

in a poem that noted, "never do anything by halves that you can do by quarters." Jean was a Quebec nationalist, even a strident one at times, but he would never venture close to anything that threatened the Canadian federation, even if it was no longer the federation originally envisioned. He also had a profound, and increasing, sense of self-worth and dignity, which was bound to lead so irascible and irreverent a soul as René into trouble.

René was constantly saying things to the press that outraged Lesage, but Lesage was patient, and knew that much of his government's popularity, especially among younger voters, depended on René. One day, however, Jean obviously thought he had to take action.

The premier was in Montreal during the middle of a strike by the liquor control board employees, and we were getting a lot of political heat from thirsty voters. He was asked by a reporter when he thought the strike would be over, and he said, "The workers should listen to me. I'm on their side. The unions are doing a lot of damage and the men should listen to me, because I am the premier of the province and I will see that they are taken care of."

That very night in the evening session of the legislature, while Lesage was still in Montreal, Danny Johnson brought this up and began to needle René. "The premier is the father of us all," he said, "and he is telling the union members to listen to him and not their leaders."

René said, "Well, I am telling them — ne lachez pas!" (Don't let go.)

A special evening cabinet meeting was called as soon as Lesage got back from Montreal, and I wandered into it completely unaware of its purpose.

Lesage began attacking René in a very hostile and personal way, complaining that he was a man without loyalty. When Jean got around to the "ne lachez pas" remark, he said it directly contradicted him (which, of course, it did). George Marler led the series of nods of approval as Lesage tore strips off René; then René started to answer back.

I could see that this was going to end in a very bad way; as Lesage continued, it seemed that somebody was going to have to go, "Why is it always you? I never have trouble with anybody else, and if we have difficulties, we iron them out in private. Nobody else ever told the unions, 'Well, you must obey your leaders.'"

I blurted out, "Ce n'est pas vrai!" (That's not true.)

Lesage whirled around and glared at me. "What have you to say?"

"René isn't the only one," I said.

Now he was really mad. "Who else?" he demanded.

"Well, it was me."

"I didn't see that in any of the papers."

"It wasn't in the papers. The woman who cleans our house told my wife that she was terribly worried because her husband worked in a liquor store, and he was on strike. Now here was the premier saying he should ignore his union leaders and go back to work, and he didn't know what to do. When Terry came to me with this, I told her to go back and tell that woman that her husband was to obey what the union leaders said, or he could be in very great trouble later on. So that is what Terry told her."

Lesage said, again, "Well, I didn't see that in the paper."

And I said, "What difference does that make?"

Lesage glowered at me, threw his pen down on the cabinet table in disgust, and said, "Time to get into the assembly."

As we started to file out of the cabinet room, René came around the table and came up to me from behind, and he just reached out and squeezed my arm above the elbow. He didn't say a word.

That evening, I got a telephone call from Dominique Clift, one of the finest journalists covering the legislature, and he said, "I hear you saved René from being kicked out of the cabinet."

I said, "I have no idea what you are talking about." What we did not need at that point was a public rehashing of the cabinet meeting.

## SEND NOT TO ASK FOR WHOM...

René was often plunged into trouble simply by giving a straightforward answer to a question, instead of treating every query as a potential trap — as a trained politician should do, apparently. Premier Lesage called me one morning at 7 a.m. and asked, "Have you read *Le Devoir* this morning?"

"No."

"Well, your friend has done it again. Quebec is going to buy out Bell Telephone. Are you in on this?"

"No, and I don't believe René is either."

"Well, the Clarendon Hotel won't put me through to René's room.

You better try and straighten this out. Let me know what it's all about. There will be questions in the assembly this afternoon."

*Le Devoir* blazoned the headline, all right. Sure enough, it implied that the province, according to René, was about to nationalize the telephone giant.

The Clarendon put me through to a sleepy Lévesque, who explained that he had gone to Portneuf the night before at the invitation of about twenty young Liberals to talk about the future. As usual, it was the question period afterwards, not the remarks (never prepared) by René that caused the fuss. He was asked, "Could Quebec nationalize Bell as it did Shawinigan?"

He replied, "Of course, it *could* be done."

A stringer for *Le Devoir* took it from there, and René still couldn't see that there was anything wrong with discussing the possibility. We had lunch that day in the parliamentary cafeteria, at twelve noon sharp, with everyone wondering what was going on.

I asked René, "If you had a billion dollars, would you use it first to take over Bell?"

"Are you crazy?" Then he looked at me and started to laugh. He recited a list of the most important problems we needed to address: "Welfare, homelessness, poverty, education…"

"Good," I said. "I will tell Jean that when Johnson asks the question in assembly, he is to point the finger at you."

Sure enough, Danny was on his feet first thing to ask about the supposed pending takeover of Bell, adding that René seemed to have lots of money for such things, even if Lesage didn't. René savaged Johnson, explained the difference between "would" and "could," and recited all the things that needed doing long before the province would even consider such action. He went on so long that the Speaker had to shut him up. Lesage really enjoyed himself.

## LESAGE PUTS RENÉ AND ME TOGETHER

René and I worked very well together, in the legislative house and out. We played some tennis together, as a pair. He was very fast, a good athlete, and very aggressive, so as soon as he could he would get up to the net, while I stayed back at the baseline, and we won some games that way. When Lesage shuffled his cabinet in the fall of 1965, he had the brilliant idea of putting us together in a more obvious way. He did this by moving René from Natural Resources to Family and Social Welfare, and myself from Revenue to Health. (René insisted on keeping responsibility for Hydro-Québec as part of his portfolio.) We immediately announced at a joint press conference that we were going to work as a team in the whole area of social welfare; as René put it, "Over the next two years, we're going to marry Health and Welfare."

One advantage of this pairing turned up quite quickly, in Drummondville. The Ministry of Family and Social Welfare had built a retirement home in the city, a really super, new facility, which, it turned out, was not much wanted. There were a lot of private retirement homes for one thing, and for another, at this time, the farm families who made up much of the surrounding population looked after their own old folks. Now this splendid facility had been built, and it looked as if it might not be used. When the matter was brought to René, he said, "Well, it looks to me as if this would suit Eric more than us. It has all the facilities for a convalescent hospital. Why don't we give it to him?"

If it is not the *first* rule of politics, it is among the *top* ones that a cabinet minister does not give up a valuable property — and the opportunities for an official opening, a ribbon-cutting, etc. — without getting something in return; but within a very short time, René had instructed his deputy minister to get in touch with mine, and the transfer took place. Of course, it raised another problem for me. I had been screaming for convalescent hospitals and now I had one, but I had to get the nuns to run it. I went over to call on a nursing order on Decarie Boulevard, and they gave me a very rough ride indeed. The provincial takeover of most of the hospital system was what was depriving them of postulants and allowing a swarm of lay people to be paid good money to do the work that the nuns did for nothing. Three of the older nuns let me know in no uncertain language that they were not pleased with me, before they agreed to look at the Drummondville facility.

I never found out exactly how it worked out. I held the Health portfolio for less than a year when we suffered a stunning and — I have to say now — deserved defeat at the polls on June 5, 1966. We had made too many changes too fast, without sufficiently informing the Quebec people of what we were doing, and they resented it. Lesage, the canny politician, was becoming a little too convinced of his own worth, and was throwing his increasing weight around a little too freely. Daniel Johnson, the Union Nationale leader, was equally shrewd, and ran a campaign that seemed to say to the voters that they could keep all the gains made under the Quiet Revolution, and still hand a rebuke to the Liberals. And Quebecers did just that.

In the run-up to this election, René and I — and Lesage, too — learned something about the limits of our power. We had drawn up a budget for the province's capital spending over the next year and had decided that we were in danger of taking on too much debt, so the limit of new borrowing was to be kept at $500 million. Lesage, René, and I met with the president of Hydro-Québec, who agreed that we certainly had the right to lay down such guidelines. But he added, "Of course you understand that this means we will have to delay the construction on Manic-5."

Because the Churchill Falls deal was still up in the air, Quebec needed to get to work right away on other sources of hydro, and Manic-5 (now the Daniel Johnson Dam), on the Manicouagan River, was the largest of a series of dams that would, coincidentally, be putting thousands of Quebecers to work as the election campaign of 1966 unfolded. This would require borrowing by Hydro-Québec over the next year of — as it happened — $500 million. If we kept the cap on, either nothing else could be done, or Manic-5 could not go ahead.

"Oh," said Lesage, and, "Ah." The premier glanced at René and me, thanked us for coming, and bade us farewell, while he remained behind, with the president of Hydro-Québec.

It did not take long to revise the capital spending plans, and Manic-5 went ahead, just as Hydro-Québec intended. Hydro engineers are always five to eight years ahead of their political masters. Within two days of the original budget decision, the premier received a letter in which Hydro-Québec stated that its capital needs for the coming year would amount to $500 million.

## THE BREAKUP

After our election defeat, I moved over to the Opposition benches, and I shared an office with Robert Bourassa, a brilliant young economist who was obviously a far better politician than I. He seemed to spend hours every day on the telephone, working a large circle of contacts all over the province — the contacts, no doubt, who would eventually become his inner team when he moved to seek the party leadership and, ultimately, the premiership.

René threw himself into the task of reforming the Liberal party. Lesage, at this point, seemed to be in the depths of despair, and not up to the task of either absorbing why we had been beaten or making the necessary changes to regain power. But there were others, including Paul Gérin-Lajoie, René, myself, Bourassa, and sometimes Pierre Laporte, who were determined to get back into office to finish the job of reform we had begun. The centre of this activity was the St. Denis Group, and it was in this band of some twenty participants that René proposed that I be supported as president of the Quebec Liberal Federation.

René had begun serious work on a new program for the party, with a group of his followers, and the splits within the party became so clear that three members of the St. Denis Group — René, Robert Bourassa, and Paul Gérin-Lajoie — were named as a sort of special committee to work out a compromise with the mainstream. When the Quebec Liberal Federation convention opened in November 1966, I was elected to the presidency, but the two men who ran with me were defeated, and the outgoing president, Dr. Irenée Lapierre, described me in a radio interview as "Lévesque's puppet" — a rather ironic title, considering what was to follow.

It was my presidency of the Quebec Liberal Federation that gave me the unpleasant but unavoidable task of ushering René out of the party, perhaps the saddest experience of my career.

In our private talks, it was clear that René's idea of a new program for the party was, in fact, effectively a separatist approach, and I could not accept it. Moreover, I was certain that the Quebec population would not follow him.

He made his position formal in a 6,000-word pamphlet he produced in September 1967, called "An Option for Quebec," which nailed the separatist banner to the mast.

One of the first calls I got when news of this hit the media was from Walter Gordon, who seemed to be in a bit of a panic, and thought the country was about to be torn apart, if not the next day, very shortly. Walter was now president of the Privy Council, as well as being a friend of Pearson's. He said, "I've just been talking to the prime minister about this, and he's very troubled." He added, "Are you with René on this?"

"Certainly not!" I told him. "But don't worry, René can't win on this one."

He said, "That's the best news I've heard in a long time. I'll call Mike right away and tell him what you said."

I called Lesage, who seemed to hesitate about what to do and whether or not we had to do anything right away about René's move, so I told him, "You have to make up your mind. We have got to get to work on this thing right away. The question is whether or not we are going to stand up for Canada."

He was not exactly overjoyed to hear it put that way, but finally agreed, and I began at once to plan a series of speeches and visits across the province to test the waters and shore up our position.

René and I were not the sort of people to hang back and keep our views to ourselves, so it very soon became clear that we had a real and irreconcilable difference of opinion on where the Liberal Federation, and the province, should be heading.

We agreed to debate the issues on *The Public Eye,* a CBC television program hosted by Warner Troyer. When I went into the studio, René was already there, early for once, standing and talking to one of his aides and one of the CBC types. He looked tired, rumpled, worried — although that might have been my imagination. This was the man with whom I had been through so much in just a few short years; not merely a political ally, but a genuine friend, who had stood by me time and again when it really counted. And now, we were about to embark on a bitter battle over issues that mattered deeply to both of us, so deeply that we could not, with all the good will in the world, put them aside.

He looked up when he saw me, gave a kind of rueful grin, and came across, with his hand held out.

"Eric," he said, "I'm sorry."

I took his hand, shook it, held it for a long time.

"Look," I said, "I'm sorry, too."

———·•·———

# Seven

# THE RUN FOR THE LEADERSHIP

*To be Prime Minister of Canada, you need the hide of a rhinoceros, the morals of St. Francis, the patience of Job, the wisdom of Solomon, the strength of Hercules, the leadership of Napoleon, the magnetism of a Beatle and the subtlety of Machiavelli.*

— LESTER B. PEARSON, 1965 SPEECH

THE CLIMACTIC CONVENTION THAT would change Quebec politics forever opened on Friday, October 13, 1967, at the Château Frontenac in Quebec City. After the usual formalities, the first item on the agenda was my report, as party president, on the past year and the current status of the party. I saw no point in tiptoeing around the main issue before us, so I made it clear in that opening address that separatism was a perfectly fair option to offer to the people of the province, but Mr. Lévesque could not expect to carry a motion advocating separatism using the Liberal party as a promoter of his plan. René was standing at the back of the hall, and I looked directly at him as I said, "Let those who want to pursue the separatist option dig their own trench." He looked straight back at me, and nodded his head.

After my speech, I handed the gavel over to Jean Tetreault, the man whom I had defeated for the Liberal Federation presidency the year before,* and who knew far more than I did about the mechanics of conventions. He did a superb job, as I knew he would, which is why we had made this arrangement beforehand.

---

* Irenée Lapierre, the party president who called me "Lévesque's puppet," did not run for re-election in 1966; Tetreault stood in his place.

The strategy arrived at — and not by me, despite much that has been written since (this was not an area in which I had any experience) — was to make the fight turn on procedural matters. Otherwise, we would be handing René a platform to drag up every grievance in Quebec from 1759 onwards. René was insisting on a secret ballot for the program resolution based on the "Option for Quebec" pamphlet, which set forth the separatist position, and which he had had passed by his own riding association. It struck me as rather bizarre that you would vote in secret on such a momentous public issue during an open political convention. But if this is what he wanted, René would have to put forward a motion to amend the agenda. All we had to do was to make sure that resolution was soundly defeated, and the battle would be over, because everyone would be able to see that we had the necessary votes in hand.

I had been up and down the country, on a Canadian Club speaking tour, and up and down the province, and I was very sure that the convention was going to lead to a resounding defeat for René. I wasn't particularly happy about it, not only because of our friendship, but because I was bound to be seen as the one who forced him out of the party, and I would pay a political price for it. The example of Dalton Camp and John Diefenbaker was not one anybody could miss.

The day before the convention, I had met with Blair Fraser, the *Maclean's* magazine correspondent in Ottawa; Charlie Lynch, Southam's top political columnist; and Tom Earl, one of the best CBC men in Ottawa. They were very hard on me for forcing this issue with René, and had some doubt as to whether he could even be defeated. I pointed out that I had criss-crossed the province and I knew how the vote would go; they were sure I was wrong. I told them that the vote against taking the separatist route would be supported overwhelmingly. They looked wise and dubious, as journalists will, but they had not been out talking to the delegates, and I had.

As it happened, René put forward his motion on procedure, and was defeated by about 850 votes to 50.

He had lost, and everybody in the convention hall knew it.

The debate raged on all that evening, as René's group kept on bringing up new points, but under Tetreault's skilful handling of the rules of debate, the rehashing of ancient grievances was not permitted to dominate the meeting.

The sting was gone, and I doubt if a single mind was changed by anything said that night.

Within minutes of the adjournment motion at the end of the evening, there were the usual meetings in hotel rooms to wheel and deal. One of the great practitioners of this sport was Maurice Sauvé, a man of great charm and even greater ambition, who was at this time the minister of forestry in the Pearson government. He wanted to be the grand conciliator, to patch up the rift between René and me. The problem was that this was not some sort of personal tiff; it was a real and fundamental difference of opinion on the future of Quebec and Canada. It could not be compromised away. Even before the convention opened, Sauvé had gone to call on Pierre Laporte, who was at this time the House leader as well as minister of labour, and Laporte said, "Go and see Eric."

I declined to see him, because I knew this had to do with Sauvé's ambitions, not the party's needs, and I also knew that, going by past performance, whatever was said under the cover of confidentiality would soon be staring at us from the front pages of the newspapers. He went back to Laporte, who agreed to a meeting in his room on Saturday morning, so I went along to that.

Pierre said, "Okay, Maurice, you've got five minutes."

Sauvé then launched into a little speech full of vague generalities and the will to compromise, at the end of which Pierre said, "Okay, Maurice, your five minutes are up." I agreed, and that was that.

However, we had another problem facing us. Paul Gérin-Lajoie was determined to push through a report, as chairman of the Liberal Federation's committee on the constitution, which called on the federal government to recognize the "special status" of Quebec. Daniel Johnson had been putting forward a version of this since he became premier, and Gérin-Lajoie seemed determined to outbid Danny on the subject.

Among other things, his report called for Quebec to become a republic, but at the same time retain its rights to Canadian citizenship under a broad special status that would reduce federal powers, or require joint federal-provincial jurisdiction, in international agreements, financial institutions, and offshore mineral rights.

The crucial section read:

> The Liberal Party of Quebec, based on the report by the Constitutional Affairs Committee submitted to the Convention of the Quebec Liberal Federation on 14 October 1967 affirms that…
>
> 4. It believes nevertheless that a new Canadian constitution, including special status and increased powers for Quebec through a new division between the federal Parliament and that of Quebec, can best serve the political, economic, cultural and social interests of the French Canadians.

These sweeping changes had never even been discussed within the party, and Paul wanted the convention to adopt his report without further ado. He wouldn't even talk about it, insisting that he would say what he had to say on the floor of the convention. Pierre Laporte and I persuaded Lesage to order Paul to come to his suite at noon on Saturday, before the convention reconvened, to meet with the strategy group to discuss this. Lesage called Paul, and the upshot, soon after in his suite, was one of those free and frank exchanges of views the diplomats talk about when they want to avoid the words "flaming row."

I said we would not allow a vote on his report until the party had at least had a chance to read it and react to it; and if he persisted, I said, "I will get up and move that it be transferred to a committee for further study."

"Oh?" he said. "And who will second the motion?"

Gérard Lévesque, a senior member of the Lesage cabinet, said, "I will," and Paul knew he was licked. And we knew that when René walked out of the party, as he was bound to do within hours, no major figures would go with him.

When the convention reopened at 2 p.m., René took five minutes to make a final speech. He used it to thank the convention for permitting him to present his argument, and went on to say that his opponents in that debate had not really given a separate status for Quebec their serious consideration, but instead had merely tried to create the impression that independence would lead to anarchy. I thought this was a little unfair; what we had said was that it would lead to instability and carry enormous economic consequences for Quebec and for Canada, but there was no point in rehashing all that.

When he finished, with great dignity, René left the platform, walked down the centre aisle to the exit, and left the convention, and the Liberal party, forever. About fifty of his supporters went with him. René tried to have his resolution withdrawn, but it could not be under the rules of order, and it went to a vote. It gained exactly four votes in favour.

However, there was still the Gérin-Lajoie matter to be dealt with. We had agreed at our strategy session that I would move it to a committee for further study, with Gérard Lévesque seconding, but Pierre Laporte beat me to a floor microphone and proposed the motion for removal for further study, including a general statement opposing separatism "in any form." That motion passed by a show of hands, reported in the press as 1,500 votes for and 7 votes against. René's backers, and there were certainly many of them, had mostly left the convention by this time.

It was done, but no one, least of all me, thought that that was the end of the matter. René was too shrewd, too determined, too charismatic a politician to write off, and I was the last person to want that to happen. What I wanted was to ensure that my party, the Liberal party, was not hijacked into support of a separatism that I knew most of its members did not support.

### I AM ASSIGNED THE SPOILER ROLE

Inevitably, I came in for a good deal of criticism for driving René out of the party, although I think the truth is that he had decided quite some time earlier that it was unlikely that he would be able to bend the party to his way of thinking; his resignation was actually inevitable. Logic insisted that he would start his own party, and he did, although it was called a "movement," at first. That did not help my case.

About a week after the events I have described, Terry and I were driving somewhere in Quebec City with Corinne Lesage and another friend, and the talk turned to René's departure. It was clear that everybody was very sorry that he was gone, and I realized that I was in for it. Sure enough, pretty soon there was a lot of talk about the fact that I had been too hard on René, and that perhaps some sort of compromise might have been worked out that would have allowed him to remain within the party. I didn't believe it for a minute.

During one of the public debates René and I had participated in together, I said, "René and I are two predictable people. I knew he was heading to this. He knew I would fight him."

René agreed. "Basically, I am a Quebecer first, and Eric is a Canadian first."

There was no middle ground between those two positions, but I knew I was never going to persuade many of my colleagues of that. The press was very severe with me, by and large; I was a roughneck, and not a very good politician (I was willing to agree with that, anyway), and I should have found a way to keep René in the party.

## OTTAWA CALLS

During all the lead-up to the provincial convention, another matter was preying on my mind, and the reaction to my role in the affairs at the convention brought it back to the fore. During the autumn of 1966, after our defeat at the hands of Danny Johnson, I was approached by Richard Nielson, one of the CBC's top producers. There were a lot of stories floating around that Prime Minister Pearson was getting ready to step down (he made it official at a cabinet meeting on December 14, not long after this) and Nielson wanted to know if I would be running for the federal job.

Paul Gérin-Lajoie put it somewhat differently. "I guess you'll be going after this, now," he sneered.

I hadn't given it much thought, but when Nielson said he was certain that I would get a good deal of support from across the country, I did begin to take it more seriously. It was clear that there was going to be a bust-up in the party — Jean Lesage was actually booed at the convention that elected me to the provincial presidency — and my political options within the province began to look narrower and narrower. I made a number of calls to see if there was any support for me, and found there was. I did not think I was likely to be elected (although this was before the unrolling of Trudeaumania made even that slim prospect beyond the realm of possibility), but I did think I should take the chance to make a clear and forceful argument about reshaping the Canadian political and economic system closer to the Confederation of 1867.

Accordingly, I worked for several months on *Challenge of Confidence,* which was a small book that embodied the main ideas I meant to promote as a leadership candidate, slated for publication by Jack McClelland of McClelland and Stewart.

So, while the battle inside the Quebec Liberal Federation was going on, there was, in the background, this other challenge still ahead of me.

I had lunch with Peter Newman of the *Toronto Star* just before the convention, and asked him what he thought of my chances in the federal race, since it looked as if I was going to become a drug on the market provincially. A few days after the convention, I got a letter from Newman that said he had been in Toronto talking to Beland Honderich, the *Star* publisher. Peter wrote: "I was astounded by the fact that he and I had quite independently come to the same conclusion — namely, that you were the best possible choice to be the next leader of the Federal Liberal Party."

(When I pointed this out a few days later to my friend Walter Stewart, he noted that the *Star* had been picking mayors for the city of Toronto since the turn of the century, and had never seen one of its choices elected. He said the backing of the *Star,* even if it lasted through the federal convention — which it didn't — was such that, with it and a dime, I could make a phone call. A cynical man, Stewart, as well as, at this time, a *Star* employee.)

*Challenge of Confidence* (which was co-published in French by Les Éditions du Jour) was launched in Ottawa less than two weeks after René's resignation, and Peter Newman wrote a laudatory column about the book and me. Peter and Dick Nielson seemed to be my principal cheerleaders at this time, and I think their enthusiasm had a lot to do with my plunging ahead.

I had a press conference in Ottawa, which was well attended by, among others, Walter Gordon, who sat at the back of the room and smiled a lot. In the press conference, it became clear that I thought Walter was on the right track in his concerns about the Canadian economy, but that I also thought he wanted to restore the balance too quickly. I said I thought it would take ten or fifteen years to restore real Canadian independence (what an optimist I was!), and I looked back at Walter, who just smiled and shook his head. Not fast enough for him, obviously.

The book called for a return to the original British North America Act division of federal and provincial powers, and a revitalized Canadian nationalism. I advocated dividing government spending powers on the basis of production and distribution, with Ottawa responsible for sustaining economic growth through nationwide fiscal and monetary policy, while the provinces looked after the distribution aspects — health, education, and social welfare. I said that medicare should be given top priority, and that a properly run medicare system was not only something Canada could afford, but was something we could not afford to do without.

In a way, this was shadowboxing; I certainly wanted to get these ideas out and debated, but the leadership race was not on yet. The Conservatives had had their leadership convention, a good deal more acrimonious even than our Quebec one, and John Diefenbaker had been ousted, mainly by the efforts of Dalton Camp, the party president. The new Tory leader was the laconic and likeable Robert Stanfield of Nova Scotia.

Pearson made his resignation announcement on December 14, 1967, and a convention was called for April 1968 in Ottawa. I was the first one into the race, which turned out in the end to be no race at all, but a waltz to coronation for Pierre Elliott Trudeau, then federal minister of justice as well as the leader of the Three Wise Men from Quebec.* He did not officially announce his entry into the contest until February 16, by which time the field was crowded with no fewer than eight federal cabinet ministers: Paul Martin, Robert Winters, Joe Greene, Paul Hellyer, Allan MacEachen, Mitchell Sharp, John Turner, and Trudeau. Sharp dropped out on the very eve of the convention and threw his support behind Pierre.

Up to that time, my major connection with Trudeau had come in the spring of 1964, when I was minister of revenue in Quebec, and he one of the editors of *Cité Libre*. He called to say that he would like to have a chat with me, and I was happy to comply. We agreed to meet in the Quebec parliamentary restaurant, but when we got there there were no tables for two, so we sat at one for four. Within a couple of minutes, Charles Taylor came by and asked to join us, and soon after that, along came René, who immediately said, "What's going on here?" and sat

---

* The Three Wise Men were the trio who came to Ottawa together from Quebec: Trudeau, Marchand, and Pelletier. In French, they were "Les Trois Colombes" — the three doves.

down. That ended any chance of a serious talk between Pierre and myself, so we agreed to meet instead after the assembly rose that night. Thus it came about that, after 10 p.m., we sat in the darkened legislative chamber debating nationalism.

Fortunately, I had read Elie Kedourie's *Nationalism,* which had come out in 1960, and had obviously interested Trudeau deeply. Kedourie was a professor of politics at the London School of Economics, and an expert on the Middle East, where nationalism is and has been a pretty devastating force from time to time. The book, which is still in print, is a classic. Pierre could have written it himself except that he believed that nationalism would always turn sour and tyrannical, whereas Kedourie's view was somewhat broader. He was able to see some positive attributes, as well as negative ones, to nationalism. My own belief is that if a nation fails to look after its own interests, no other nation will. I was certainly more nationalist than Trudeau, but I could see at once the power of that illuminating intellect, even if I didn't always agree with it.

Not long after Pearson's announcement, while he was in the West Indies on holiday, the Liberals lost an important vote on a tax measure in the House of Commons, a gaffe that should have led to an immediate election. The defeat was brought about by a series of blunders; not only were the Liberals in a minority position, many of their own members (including Walter Gordon) opposed the tax measure under discussion. Somehow after the defeat, Pearson, hustling back to Ottawa, and with the support of Louis Rasminsky, the Bank of Canada governor, was able to talk Stanfield, the new Tory leader, into allowing an adjournment. The government regrouped, and remained in office. The effect of all this was to convince many of the Liberal faithful that the party's old guard was incompetent; it was time for a radically new kind of leader. Translation: Pierre Elliott Trudeau.

I had sounded out Jean Lesage before taking the plunge, and he had advised me strongly not to do it. He said I had no hope of winning, because I had no position in the federal party, and indeed many of the federal Liberals were mad at me because of the way I had shown them up over the U.S. corporate guidelines. About half the delegates, he told me, would be unelected appointees of the Liberal party machine, and they were going to be picked by, and committed to, the cabinet ministers, who were going to have a lot more clout with the delegates than I.

I thanked Jean for his very wise counsel, and paid no attention to it. Something happens to you when one of these contests kicks off; I kept assuring myself that I had no possible chance of winning, that I was running merely to get my ideas out into the marketplace of public discussion, but at the same time, in the back of my head, was a "what if?" What if? — the most illusive and seductive phrase in politics. At the same time, I felt that I had to do something about the widening gap between Quebec and the rest of Canada, and the best avenue available to me was a leadership campaign.

A number of books have been written about that leadership campaign, and I have no great insights to add to them. I persuaded my son, Tom, to take a leave of absence from his senior job with the investment firm Nesbitt, Thomson. This was graciously granted by Deane Nesbitt, with full pay for the three-month period. So, my son became chairman of the Kierans for Canada Committee. Then I called Charles Denis, by this time working in the Ministry of Education in Quebec City, and said, "Let's form the old team and go for the Liberal leadership."

He wanted to know what my chances were, and I told him, "I think I can pull it off." He agreed to handle the French media for the campaign, while Richard Gwyn, then working for *Time* magazine, handled the English-language media, mostly from behind the scenes.

One of the highlights of the campaign, for me at least, was a speech I made to students at McGill, with less than two weeks before the convention, on the subject of Canadian foreign policy. Many students at this time were becoming increasingly hostile to what they saw as Canada's, and especially Lester Pearson's, complicity in the American war in Vietnam, and most of the candidates skirted this issue. I saw no reason to do so, and said:

> The Vietnam War is wrong, period. The Canadian government should publicly declare that we oppose the war and the continuation of it by either side. We should halt all arms sales to belligerents.

Well, at least that was clear, which was more than you could say for most of the other candidates' statements. I also declared that Canada should withdraw from NATO and NORAD. This speech received a fair amount of praise from non-Liberal commentators, but it was not exactly what the party insiders wanted to hear. They had, after all, been the architects of our approach to date. That policy was a monument to hypocrisy. We were, on the one hand, one of three nations on the International Control Commission (the others were India and Poland), a body specifically set up under the United Nations to block the shipment of arms to Vietnam. On the other hand, and at the same time, we were selling as many explosives, bombs, and military hardware as we could to the United States, under the Defence Production Sharing Agreement. No one wanted me to point this out; Trudeau did one of his famous dances all around the subject, and left it at that. Wise fellow.

My leadership campaign cost $194,000, of which $40,000 came from outside sources and $154,000 from my own resources. I had many occasions to be grateful for the fact that Canadian Adhesives, which I still owned, was turning over a nice profit every year, or I could never have done this.

Terry was wonderful throughout, as was Tom, as was my daughter, Cathy. If they thought I was crazy, they never allowed a hint of discouragement to escape their lips.

## MY, AHEM, LEADERSHIP STRATEGY

My strategy, if you could call it that, was to bypass the party machinery — which was never going to work for me, anyway — and to cross the country and talk to as many delegates and potential delegates as I could, to convince them that I was a new man with new ideas. And that is what the Liberal party needed at the time.

They agreed, but they had their eye on another new man, Pierre Trudeau, who became an instant and overwhelming media favourite because of his wit, quick mind, and, let's face it, sex appeal.

The convention was held in the Ottawa Civic Centre; Trudeau went down, with his entourage, in a privately leased railway car, which was attached to the regular Montreal-Ottawa noon train. I drove. The convention was marked by the usual nonsense — girls with pom-poms; hospitality suites (Trudeau had eight of them); press releases by the score; saturation media coverage; hopelessly crowded conditions on the floor for delegates and onlookers; and a lot of pointless backroom meetings to divvy up delegates, who, in the end, often refused to be divvied up, and voted as they meant to anyway.

The voting was done on an IBM "Votamatic" machine — apparently invented by Rube Goldberg — which was to collate the results from thirty-seven scarlet booths, where the delegates voted alphabetically, and very slowly.

The first ballot took more than an hour to cast and count, and when the results were announced at 3:16 p.m. on April 4, Trudeau had 752 votes, and I had 103. I was last. It was time to withdraw, which I did, while refusing to deliver my delegates to anyone else. "I am not having any discussion other than a friendly one with other candidates," I said. My votes had come mainly from Quebec, and from British Columbia, where Pat McGeer and Art Phillips had been towers of strength.

I went back to my seat in the stadium, in the box over the rink, and a reporter came up to me and said, "Just before the announcement of the results, I saw your face pale as if you had been shocked. Did they tell you the results before the announcement?"

I said, "No, what I just heard was that Martin Luther King had been assassinated in Memphis, Tennessee."

A few minutes later, in the box next to me, where Paul Hellyer was sitting, Judy LaMarsh came up and said, "Don't let that bastard win it, Paul...He isn't even a Liberal." She wanted Hellyer to go to Robert Winters, to block Trudeau, but Paul insisted on hanging on for another ballot. It would have made a great deal of difference if he had gone to Winters, a very able minister under St. Laurent and Pearson; I firmly believe that with Hellyer's backing, Winters would have won overwhelmingly.

It took four ballots to congeal, and there was a lot of back and forth between and among the candidates as the survivors tried to get those dropping out to align themselves with their camps. Just before 8 p.m., party president John Nichol announced the results of the fourth ballot. He got as far as "Trudeau, 1,203..." — enough for a clear win — and the roar of the crowd drowned everything else. (John Turner and Robert Winters were the only ones left by this time; Turner received 195 votes and Winters 954.)

It was over. Pierre Elliott Trudeau was the new Liberal leader and

Canada's fifteenth prime minister. He was a man of great ability — one of the singular minds of our time.

## DOING THE "JOIN THE CABINET" DANCE

Terry and I went down to Bermuda for a couple of weeks for a rest, to play a little tennis and think about the future. When we came home to Montreal, Jean Marchand called a couple of times to ask me what I intended to do. He was Trudeau's Quebec leader, and with an election coming on had some safe Liberal ridings at his disposal, but I wasn't at all sure I was interested.

I went to see Paul Desmarais to talk about a paper and chemical distributing company, one of many units in Consolidated Paper, which Desmarais controlled. Although it was a subsidiary of his own major firm, Desmarais didn't know the company. It was quite a lot like my old Hygiene Products, so I felt some confidence that I could make it work. Desmarais said to let him think about it, and to call back in a couple of weeks, but I never did go back. It would have required an investment of somewhere between $5 million and $7 million, and while that was a concern it wasn't the main factor; I never pursued this opportunity because other events intruded.

The afternoon of the day I saw Desmarais, there was another call from Jean Marchand. He said, "Pierre's going to be in town, and would like to see you."

Obviously, I thought this presaged the offer of a cabinet post, but Trudeau was not at all like Lesage, and when we met at his hotel there was no straightforward offer at all. Instead we danced around with talk about the Université de Montréal from him, and of McGill from me. This went on for about forty minutes, and then I got up and he got up, and we shook hands and said goodbye.

About a week later, Marchand called again, madder than hell.

"What did you two talk about?"

"Nothing much," I said.

He said, "Look, I'm coming to see you."

"All right, meet me at the MAAA [Montreal Amateur Athletic Association] about five o'clock."

"Fine."

The upshot of that was that he offered me a choice of one of three ridings in the Montreal area. They were Duvernay, an overwhelmingly French riding in Laval; Argenteuil and Lake of Two Mountains, off the island towards the northwest; and Compton, in the Eastern Townships.

I immediately said I had no interest in Compton, about which I knew almost nothing. He said, "Well, it is about 35 per cent English." Argenteuil and Lake of Two Mountains was about one-quarter English, and Duvernay, about 5 per cent. I agreed to take a look at the latter two ridings, and went first to Argenteuil. It was a very strong Liberal riding, and when I went out there to talk to the members of the nominations committee, one of them said, "We can guarantee you the nomination, but first, come with me."

He got up and I followed him into another room, where there was a refrigerator. He opened the door of the refrigerator and said, "That will hold about $20,000, and we want it full before we go any further."

I just turned on my heel and walked out the door.

When Marchand called to find out what had gone wrong and I told him I was not into refrigerator politics, he wanted to know, "What's the big deal?" I thought it was a very big deal, and that was very nearly the end of my career in federal politics.

However, I then got a call from one of the senior executives of the riding association in Duvernay, who had been in touch with Marchand. There was no talk of money. He said, "If we can get Marchand to come down and speak at the nominating convention, it's all over. Would you come?"

So I naturally phoned Jean, who said he had already agreed to be the main speaker.

I said, "I thought Maurice Sauvé was going to run in Duvernay?"

Jean replied, "We don't want Sauvé; you can't count on him. Besides, there has been an extensive poll in the riding, and it looks as if Sauvé is going to withdraw." This poll showed that Robert Cliche, the NDP Quebec leader and a very engaging politician, would beat Sauvé badly. Jean said, "Cliche has been living in the riding for about twenty months, and the NDP think they can make a breakthrough in Quebec. Pierre does not want that to happen."

I thought about it, and decided to go for it; and everything went as advertised. Jean Marchand came down to make the main speech at the nomination meeting. It was not so much a speech as a benediction, and I was duly nominated, unopposed. However, by this time, the federal election was scheduled for just a month away, on June 25, 1968, so I plunged into what the newspapers always call the whirlwind of campaigning. I began to see that the hackneyed saying had some merit. Cliche was a charismatic lawyer, a strong orator in either official language, and a hard worker.

Claude Ryan wrote an editorial in *Le Devoir*, in which he said it was a pity that two such deserving candidates were running against each other, since only one of us could go to Parliament. But Cliche was no more inclined than I to bow out, so we went at it, hammer and tongs. René backed him, with his newborn Mouvement Souveraineté-Association. It was one of their first electoral tests. René said of me, "With his constitutional ideas in a riding that's 95 per cent French, Eric has to be beaten." Well, at least he was still calling me Eric.

Cliche treated me as a carpetbagger, and claimed that my workers "needed a road map to find Duvernay," which was a pretty good line. He also claimed that my organization was made up of "mercenaries" who had endless amounts of money to throw around. Actually, the campaign cost $34,000, about half of which came out of my own pocket.

I went up and down the riding, knocking on doors, attending coffee parties, making speeches. I did not kiss any babies; I did talk about what I thought were the key issues, which included a reordering of economic priorities and a restructuring of federalism. I went into every mall and gas station that crossed my line of sight, shaking hands, asking questions, and smiling.

The race was obviously a close one, but about ten days before balloting I ran into Evelyn Dumas, one of the finest reporters in the province, who said, "I think you're going to take it." She also sent me a telegram that said, "We're counting on you," which was encouraging.

At the time, I didn't really care if I won or lost; however, I did want to make a good showing in an overwhelmingly French riding. If I then lost, I could go back to business with a clear head and a clean conscience, having done my best against an extremely well-known opponent, and a pretty smart candidate.

My parents wanted me to lose. My father, who was in failing health, told me he didn't want to see my name in the papers anymore.

I went to one of the printing firms I had worked with years before and asked them to make me up postcards to cover the whole riding. They had a very good picture of me and a slogan, in English and French, that read, "Duvernay, vaut-il un ministre?" (Does Duvernay deserve a minister?) Well, you could read this in two ways: I had been in the Quebec cabinet, or I was going to be in the Trudeau cabinet. (The latter was far from certain, though; I already knew that Bryce Mackasey and Jean-Pierre Goyer, who had been tireless workers in Trudeau's leadership campaign, did not want me in the cabinet. They were not anxious for competition from another Montreal candidate for a cabinet post.)

For some reason, this postcard sent Cliche into a wild rage when it began to hit homes about five days before the election. He called a press conference and attacked me in very intemperate language, calling me "deceitful" and "unfair." Up to this point, he had been getting very good press, but this turned quite a few people off, because it more or less destroyed the image he had built up of sweet reasonableness; he looked instead like someone who couldn't take pressure.

It was still a very close race, but this incident gave the Quebec central office the idea that if Trudeau came into the riding and made a strong speech, it might just do the trick. All of a sudden, the central office flooding us with money for pamphlets and advertising; and we began to gain real momentum after a radio debate among the riding candidates in which I was able to hold my own with Cliche in both languages.

Sure enough, Pierre came to make a speech to a crowd of about 5,000 people, and threw out rather broad hints that I was the sort of fellow who was needed in the cabinet, for which I was duly grateful. Before he left, he let me know why he was being so helpful. "I don't want Cliche there; I don't want any leader of the NDP in Quebec to have a seat in the House of Commons."

On election night, I was in the riding office, and my lead was beginning to build slowly, when somebody came and told me the prime minister wanted to talk to me. I naturally rushed to the phone. Pierre said to me, "I've heard you've won, and I am just so happy. Stick around. I assume you are not going anywhere in the next week or so?"

I said no, I would stick around.

## A TIME OF GRIEF AND HOPE

Trudeau announced his new cabinet on July 5, but the period between the election on June 25 and that date was one of turmoil for me. My father, who had been having increasing heart problems, was gravely ill.

There were all the usual rumours floating around about the cabinet, and phone calls from various people, including Doug Fullerton, who was sure I was not going to be included, and Peter Newman, who was sure I was, and then sure I wasn't.

This did not seem so important to me when my father died on July 3.

It was during his wake that I received a telephone call from Ottawa. Trudeau came on the line to say, "I want you in my cabinet as postmaster general. Oh, yes, and future minister of communications."

My father's funeral was set for Saturday morning, and the cabinet swearing-in was at two o'clock on the same day. My sister Kathleen and her husband, Bob Howland, chairman of the National Energy Board, had come down from Ottawa, and Bob drove me straight from the funeral to Ottawa. We had a bite to eat at the Château Laurier and then went to 24 Sussex Drive for the swearing-in.

It was, of course, a very solemn occasion, but I went with somewhat mixed feelings. There was my father's death to think about, for one thing. For another, I was not at all sure what I was getting into. The Post Office was not exactly the portfolio of my dreams; it certainly did not touch the major economic issues that I wanted to grapple with, and it was a very troubled institution, which appeared to be on the verge of a strike.

Well, I always said I enjoyed a challenge, but I had little notion what a mare's nest I was walking into. People were beginning to ask, "What makes Eric run?"

# Eight

# POSTMASTER GENERAL

*There's a solution to the Post Office problem. It could be*
*ordered that Post Office workers receive their cheques by mail.*

— ALLAN FOTHERINGHAM, 1978

**I** HAD NO REAL IDEA of what I was getting into. Terry and I drove down
to Ottawa, on a sunny day in early July 1968, so I could take up my new
position as postmaster general and putative minister of communications.
On the way, Terry made me promise that I would remain silent in cabinet for at least two weeks, which I did.

I asked Richard Gwyn, who had been helpful to me in the leadership
run, to be my executive assistant, and he agreed. It turned out to be one
of my better moves. Later I hired André Houle, a young Radio-Canada
journalist, to work as a special assistant on postal matters; and Frank
Howard, who had plunged me into all the fuss about the U.S. guidelines
back in 1965, to come as information officer in the Communications
Department. I felt I was well served.

Terry found us an apartment in a large building in Rockcliffe, where
a number of journalists and politicians were established, on the eleventh
floor. When I came home at night, I would have to go right past the
apartment where Paul Martin, Sr., lived. If his door was open, I was
expected to drop in and trade political gossip for an hour or so with Paul,
which was interesting, but interfered with my early-to-bed–early-to-rise
routine. Sometimes, I slipped by, feeling guilty.

Within a week of my arrival, the vice-president of public relations for
Air Canada came to see me with the news that he was arranging for me to
go to Russia, where they had just reached an agreement with Aeroflot
to exchange planes for postal services. We would carry their mail; they
would carry ours. That was fine, but it didn't need my imprint.

I said, "Why would I want to go to Russia?" The subject was dropped.

Then the deputy postmaster general wanted me to go to Nigeria to a meeting of postmasters of the world, and he pretty well told me I had to go.

Again, I said, "Why?"

Well, it turned out they were trying to come to an agreement on the postal rates for the international shipment of parcels, so I said, "I don't think I am much use for that."

We had a department in which morale was appalling, we were on the verge of a strike, and we were running a huge deficit; and it was pretty clear that as far as the top bureaucrats were concerned, the best thing to do was to get the minister out of town and keep him there. I declined to play.

I will come back to the postal problems in a moment, but it might be useful background to look at the way the cabinet into which I was so hastily thrust worked.

## AT LUNCH WITH TRUDEAU

Every Thursday morning, members of the ministry would emerge from their House of Commons offices (mine was on the ground floor of the Centre Block) and head towards the cabinet chamber, a long, dark room just off the Rotunda Gallery on the second floor. Room 205S. At 10 a.m., we would all trail in and make for one of the thirty straight-backed, leather-upholstered armchairs set around the large oval table that dominated the room. Ministers would sidle into their own appointed places, its boundaries marked by note pads, pencils, and a pile of cabinet documents, most bearing the impressive notation: SECRET.

A moment later, the prime minister would enter, having covered the sixty metres from his own third-floor suite, room 307S, in a few dozen purposeful strides. His place at the long, oval table was halfway down one side. He was flanked on his right by the newly minted Senator Paul Martin, who was government leader in the Senate, and on his left by Public Works Minister Arthur Laing. The other ministers ranged down the table on either side of him in order of seniority of service.*

---

* I am describing the main cabinet room, which was actually being refurbished when I first moved to Ottawa. For the first few months, we were jammed into a room in the East Block.

I sat directly opposite Trudeau, sandwiched between Transport Minister Donald Jamieson and Minister Without Portfolio Robert Andras. Low seniority brought us near the tail end of the line of precedence, which happened to be opposite the prime minister. He would glance quickly at the two agendas prepared in the Privy Council Office the day before; one list noted the four or five major items on the agenda for this meeting, the other gave the twenty or thirty decisions taken by the eight standing committees of cabinet during the past week. Beside each agenda item were the names of ministers who had indicated that they wished to speak to specific points. For the first couple of weeks, my name was never on these lists; after that, I tended to wade in whether it was on or not.

At the beginning of my second week, Michael Pitfield, who was then deputy secretary to the cabinet (that was his official title; his real title was friend, confidant, and adviser to Trudeau) came to ask me if I was free the next day, because the prime minister would like me to drop around to 24 Sussex Drive for lunch.

Well, yes.

At that luncheon, Pierre said he was expecting to hear more from me in cabinet, and I told him about the undertaking I had given to Terry. He smiled. "Well," he said, " I want to hear your opinions in cabinet, not only about matters that touch Quebec, but also with reference to other subjects, such as NATO."

There was a bit of a pause there. He knew that I had said in my campaign for the leadership that I wanted Canada out of NATO, so this had to mean something. It turned out that Trudeau wanted us out, too, but he didn't want to say so. I said, "Well, my view is that the Germans are a lot richer than we are right now, so I do not understand why we are spending hundreds of millions of dollars to keep troops over there, when the money is badly needed back here." He repeated that he wanted a thorough discussion on this issue.

At this time, there was a lot of argument going around on the subject of NATO. Our External Affairs people were sending in reports that came before cabinet complaining that Canada wasn't pulling its weight within the alliance. (This was the U.S. view, which turned out to be the view of our Department of External Affairs — now Foreign Affairs and

International Trade — on an astonishing number of occasions.)

Stories were appearing that there was a split in cabinet on the issue, although in fact it was more of a splinter than a split. I wanted us out of NATO, and so did Donald Macdonald, who was then House leader and president of the Privy Council. Then there were the hawks, people like Mitchell Sharp in External Affairs and Léo Cadieux in National Defence, who thought we should step up our involvement and our spending.

However, many of my colleagues had little or nothing to say. Gérard Pelletier, for example, hardly spoke in cabinet, although he was both secretary of state and one of the Three Wise Men. Jean Marchand, who did speak up quite often, had little to say of substance about NATO; I assumed that, like Trudeau, he wanted to see how an anti-NATO stance would play politically before making any pronouncement. As far as I could tell, there were perhaps five ministers who wanted us to either pull out or lessen our contribution to NATO, and twenty who felt that things were just fine the way they were or that we should be contributing more.

When I let my views be known in cabinet, some of the others allowed that it would be nice to see some diminution of our expenditures overseas, but nobody wanted to step on the toes of External Affairs or National Defence, so it wasn't really much of a debate, or a split.

That was one of the most notable differences between the Lesage cabinet and the Trudeau one. In Quebec City, you were encouraged to speak up about anything; you were a member of the decision-making body, not just the Minister of Torn Pants, or whatever. If you didn't agree with what somebody else was saying, you didn't allow the fact that it was not your portfolio to muzzle you. As a result, we had some ding-dong battles, but — and this was another major difference — when the issue was decided, the battle was over. As Lesage said, you defend the decision, or quit.

In the Trudeau cabinet, carrying grudges was a major occupation, and when you spoke up about somebody else's portfolio it was resented. You were never told to mind your own business, because that would not be polite, but the words hovered in the air, palpable though unspoken. If you were horning in because it affected your riding or your region, that was all right — "That won't play in Moose Jaw" was the accepted formulation — but for the postmaster general to tell the secretary of state for external affairs that he was off base was frowned upon. There were six major portfolios in cabinet that were either directly economic or heavily involved with economic issues. This was the one area where I felt I had real competence and could make a true contribution; only the wildest optimist would have expected me to curb my tongue for long.

Trudeau began with a willingness, even a desire, to have wide-ranging discussions; he was equally objective towards, as well as tolerant of, views that he did not agree with and those that he did agree with. Before long, he became very concerned with the limited contributions of many members of cabinet. For instance, when I had lunch with Pelletier and two or three other cabinet ministers, Gérard had very strong, intelligent things to say about NATO — and you knew that his views were shared by the prime minister — but when the issue was on the agenda, he was the silent tomb.

Then came a request to go out to Nanaimo, British Columbia, where Tommy Douglas, a man I greatly admired, was attempting to regain a seat in Parliament. The NDP leader had been defeated in his own Saskatchewan riding in the 1968 election; then Colin Cameron, the NDP member for Nanaimo-Cowichcan-the Islands, died suddenly, and a by-election was called in January 1969. I was sent out to make a speech to the faithful at the Tally Ho Inn in Nanaimo on January 25. It was actually Marc Lalonde, then Trudeau's principal secretary, who approached me.

The Liberal riding association for the area had already approached me on this subject, and I had turned them down, but Marc, with whom I was at that time on what might be called a semi-friendly basis, said, "I want you to know that the prime minister is not telling you to go, but he would like to answer a request from the riding." Or to put it another way, the prime minister was not ordering me to go, but go. So I did. Before I went, I wrote my speech, with the help of Richard Gwyn, my executive assistant.

It was a pretty straightforward speech, not hard to understand, and it dealt very largely with NATO (a subject on which Tommy Douglas felt at least as strongly as I did, and on the same side). I wrote that instead of being a genuine deterrent against a genuine threat, the alliance had become "a self-justifying deterrent against a non-existent military threat." I went on to describe the Warsaw Pact and NATO, both dominated by sterile military bureaucracies, leaning on each other for support:

The real battle is not the waning ideology of imperial communism versus consumer capitalism; it is the waxing tensions of the world which, in a mirror image of our own society, is increasingly divided into haves and have-nots.

I said to Trudeau, "I'd like you to have a look at this before I go out there." He looked it over for a few minutes, and then looked up and said, "Who wrote this, Karl Barth?" *

I said, "The hot parts were written by me and the filler by Richard." He grinned and gave it back to me.

I delivered the speech, which went pretty well — Nanaimo was a hotbed of peaceniks at this time — and when I came back, there was a donnybrook in cabinet. Léo Cadieux, the national defence minister, told me that the reaction in Brussels, NATO headquarters, was "deplorable," and accused me of breaking cabinet solidarity. Trudeau reminded him that the cabinet had not yet taken an official vote; we were leading up to that, and ministers had the right and duty to make their views known in public.

Cadieux was getting quite emotional as the debate went on; he had a bunch of files in front of him and he kept turning them over, and out of one of them came shooting a picture of me as an officer in the Canadian Officer Training Corps. This brought a smile from the prime minister, and I assumed it meant that the RCMP had opened a file on me, and given it to Cadieux.

When a decision was finally made in cabinet, it came from the Priorities and Planning Committee, which Trudeau chaired, and it simply made a cut in the number of troops overseas, while keeping Canada firmly within NATO.

I learned a fair amount from this exercise, including the fact that Pierre was a pretty shrewd politician, when it came right down to it, and that I had not made any friends in cabinet. Pierre was a good chairman, an incisive summarizer of discussion, and a ready listener; but if the matter was not something that he felt strongly about, he would simply defer to the minister in charge. Votes weren't taken, by and large; the ministers

---

* Karl Barth was a Swiss Protestant theologian, a bitter opponent of Hitler regime in Germany, and the author of the Barmen Declaration.

would make their points, and then Trudeau would summarize the debate and give the "consensus," which would basically be the decision he had made, and from then on, government policy.

However, his lack of attention to detail meant that policy issues were often decided by the people around the prime minister — the senior bureaucrats and advisers who made up what came to be called "the Supergroup," whose most powerful members, like Pitfield, Lalonde, and Gordon Robertson, had never been elected. The prime minister and cabinet listened to you with respect, but then the ministers would go back to their departments and do what their experts, the same old experts, had told them to do in the first place. It was like a procession. When the pope gets down off the altar at St. Peter's and walks down the aisle, the one thing you know is that he is going to get to the end of the aisle. You can argue and argue, but in the end the procession goes on its way. The senior mandarins were the great processioners of all time; they called the role, lined up the marchers, lined the route, and determined the finish line; then they told the public that decisions were reached in cabinet.

Moreover, the decision-making process was not a controlled, efficient progression, but ad hoc, scrambling, and nearly always attuned to "How will this look in June 1972?" which was the putative date for the next election.

Trudeau had come in on a platform of a "just society" and a new kind of politics, but it had a rather familiar ring to it. In fact, the idea of promoting more equity was completely abandoned in September 1968, when the Throne Speech announced that the coming year would be a period of reassessment of government priorities and expenditures. The pause that refreshes. Good housekeeping.

This wasn't new politics. John A. Macdonald would have lifted his glass to it.

Shortly after I went to Ottawa, I decided to find a new advertising agency for the postal department, and since the prime minister had made much of the fact that he was going to take patronage out of politics, I decided on Harry "Red" Foster, a Toronto Tory, to design the new campaign. We had received nine bids in a tendering process in which I'd given my word that it would be open to all; his submission had been by far the best for the job. The contract went into the Treasury Board, and disappeared for months. I told Foster to go ahead, that he had a contract, and he said, "Yeah, but will I get paid?" My reply was to keep on sending in his bills. Something would have to give, and it wouldn't be us. Harry thought that was wonderful. And he did get paid.

I was hauled before the cabinet committee in charge of advertising and they kept saying, "These people aren't even our friends!" So I said, "Look, in a way I'm doing you guys a favour. We're always telling everybody that we keep patronage out of the Liberal government — and it is just coincidence that every one of twenty-two other contracts has gone to a Liberal firm. Well, here's the living proof, a Tory firm with the Post Office contract." They weren't very pleased, but they eventually bought it.

## THE POSTAL STRIKE

Two weeks after I took over the Post Office portfolio, the first legal strike in that department broke out (there had been plenty of illegal walkouts), and I must say I had some sympathy for the strikers. They had been working under dreadful conditions for decades, with lousy wages. Between 1959 and 1965, they had had only one hourly pay increase, from $1.39 to $1.59. The mail was truly being delivered on the backs of the postal workers and their families. Then an illegal strike occurred in 1965, which lasted seventeen days and earned a jump to $2.50. This strike put a more radical leadership in charge of the unions, and showed the workers that the law didn't matter much, which was not a help to me. Among the problems I faced was the fact that the postal employees did not work for me; all the contracts went through the Treasury Board. Also, the government was so used to using the Post Office for patronage instead of service, and so used to keeping postal rates low to assuage the voters, that we were running a deficit of $70 million a year. Stamps cost four cents, and the mail was moving, but the Post Office was not a happy place to work for.

One of the first things I did was to order a study of the whole system. This study noted that 80 per cent of first-class mail in the country originated with large corporations, for example, Bell Canada, which sent out bills once a month. The average family mailed four envelopes a week, while half of all our stamps were sold to just 300 private companies and the federal government. In second-class mail, the situation was even worse; the rates were subsidized by nearly 80 per cent, which meant that newspapers and magazines were paying about one-fifth of what it cost to deliver them. We were projecting a deficit of $100 million for 1968, and $47 million of this was due to second-class mail subsidies.

At the same time, we had five post offices within a three-mile radius in a village in Nova Scotia, and another post office whose only customers were the members of the postmaster's family, all of whom were, no doubt, loyal Liberals. It was no surprise that costs were going up and losses mounting. Situations like this were common all over Canada; they dated from the days before automobiles were sold, so it made sense to have postal outlets very close to one other.

Before I could even begin to grapple with this, there was the strike to settle. Bud Drury, as president of the Treasury Board, had been trying to reach a deal with the unions but was getting nowhere, and he came to me and said, "Look, the union leaders would like to meet with you."

So I went to a meeting in August 1968 and said, "I agree that you people have been getting a bad deal for years. The people of Canada have been getting their mail on the backs of people like you, and I am on your side. The problem is that the government has set a maximum of 6 per cent for any wage increases this year, and it is not going to be broken. But I intend to play catch-up as best I can.

"You can settle now and know that someone who is on your side will be going to bat for you, or you can stay out on strike, but you will not end up with more than 6 per cent."

They huddled together for a while, and then we shook hands. The strike was over. Of course, my problems were just beginning.

Great Britain had decided to go to a public corporation for its postal services, and this seemed to me to make good sense. One reason for this was that a Crown corporation reduces the problem of political interference. I agreed.

You could not make long-term commitments for the kind of technological revolution we were facing even then. The money would just vanish. We had workers in Montreal and Toronto fainting on the job because the plants were so hot. In Montreal, at any given time between three and five o'clock in the afternoon, you would have half a dozen employees on the floor of a stone masonry building with walls three feet thick. They had been promised air conditioning for years, as had the main Toronto post office, and for years the money kept being whisked away for other departments.* If you had a Crown corporation, the financing would be committed over a period of years, and you could plan for the increases in productivity that would have to come about if the operation was even to stay in business, much less improve. In theory, a Crown could sue a government that did not pass over the money that had been allocated, and in fact you could make a Crown pay its own way (as the Post Office eventually did, and does).

I managed to get stamps raised by two cents, to close about 900 inefficient post offices, and to cut back delivery in non-rural areas to five days a week. But every step was a battle, not only against the unions, who regarded any change as a threat, but against my colleagues in cabinet.

Closing post offices was political dynamite, and hurt me in the long run, because it made my colleagues wary of me at best, hostile at worst. However, what I could see was that a century of running the Post Office on the basis of preference, patronage, and politics had left us with a system that delivered letters more slowly than it had in 1930, and was headed for a deficit, if nothing was done, of $130 million in 1969, and rising. As Allan MacEachen once said to me, "This is all very sensible, Eric, but does it get us re-elected?"

If we didn't act now, then when?

The same reasoning moved me to bring the post offices under the Public Service Commission, so that postmasters could be appointed, and retained, on some grounds other than party membership. Again, my colleagues reeled back in horror. About the only credit I ever got for this was in Jeffrey Simpson's *Spoils of Power*, in a section where he lamented the fact that the Trudeau government appeared as wedded to patronage as any of its predecessors:

---

* If another department had serious reasons for requesting a supplementary estimate, the Treasury Board would search other areas to see what could be postponed for a year. The Toronto or Montreal post office air conditioning could be put off for another twelve months. Year after year after year. The point about a Crown corporation was that its spending would not be a budgetary item. It would be an investment by the government, and would not appear in the Estimates, to be plucked away.

One important patronage reform, largely unheralded at the time, did mark the first Trudeau government — Postmaster General Eric Kierans placed the appointment of postmasters under the public service commission. Kierans, a minister who believed in applying the principles of business efficiency to the post office, eliminated at a stroke one of the federal government's oldest bastions of local patronage, one that had served and bedevilled ministers since Confederation.

None of these reforms was as important as remaking the whole postal system into an efficient organization, and that could be accomplished, I was certain, only by making it a Crown corporation. I got cabinet approval to do this in October 1968, and I thought, There, that's done, but of course it wasn't. The Privy Council Office (PCO) stepped in and decided to slow it down. First thing I knew, my deputy was telling me that he had been talking to the PCO and we ought to have a study — another study, not the one that had already said we needed a Crown corporation — to reinforce my position. It would give me backup when I was debating the matter in the House. Like an idiot, I went along with this, and pretty soon the place was swarming with consultants getting in the way and questioning everybody from senior engineers to office help. Nine months later, back came the report: What the post office needed was a Crown corporation.

This got fed into the hopper, but two years later, the Department of Justice had not even begun to draft the necessary legislation. So we had more strikes, and more deficits, and no money to do the jobs that needed to be done. We were running a 1960s operation on the technology of the late 1800s. When I took over, the annual budget for training and education in a $600-million-a-year transportation operation was $35,000. I managed to get that up to $1.5 million before I left, but it wasn't nearly enough. If you were going to go to postal codes, another of the innovations I managed to shove through, and high-speed readers and modern transportation systems, you needed expert training, and continuing education.

What we had was pitiful.

## LES GARS DE LAPALME

This brings us to the tragic affair of *les gars de Lapalme* (the Lapalme boys), which was hopelessly bungled. The director of transportation for the Post Office when the trouble began had never been to a course in finance, much less personnel relations, and he was supposed to settle complex issues that had confounded experts.

Briefly, what happened was that a long-simmering dispute within the Montreal postal system came to the boil. The employees who moved the mail from the central post office to the green relay boxes and the red mailboxes on the corners of most of the Montreal district, although they drove red trucks with the postal insignia on them, did not work for us, but for a company called Rod Service Limited, which was run by an ex-wrestler named Rod Turcotte. Year after year, his company got the contract, worth $3 million in 1968, without any public tender, even though the postal act specifically required competitive tenders for all contracts. There was a loophole in the law that allowed the postmaster general to make "temporary arrangements for the conveyance of mail" until a contract was signed, and these temporary arrangements had gone on since 1938, with various companies. Invariably, those with the right political connection got the business.

Rod Service Limited was a poor employer, offering long hours and low pay, and in 1965 a union was certified to represent the workers. The union was affiliated with the Confédération des syndicats nationaux (CSN), and it staged a three-day strike to get its first contract. Two other strikes occurred, in 1966 and 1967. Then, at the end of January 1969, Rod Service laid off 96 of the 457 drivers, and all Rod workers immediately went on strike, tying up Montreal mails.

Then a new company appeared, G. Lapalme, Inc., a firm owned by two brothers, Gaston and Guy Lapalme, who had had lucrative contracts hauling loads for the Quebec Liquor Board. It hired the former Rod Service drivers and on April 1, a one-year agreement was signed with this new company. I was pretty fed up by this time with the turmoil, the patronage, and the blatant illegality of proceeding with contracts that were never tendered, and I finally got cabinet permission to inform the company, which I did in late September, that new contracts would be called for in April 1970 (this met the requirement to give the company six months' notice).

We then announced a call for tenders, and when they came back in January 1970 G. Lapalme had not submitted a contract bid, so five contracts were drawn up and signed with five other companies covering the Montreal area. I cleared this with cabinet before these contracts were signed.

That was when the famous *gars de Lapalme* sprang into being, claiming that I was trying to dump them and bring in cheaper labour. Not true. I was trying to obey the law and bring in productive labour. We had one meeting at which Frank Diterlizzi, the man who had run the drivers since the old Rod Service days, disagreed loudly about what should be done. The union began a series of strikes, shutdowns, and violence that paralyzed the postal service. They brought in goons to intimidate anyone foolish enough to drive a postal truck, poured glue in the locks of postal boxes, smashed up trucks, beat people up. This was not incidental violence; it was a major campaign of lawlessness, which forced us to reroute mail around Montreal to keep it moving to other parts of the country, while service within the city became chaotic.

Finally, Jean Marchand, who of course had a very strong union background, and who seldom got involved in cabinet tussles, decided to join in. He leaned across at one cabinet meeting to ask me, "How are you getting along with the Lapalme boys?"

I said, "Well, I'd get along a lot better if I didn't have three of my colleagues undermining my position."

Trudeau said, "That's a serious charge. Are you prepared to substantiate it?"

I started with Marchand. I said he had been on television the night before with a labour leader, promising that the situation with the Lapalme workers would be settled shortly, which, I said, was "completely misleading." I pointed out that the current demand from the CSN was that the drivers should become full-fledged members of the public service as part of any settlement. The CSN would then have a foothold in the government sector, which would immediately be followed by a full-fledged strike of all postal workers, 25,000 of them.

"If you want to risk that," I said, "go ahead and settle."

Marchand started to shout that I was all wrong, but Trudeau cut him off. "Who's next?" he said.

I replied, "John Turner." He was then the minister of justice and solicitor general.

Trudeau's eyes sparkled. "What has he done?"

"It's what he hasn't done that matters." One of the top officers in the Montreal police had come to see me in Montreal. He was the chief of the motorcycle brigade, and he had said to me, "Mr. Minister, we're going to stop arresting the strikers. By the time we get them to the station, their lawyer is there and gets them out. Don't blame this on the provincial government; what is being destroyed is federal Crown property. This has been going on for weeks, and we haven't been able to keep a single person behind bars overnight."

I told the cabinet, "Mr. Turner knows this; it is his officials who make these decisions."

The prime minister turned to Turner and said, "Have there or have there not been any charges laid?" The answer was no.

Trudeau said, "Next?" and I said, "Bryce Mackasey." It was clear to me that Mackasey was leaking stories to the press. The most blatant example was a story by John Gray of the *Montreal Star,* which could have come only from Bryce Mackasey, and which did a good deal to both undermine my position and make clear that Bryce was on the side of what was, from my point of view, organized thuggery. Mackasey claimed he had a right to interfere as minister of labour, but I said, "This is a matter between Lapalme and the Post Office," and I did not want his interference.

Trudeau said, " I think you have cleared the air a little, and I hope you will see more co-operation in the future."

Well, that just made Marchand madder than ever, so the prime minister called the two of us to a meeting in his office. He said, " I can't have two of my prominent ministers from Quebec fighting," and I said, "Well, if you forget that this is an ordinary union struggle and see that what it is really about is the demand that the drivers be admitted to the public service, you will see what I am talking about. If you want to risk a major strike, this can be settled now."

He turned to Marchand and said, "I don't really see what we can do but follow the advice of the postmaster general. Why is the violence escalating?"

All Marchand would say was, "Well, if you want to go along with Eric, I quit."

So Pierre turned to me and said, "You know, Eric, three of us came down to Ottawa together to do a job, and we can only do it if the three of us stick together."

That was plain enough. I replied, "I suppose that lets me out." And out I walked.

The upshot was a special cabinet meeting called for 5 p.m. later that week, and at that meeting the only ones who supported me were George McIlraith, the solicitor general, and Jean-Pierre Côté, the minister of revenue. That meeting passed a resolution to recognize the drivers as the bargaining unit under the new contracts. In other words, the five companies would have to hire them, whether they wanted them or not.

The next morning, March 17, I put my resignation on Trudeau's desk. It was the day of the Priorities and Planning Committee meeting, and when I went to his office his secretary told me where he was, and that if I wanted to see him he would come out of the meeting.

I said, "No, I just want to leave this envelope on his desk," and walked out.

There is a protocol to this sort of thing — well, to everything in Ottawa, I guess. If a minister submits his resignation and the prime minister reads it, it becomes the first order of business in the House of Commons that day, no matter what. The solution, obviously, is to not read it. I had not been back in my own office long, before there was a call from Trudeau.

"I want to see you, right now."

I went to his office and told him, "Look, we have signed agreements with five companies in Montreal, and I am now being asked to repudiate these, and my position is just not tenable."

He said, "There has to be some other way."

I went back to my office, and he called me there shortly thereafter to say, "I'm calling another cabinet meeting in which we will reverse the decision of last night, and I'm asking a good friend of yours, Carl Goldenberg, to be the conciliator on this thing." Goldenberg spent exactly one week studying the matter, and came down with a report typed on five pages. I strongly suspected — and he just as strongly denied — that it was vetted before release by Marc Lalonde. Marc had telephoned me two days earlier and left a message to call him back; when I did, his secretary told me that he was over at the Château Laurier, closeted with Goldenberg, and I drew my own conclusions. Two days later, the report came down.

This document was highly critical of me, and said that the Lapalme boys should be given the jobs, but within the public service. The five contracts should be cancelled (and were bought off, to the huge relief of the companies involved), and the Post Office itself should handle the transport of mail within Montreal. Goldenberg entirely renounced my handling of the affair and, in my view, proposed to reward *les gars de Lapalme* for their violent and outrageous conduct. He said, on the one hand, that "violence must not be condoned"; then he went on to condone it:

> The Lapalme employees lose their status and rights as employees under their collective agreement on the expiry of the agreement and of the Lapalme contract of March 31st. This has created a state of fear, insecurity and demoralization which has led to destruction and violence.

Another way to put this would be to say that any time members of a labour union feel they are likely to lose bargaining rights, it is to be expected that they will conduct a campaign of terror, which must therefore be the fault of somebody else.

I couldn't resign again, which would have seemed petty and childish, but I could and did step back and let Bud Drury and the Treasury Board negotiate with *les gars*. That worked out about the way you would expect. The truckers refused to accept an offer based on Goldenberg's report, because it did not propose certifying the union — the report did not do so despite the fact that, by Goldenberg's own argument, this was bound to lead to violence, apparently justifiable violence. *Les gars* then began another series of demonstrations marked by outbursts of thuggery, this time invading Parliament Hill, where, on one notable occasion, they stopped the prime minister's car. Trudeau's contribution to labour relations was to push the button to lower his car window, thumb his nose at the pickets, and shout his contempt.

This new campaign involved attacks on 662 trucks, seven dynamite bombings, damage to 1,200 post boxes and 492 relay boxes, and injuries to seventy-five people. Oh, yes, and finally 142 arrests. Still, there was no settlement.

In October 1970, the October Crisis — of which more will be said in the next chapter — subsumed the postal chaos, and the Front de libération du Québec (FLQ) made as one of its demands a promise that all of *les gars* would be hired within the public service. This was rejected, and the union slowly disintegrated.

### THE TREASURY BOARD IS PISTOL-WHIPPED

While struggling with the Post Office, I was also serving as vice-chair of the Treasury Board, under Bud Drury, and this proved an illuminating experience, to say the least. I liked and admired Charles Mills "Bud" Drury, certainly the hardest-working member of the cabinet. All kinds of requests, or demands, came before us for money that was outside the main budget, and they had to gain our approval.

One of these was a request to buy approximately $83 million worth of machine pistols from Scandinavian armament manufacturers. Apparently, when the Americans earlier approached the manufacturers, wanting to buy similar weapons for their defence department, they were in effect told, "Why not get them from Canada? They have millions of dollars' worth of these in inventory, unused. We have shut down that line, and will be producing a new, improved model." The money was to replace the guns that we would provide to the Americans.

This was being shepherded through by Simon Reisman, later the architect of the Free Trade Agreement, who at this time was one of the most influential figures in the Department of Finance. He simply dumped the request before us and expected us to comply. However, I had gone through the documentation the night before the Treasury Board meeting, and concluded that these weapons had never even been unwrapped, and we had bought them five years earlier. Why did we need to spend millions more to replace them?

I asked, "How many of these pistols have we actually used?"

He didn't know, so there was a pause until an aide replied, and the answer turned out to be that none had been used. Only one carton had ever been opened, to make sure they were of the make and model that had been paid for.

I was beginning to enjoy myself by now, but Simon wasn't. I asked, "If you haven't even opened the boxes, what's the need for an immediate refill?"

Bud intervened and said, "That's a very valid point. You can ship them to the States if you want, but without any guarantee of replacements."

The item was dropped from the agenda for that meeting, but it kept coming back, again and again, until it came up at one meeting when I was away, and it slid right through.

Reisman had won; a totally unnecessary expenditure had been approved.

In another case, Bud called me at home one night to warn me, "There is going to be a tough one tomorrow. John Turner wants a special job and salary classification for his lawyers in the Department of Justice." The justification for this was that you wanted the best lawyers you could get in the department that was going to draft legislation; but this request came in the middle of the government's much-publicized "war on inflation," and giving one group of government lawyers a big, fat raise was not a good idea, politically or practically. There was also the problem that you were saying, in effect, that the other government lawyers were inferior to John's troops.

Before the Treasury Board, Turner presented a well-argued case, which he delivered at great length. I replied, and we went back and forth for a long time. It was clear that he had a valid argument; it was also clear that we couldn't accept it, both because of the government's strong stance on inflation and because paying a premium to lawyers in the Justice Department would immediately drain all the other departments of some of their best brains.

He was extremely bitter when he couldn't get his way, and those blue eyes of his did their best to bore a hole right through me.

Then, I had to deal once more with John Doyle, who was still forging ahead in Newfoundland with deals that the taxpayer financed, while he somehow wound up with the benefits. This time, he wanted more than $17 million in public funds to build infrastructure for a linerboard mill at Stephenville, Newfoundland. It was a very complicated deal, and a typical Joey Smallwood arrangement, under which a subsidiary of Canadian Javelin, Doyle's company, got the rights to a timber tract covering an area roughly twice the size of Belgium, for nothing. The timber would provide the raw materials for the mill.

I could see that I was not going to be able to block this one, because it clearly had the backing of the senior mandarins, so I called in my friend Walter Stewart and asked him to have a look at Doyle. The result was an article in *Maclean's* magazine in January 1969, entitled "John Doyle Gambles With Millions: Heads He Wins, Tails You Lose." It pointed out that Doyle was a fugitive from justice (as we saw in chapter 4, he had been convicted of using the mails illegally for purposes of stock transactions in the United States); that he owed Revenue Canada millions of dollars for unpaid taxes that went back nearly two decades; and that, if the scheme succeeded, all the profits would flow to his companies, whereas if it failed, the losses would be borne mainly by the taxpayers of Canada and Newfoundland. The request for funds did not go through.

That was one of my few victories. The way it worked in general was that a department would send a demand to us for supplementary spending for its budget, along with a heavy file of well-nigh incomprehensible documents to read the night before a Treasury Board meeting.

On one occasion, I told John Munro, the minister of national health and welfare, when he came before us with a request for a $500,000 supplementary, "You're running a budget of more than $4 billion, and if you can't squeeze $500,000 out of that somewhere there must be something wrong."

He didn't speak to me for six months.

I wanted to say, "Remember, John, this isn't your money," but I presumed he knew that.

## THE CASE OF THE CPR ARCHIVES

One day not long after I had taken over the Post Office, the prime minister asked me to assume the additional responsibility of revenue minister, temporarily replacing Jean-Pierre Côté, who was about to undergo heart surgery. I agreed, of course.

Within days of taking on what I had expected to be a simple job, it became complicated. The director of legal services in the Department of National Revenue (or Revenue Canada) called on me to discuss a dispute with the CPR that had to be resolved swiftly. It had been waiting for a cabinet decision for months, and was now in danger of being proscribed because of the time lapse. The CPR had sold its vast forest holdings on Vancouver Island some years earlier for approximately $65 million. In its books, the railway showed this money as a capital gain, which at that time in Canada was not subject to tax.

However, some of the eagle-eyed accountants in Revenue, looking over this transaction, concluded that it was not a capital gain at all; it was "an adventure in the nature of trade," which is taxable. Their reasoning was that the CPR had been working similar land deals in a whole string of transactions stretching back to the 1880s. They were cashing in the huge land holdings that came to them as part of the deal for building the first trans-Canada rail route, and that, the accountants said, was an adventure in trade.

The matter had been raised with the previous minister of finance, Mitchell Sharp, and had been languishing on the desk of then prime minister Lester Pearson for some time, but no action was taken. And if we didn't act now, it would be too late.

I thought, frankly, that the department was going to have a tough time in court, suddenly raising questions about a practice that had gone on for some time, but I was sympathetic to the argument and thought it worth pursuing. I promised to raise it with cabinet, along with another similar issue that had to do with the Montreal Expos. Canada's only major-league team at the time had applied for the right to depreciate the cost of acquiring baseball players, which struck me as rather odd, even if all the American teams were doing it.

When I went to see Côté in hospital, he made it clear that he wanted to handle the Expos' issue himself, and he did. (He allowed the depreciation.) But the more pressing matter of the CPR he asked me to present to cabinet as soon as possible. He, too, agreed with the department. The next Thursday, cabinet day, I asked the prime minister for a few minutes at the beginning of the meeting to put the case, thinking that it was really just a matter of explaining the issues and receiving a go-ahead.

Instead, Mitchell Sharp, who was now secretary of state for external affairs, exploded in a rage. He said that I, as a temporary revenue minister, had no right to take such action, and when I pointed out that I had the approval of the minister, he said that made no difference.

Finance Minister Edgar Benson, Mitchell's successor, didn't seem to know much about this, but opined that "we could use the money."

We got into a long, hot, and complex discussion about the difference between capital gains and adventures in trade, while Trudeau was getting restive and the rest of the cabinet was sinking in gloom. Then, Minister of Defence Production Don Jamieson, who always had a knack for defusing these situations, asked the prime minister for permission to put a question to me. Trudeau said, "Go ahead."

"Eric," said Jamieson, "when you were talking to the minister, was he out of the ether yet?"

This snapped the tension, and Trudeau ended the debate, saying, "If Eric has been good enough to take on these additional responsibilities, and the minister agrees with his decision, he should be allowed to go ahead."

I told the department to go to court.

Two weeks later, the director of legal services came to see me again, just before another cabinet meeting, with information he thought the cabinet ought to have. The CPR would be sending an official to Revenue Canada's Montreal office that day to turn over a cheque for $34 million, to stop the court proceedings.

I was stunned. "Why would they give up like this?"

The answer, I was told, was that Revenue Canada had assembled a lot of information on all these deals, and they were going to pry the necessary confirmations out of the CPR archives in court. To keep the vaults closed, the railway lawyers handed over $34 million. The CPR archives, fundamental to understanding a crucial period in Canada's history, are still closed to historians, and everyone else.

Needless to say, none of this did me any good at the time; all that came across was that I was not a team player. I was beginning to feel that I did not exactly have a brilliant future in federal politics, but my attention was quickly captured by another problem, which involved Terry, and a valuable collection of stolen art.

## THE CASE OF THE CAPTURED KRIEGHOFFS

When I first began to work seriously on my French, Terry took up the same studies and did very well. She belonged to a French-speaking association in Quebec City, known as the Société d'étude et de conférence, which required the members to annually submit a paper on a subject of their own choosing. Terry, who had a great interest in art and became a gifted sculptor, chose to do her paper on Cornelius Krieghoff, the painter whose works on life in nineteenth-century Quebec are very valuable. This study was so well prepared that it won first prize for the best paper in the entire province by a member of the Société d'étude. Terry told me that when she got the telephone call announcing her win, the chair of the contest could hardly conceal her astonishment that it had been written by "une Anglaise." Terry was the first anglophone ever to have been awarded the first prize in the association.

As a result of this, or so we presume, some years later Terry was contacted by phone, at our apartment in Ottawa, by a man who said he knew of her interest in Krieghoff, and wanted to know if she wanted to buy some Krieghoffs — in a very private deal. It was not hard to figure out where these must be coming from; there had been a break-in at the Musée du Québec, and a number of Krieghoffs, part of the estate of Maurice Duplessis, had been stolen, as my wife well knew.

Terry immediately contacted the RCMP, who told her to go ahead with the arrangement, and they would stake out our Ottawa apartment. However, the mysterious caller did not turn up for the appointment, and called again to say he would go through with the deal only if it could be done at our house on Queen Mary Road, in Montreal. Terry agreed. At this point, the RCMP turned the case over to the Quebec police, who were extremely friendly and efficient. When the call from the thief came to her, it was, naturally, on a day when I was back in Ottawa, and I played no part whatever in what followed.

Once the time for a meeting was set, the Quebec provincial police officers installed a microphone in our fireplace and Terry was instructed to get the villain to sit down close enough to it that they could pick up his voice, and get the evidence they needed to use in court. Terry was nervous — who wouldn't be? — but she did her job perfectly, and in due course the man appeared and they dickered over the price for the paintings. As soon as he had made clear his part in the robbery, two police officers came bounding down the stairs (there was another officer in concealment downstairs) and he was arrested.

Terry, her nerves ajangle, phoned our son, Tom. He came charging over, barged into the house, and found Terry sitting at the dining-room table, with two large, burly men.

"Who the hell are you?" he demanded.

She had to explain to Tom the Krieghoff robbery, and how instrumental she had been in the capture of the principal thief — a capture that led to the subsequent recovery of the paintings.

### I AM SHUFFLED

On July 30, 1970, after three days of discussing the tax reforms recommended by the Carter Commission (of which we will learn much more in the next chapter), cabinet dispersed for the summer break. There were no reforms; the ministers had been well briefed on the opposition, political and bureaucratic, to the changes. I was feeling very frustrated, and then I read in the newspaper that my cabinet post was to be changed; I was to go to Manpower and Immigration (M&I), then being run by Allan MacEachen.

The prime minister invited me to his office and thanked me for the three-day battle I had put on for the reforms; the members of cabinet had all learned a lot, he said, but were not ready for so much change. After some small talk, I mentioned the news item about various cabinet changes, including myself going to M&I. He appeared genuinely surprised and assured me that he was delighted that I wanted to stay in the Post Office.

A week later, I was called in again, while the country was still waiting for the announcement of cabinet changes, and Trudeau explained that there would be no chance of tabling the Crown corporation legislation regarding the Post Office in the coming year, because there was so much social legislation coming forward, with which I would be very pleased. He had therefore concluded that I would be more useful in Manpower and Immigration. I reminded him that we had talked about this a week earlier, but he went on to say that a further reason for moving me to another portfolio was that the Crown corporation legislation would prolong the House debates for months, and nothing would get through.

I replied that if he thought that I was confrontational in the Post Office, M&I would not be any better; and I rhymed off a number of problems that would have to be addressed there. I explained that I was an avid reader of the auditor general's reports, which were my bedtime reading, and the auditor general had had some very pointed things to say about the way Manpower and Immigration operated.

Then there was some discussion about my moving to Health and Welfare, but I said no, because I had made too many speeches against the federal takeover of this provincial field when I was Quebec's minister of health. We went over other options, and it was finally agreed that I would yield the Post Office to Jean-Pierre Côté, who would become an associate minister of the department, and I would retain the Communications portfolio. Even then, it was not over. The prime minister called me in before the announcement, suggesting instead that the title "Minister of Communications" go to Côté, and that I could be an associate minister in charge of Communications. I said no. The grounds for the alternative proposal were that Jean-Pierre could use the greater salary, which would make little difference to me.

The day before the change by which I would be stripped of the Post Office was announced, Allan MacEachen invited me over to Manpower and Immigration to show me around. When I asked why, he said he wanted to introduce the new minister to his officials. He must have taken the earlier newspaper speculation very seriously indeed.

At the luncheon meeting after the cabinet shuffle, the newly minted minister of national defence, Donald Macdonald, rushed over to tell me that he was scheduled to meet with the armed forces' chiefs of staff.

"What will I tell them?" he asked. "They know where I stood on NATO."

"Take the offensive, Don," I replied. "Just tell them, 'Cheer up, chaps; it could have been worse. You could have got Kierans.'"

He doubled over with laughter.

## GETTING TELESAT OFF THE GROUND

With the postal portfolio taken away from me, I was left to concentrate on the building of the Department of Communications. This was a new department, established in 1969. It had been promised in the Trudeau campaign without a great deal of thought as to what it would actually do. For example, although it was the federal Department of Communications, it had absolutely nothing to do with either the CBC or Radio-Canada, the two most important instruments of public communication in the country. This was a distinct drawback; on the other hand, happily,

I had a deputy minister, Allan Gotlieb, who was not only a talented lawyer and an expert on the Canadian Constitution with a background in External Affairs, but also someone very much attuned to modern technology, and the ways of the Ottawa bureaucracy.

Gotlieb was my choice in part because I had first encountered him as a member of a committee on reviewing the Constitution. The committee was chaired by the prime minister, and I was a member; there were senior civil servants as well as outsiders on the committee. Trudeau obviously had strong views and so did I, especially on the abuse of the spending power by the federal government. Allan Gotlieb distinguished himself by being, as far as I could discern, the only adviser willing to challenge the prime minister directly.

While the planning for the new department was still in its early stages, in late 1968, Trudeau called me in and asked me with whom I would like to work. I said, "The naming of deputy ministers is your prerogative," and he replied, "I wouldn't want to give you someone you couldn't work with." When I mentioned Gotlieb and why I admired him, and assured Trudeau that we were not long-time friends, it became clear that the prime minister also favoured this appointment. The problem was that he would have to be jumped two ranks from his position in External Affairs, and that might produce a discipline problem for Gordon Robertson, the secretary of the cabinet. But that was soon worked out and Gotlieb became the deputy minister of the soon-to-be-formed department.

He did much of the work of setting up the new department. Our first challenge had to do with launching a communications satellite, something that had been recommended by the Science Council of Canada in 1967 as an absolute must. It would bring the north into instant touch with the rest of Canada, help to develop resources, and open the door to further development on the technological side in what was coming to be called the "revolution" in communications. Which, in fact, it was.

The Science Council had made much of the fact that the Americans were working on a sophisticated system, but Canada had a head start on them, partly through work done by the National Research Council of Canada. The chance existed that, for once, we might beat the Americans to the punch.

What I had to decide was who should build such a satellite, and who should operate it. The second problem was easy; Telesat Canada, established in 1969, and jointly owned by the federal government and a consortium of telephone companies, would do the job. In turn, Telesat would contract the building of the satellite to a private company, and it was my responsibility to choose the company. In May 1969, cabinet authorized me to open talks with RCA of New York and Montreal and with Northern Electric of Ottawa for the prime contracts for the first satellites and the ground stations to serve them.

RCA would be the major recipient of a "directed contract," one not open to competitive bids, for the satellite, and Northern Electric would get many of the subcontracts. Then I discovered that RCA had never built a satellite, whereas Hughes Aircraft Company in Los Angeles had been building them for years. Not precisely this satellite, which would carry a lot of advanced technology, but many versions not that far from it. At the time, the heavy Intelsat satellite, built by Hughes, was carrying enormous traffic across the Atlantic.

We were going to reinvent the wheel; we were going to build, from scratch, an advanced piece of equipment that was already, so to speak, sitting on a shelf in Los Angeles. Not only was the RCA option bound to be much more expensive, it was much riskier. The obvious thing to do was to find out from Hughes how much they would charge to do the job, and the answer that came back was astonishing.

RCA's offer was to put up two satellites, each of which would carry six channel transponders, for a cost of $63.5 million "open." In other words, if the cost came back higher than that, we were to pay the difference, not RCA. Somebody in the department came across a letter from RCA in New York to the Canadian branch indicating that it was to be done strictly on a "cost-plus" basis, and that not a cent of the American corporation's money was to be used. The $63.5-million figure promised a satellite in thirty-six months after a starting date of July 1, 1970.

The Hughes offer was for two satellites, each with twice the capacity, for less than half the cost — twelve channels instead of six, $32 million instead of $63.5 million. And the $32-million figure was firm; any cost overruns would be carried by Hughes, not us.

When I announced that I was going to go with Hughes, you would think I had sold the Canadian flag off Parliament Hill. Newspaper editors threw up their hands in horror that Kierans, a supposed nationalist, would sign on an American company. My cabinet colleagues reacted as if I had put out the Centennial Flame. RCA was in Montreal; ergo, I was wrenching jobs away from Canadians — French Canadians, at that. And this was at the very time when the forces of unrest in Quebec were looking for symbols of this sort. There were twenty-eight members of cabinet; had it been a question of voting at this point, the result would have been twenty-seven to one. The Montreal cabinet ministers, led by Marchand and Mackasey, were particularly vehement, but other opponents included Joe Greene from the Ottawa Valley and Herb Gray from Windsor.

I continued negotiations with Hughes. It sent up a team of three engineers to deal with the Canadian spinoffs — a crucial element in any technical contract — which we set at approximately 30 to 32 per cent of the total budget. Northern Electric and the Ottawa-based Spar Aerospace were both represented at this meeting, which also included Allan Gotlieb and David Golden, who was the newly appointed president of Telesat. It was quickly evident that the Americans were impressed by Larry D. Clarke of Spar, which did get most of the Canadian elements of the contracts.

While the contracts themselves were moving along, things were not going so well on the political front. We were being killed by all the negative publicity, so Richard Gwyn, my executive assistant, arranged for me to go and talk to the editorial boards of some of the newspapers that were screaming the loudest — the *Telegram,* the *Star,* and the *Globe and Mail* in Toronto, and *Le Devoir* in Montreal.

It turned out to be quite a lot of fun. I saw the three Toronto newspapers in one day, and it astonished me how little they knew about this matter on which they had pronounced so strongly. All I had to say to them was, "The fact is that RCA has never built a satellite. What they build in Montreal are record players and music products, and if you think that is a suitable background for this, think again. If we put up a satellite for $63.5 million plus and it flames out, what will you be writing then?" (Actually, that was easy; they would be writing that I should have paid no attention to them and gone to Hughes.)

The *Star*'s editorial board was dominated by Peter Newman, and he quickly took my point. At the *Telegram,* nobody mattered but the publisher, John Bassett, who knew enough about money to know that paying twice as much in an open-ended contract instead of half that for a firm price made no sense. Yardley Jones, the *Telegram*'s cartoonist, and an eloquent debater, also sided with me; the newspaper soon changed its editorial stance.

However, at the *Globe,* Richard Doyle (later Senator Doyle), who had written the paper's "shocked and appalled" editorials, was very much harder to move. In fact, I think he was embarrassed. It quickly became clear that he hadn't any idea of what was really going on, and didn't want to say so. Jean Howarth, one of the editorial writers, asked some bright and interested questions, and Doyle sucked on his pipe and sulked. He did hint at one point that "there may be more to this than meets the eye," but that was all. Thereafter, the subject disappeared from the paper's editorials.

The next morning I was down in Montreal with the editor of *Le Devoir,* the redoubtable Claude Ryan, who kept asking me question after question about lost jobs in Montreal, and dismissing the notion that the extra cost ought to matter. After about an hour and a half of this, I said, "Claude, I'm going to do something I shouldn't do. I have the working papers here on the RCA project. Now, you have just been telling me that it would be a great thing for Montreal and give French Canadians a full role on the frontiers of science. Your editorials talk about the 1,500 French Canadians you say RCA would employ. Well, here is the list of employees they are planning to hire."

I handed him the list. There were 156 names on it. "Go down that list and tell me when you find a French Canadian name." He finally did; it was the 156th name.

He looked up at me, very fierce, and said, "Vous êtes un mauvais ministre." (You are a poor minister.)

"Comment?" (Pardon?)

"If you had been a good minister, you would have seen that I had this information before I wrote my editorials."

I was too stunned to make any reply to that.

When the editorials calmed down, the pressure came off the ministers, but there was still a lot of grumbling. On the final day for a decision,

Trudeau gave me the whole morning to make my case, and when I was done, all anybody asked was, "Why doesn't Northern Electric get more of the contract?" I said that my understanding was that the previous administration (the Pearson government) had given Northern Electric $83 million — "Does anybody remember what they did with it?"

I had prepared a memo for the ministers, which pointed out that RCA would give no guarantees whatsoever with regard to cost performance, patents, or delivery, and I told them in cabinet that "if we go for the RCA contract and there is a flame-out" we were going to have a lot of explaining to do.

There was no vote. The prime minister summed up the "consensus," which was that Hughes could do the job faster — and speed was very much an element in this affair — and with less risk, and that was that. The ANIK A-1 satellite was completed by Hughes on time and on schedule, and launched well before any American system of comparable sophistication was ready.

However, by that time, I was long gone, a process helped along by my entanglement in another matter of public policy that got me into trouble with my colleagues, the Mackenzie Valley Pipeline.

## JOE GREENE'S PIPELINE GETS PLUGGED

The Mackenzie Valley Pipeline was a project that Energy Minister Joe Greene and Northern Affairs Minister Jean Chrétien were determined to shove through. The Americans had found huge quantities of oil on Alaska's North Slope and were debating about routes to bring it to market. Greene and Chrétien decided that the best way was through Canada, right through the environmentally sensitive Mackenzie Valley. Mitchell Sharp was another enthusiast for the pipeline, which, it was claimed, would provide thousands of jobs for Canadians. In mid-March of 1971, Greene and Chrétien invited a group of American oil executives to Ottawa to pitch them on the notion of bringing the oil down the Canadian route. (The major alternative, and the one eventually adopted, was to ship it by sea.)

I decided to attack the proposal on economic grounds, the only area where I could claim expertise. In late March, I called David Crane, then with the *Globe and Mail*. He turned up the next day, and I told him that the Mackenzie Valley project would cost somewhere between $3 billion and $5 billion, would create few permanent jobs, and would be of far more benefit to the Americans than to us. "We would be pushers of oil, gas, and other resources, comparable to the hewers-of-wood-and-drawers-of-water image of Canada of a century ago." Moreover, the money would have to be raised outside Canada, and that would have an immediate effect on the Canadian dollar, driving it up. This would make our exports less competitive and, once more, redound to the advantage of the United States, not Canada. I said, "It's not a question of their murdering us. We'd be killing ourselves."

The story naturally made headlines, and the opposition parties, especially the NDP, were delighted. Joe Greene et al. were not so pleased. When Greene was asked in the House whether I had consulted him about the matter before giving an interview, he slouched in his seat and said he regretted he had no right to check the speeches and interviews of other ministers.

Trudeau was calm about the brouhaha — not because he thought the pipeline was a good or a bad idea, but because he believed in different views being aired in public before a cabinet decision, and not after. The pipeline was a very bad idea, both economically and environmentally, as a subsequent inquiry, the Mackenzie Valley Pipeline Inquiry, found. That examination, led by Justice Thomas Berger, put a moratorium on the whole plan for a decade. As I write this, it is under discussion again; but any such scheme today will be guarded by far more vigorous environmental conditions, and will provide far more benefits to Canada. Moreover, it is unthinkable now that anything of this sort can simply be dumped on the Native population, with no consideration as to how it will affect their lands, their hunting rights, and their way of life.

Jean Lesage had made me a follower of the belief that you had your say in cabinet on each and every issue, because you were going to have to defend the decisions taken in public, or leave the government. This is why I was so involved in areas outside my own particular portfolio, such as the Mackenzie Valley proposal.

By the time it became clear that the pipeline would not go ahead, the issue was of much less importance to me. As a result of other issues, which will be discussed in the next chapter, I had already resigned from the Trudeau cabinet.

## Nine

————— •◆• —————

# RESIGNATION

*I left Ottawa in 1971 because I could not live with a government whose economic policies were inducing unemployment.*

— TOM KENT, *A PUBLIC PURPOSE*, 1988

I DID NOT LEAVE THE federal cabinet of Pierre Elliott Trudeau because of the October Crisis. Perhaps I should have, but I didn't. For thirty years I have said very little on that lamentable period of Canadian history, and you will see that I had very little to be proud of throughout the whole affair. It is time to tell that story now, for the first time, from my perspective; then I will go on to talk about the economic issues and issues of governance that sent me out of politics. Readers can decide for themselves whether I waited too long to walk away.

### THE OCTOBER CRISIS

On Monday, October 5, 1970, at 8:15 a.m., two men gained access to the home of British trade commissioner James Cross, in Montreal's Westmount, on the pretext that they were delivering a birthday gift. What they carried, however, was not a gift, but revolvers; they handcuffed Cross and bundled him into a waiting taxi, and a bystander heard one of the men say, "We're the FLQ." Soon afterwards, the police received a ransom note containing a list of seven demands, which included publication of a manifesto from the Front de Libération du Québec. The ransom note also demanded the release of twenty-three "political prisoners" — whose numbers included convicted terrorists; $500,000 in gold; and the rehiring of *les gars de Lapalme,* as mentioned in the last chapter. They had written out a list of "enemies of the people," on which I ranked in the first ten. They also wanted a plane to fly them to either Cuba or Algeria, with their gold.

The next morning, at a meeting of the cabinet's Committee on

Priorities and Planning (I was not a member), Trudeau made it clear that Canada would not give in to these demands, but would keep negotiations open to save the life of James Cross. A message went back to the FLQ (these messages were always left in a telephone booth that the kidnappers would indicate to one of two Montreal radio stations, with the location passed on to the RCMP), rejecting the demands but asking to speak to the kidnappers. They replied that Cross would be killed if their demands were not met by 8:30 a.m. on Wednesday. A series of pre-dawn raids that day resulted in thirty arrests, but no clues as to the whereabouts of the trade commissioner. The 8:30 a.m. deadline was ignored.

The afternoon of Wednesday, October 7, the kidnappers sent along a handwritten note from Cross to prove that he was still alive. That evening, External Affairs Minister Mitchell Sharp, at a news conference, asked that a mediator be named by the FLQ to deal with the federal authorities. The man named was Robert Lemieux, a Montreal lawyer.

On Thursday, October 8, at 10 p.m., Radio-Canada met one of the key demands, broadcasting the FLQ manifesto, in French. It was also printed in major newspapers the next day, and turned out to be a nearly illiterate hodgepodge of demands, complaints, and threats.

On Saturday, October 10, Pierre Laporte, a friend and ally from the Lesage government, now labour minister in Robert Bourassa's government, was seized at the point of a machine gun from outside his home on the South Shore, near Montreal. This crime came shortly after Jérôme Choquette, Bourassa's justice minister, had refused to release the prisoners demanded by the FLQ and offered instead to trade a safe conduct to Cuba for the release of Cross. The abduction was immediately described by the media as "an instant response" to Choquette's statement, but it could not have been. The abductors were driving around Laporte's home while the justice minister was speaking. This was the work of an entirely different group of FLQ supporters, who had decided that the seizure of Cross was a mistake; what was needed was a French Canadian hostage. However, the coincidental timing made it appear as if the terrorists were a highly organized, incredibly swift-moving organization.

That night, Premier Robert Bourassa moved into a guarded suite on the twentieth floor of the Queen Elizabeth Hotel in downtown Montreal. This was later made to read that he spent the crisis "cowering in his bunker," although how you got a bunker on the twentieth floor of a hotel was never explained. I knew Bourassa, and I don't believe for a minute that he cowered anywhere. If he went into safekeeping, it was because the police officials responsible for his security told him to do so — how could he have refused?

On Sunday, October 11, while senior officials from Ottawa and Quebec held a series of meetings to plot strategy, Robert Lemieux was arrested, charged with "obstructing justice," and thrown into jail. That night, Premier Bourassa made a speech which seemed to indicate that he was willing to negotiate with the kidnappers; then Lemieux was released from jail and asked to act as their spokesperson.

This was the Thanksgiving weekend; it led to a pause of two days while the police scrambled around, senior bureaucrats met, and not much happened.

On Wednesday, October 14, Bourassa called René Lévesque, who, with Claude Ryan, was pressing the Quebec government to at least consider releasing the prisoners. At this time, René was the leader of the Parti Québécois, formed in October 1968 out of his Mouvement Souveraineté-Association and the Ralliement national. He was also the voice of reason.

Ever blunt, René asked the premier, "What the hell's going on? Are you negotiating or aren't you?" Bourassa replied that they were, that he was being kept "fully informed" by the prime minister, and that Trudeau was willing to confirm safe conduct out of the country in return for the release of Cross.

"Jesus Christ!" René exploded. "That's what Choquette said last week!" Bourassa told him that he had a serious split in his cabinet about what action to take, and, he added, "I have the police on my back."

The next day, Thursday, the federal cabinet gathered for its regular cabinet meeting, and it was one of the strangest sessions I ever attended. Trudeau, as usual, was calm, fully in control. Very, very impressive. However, he had very little information to give us. John Diefenbaker, the leader of the Official Opposition, and, before this, ever the defender of civil rights, had asked pointedly in the House whether the government was willing to impose the War Measures Act, a draconian piece of legislation that had been used, and abused, during the Winnipeg Strike and against Japanese Canadians during the Second World War.

Now, it became clear, it was to be imposed again. But the case for imposition was, even within the cabinet room, fuzzy, ill defined, and supported by almost no concrete evidence.

Around the long, oval table in room 205S, the cabinet ministers are gathered, hunched over a pile of documents provided by the Privy Council Office; but we aren't looking at those. We are, instead, looking down the room towards a telephone booth where Marc Lalonde, not a member of the cabinet, but the prime minister's principal secretary, is talking on the telephone to Jérôme Choquette, and every time he comes back from the booth, it is to tell us that "things look very bad, very bad indeed."

When the ministers ask questions, they are answered by Lalonde, not the prime minister, and what he tells us is that Quebec is ready to explode. If swift and stern action is not taken at once, the best information from the best experts is that there will be riots, political assassinations, chaos. There is no question that Lalonde was the dominating figure that morning.

The FLQ had been in existence for six years at this point — this is not something I knew at the time, but it is useful, I think, to consider the background against which we were making our decision. During those years, there had been 200 bombings in Quebec, either by the FLQ or other criminal groups, and a number of holdups to gain money to further terrorist aims. These bombings and holdups had resulted in six deaths, none of which had been a planned assassination.

In contrast, in the fifteen months ending April 30, 1970, there had been 4,300 bombings in the United States, resulting in forty-three deaths and 384 injuries. New York City at this time had a bombing on an average of once every other day.

In our immediate crisis, we had had, so far, two kidnappings. No one in New York was proposing the elimination of all safeguards against unlawful arrest, but that was exactly what we were doing.

## THE CALL FOR "ALL-OUT WAR"

Of course, we were as swept up in the hysterical coverage of the FLQ activities as everybody else. Ontario's Premier John Robarts was calling for "all-out war" on the terrorists; newspaper editorials were screaming for drastic action; and police officials were warning us that there was a connection between the FLQ and the militant Black Panther movement in the United States. Later, this turned out to mean that there had been one report in which an informant had two years earlier said there was such a connection.

During our cabinet meeting of October 15, in the two hours before lunch, cabinet members talked around and around the subject, but came to no firm conclusion. I did not speak.

When we broke for lunch, I went back to my office on the ground floor, where Richard Gwyn and Allan Gotlieb were waiting for me. There were both reluctant to see the imposition of War Measures, but both insisted that if that was how cabinet was going to go — which it clearly was — it was my duty not to break ranks.

I was heading back up the stairs to the cabinet room when Jean Marchand caught up to me. He said, "How are you going to go on this thing? The prime minister is worried; he thinks you have some doubts. You didn't say anything this morning."

I said, "I don't know. I won't know until I speak this afternoon."

When we got back to the meeting, I was the first on the list, and I said, "I intend to support the imposition of the War Measures Act."

As soon as I said it, looking directly across the table at Trudeau, he raised one hand, in a sort of gesture of triumph, and brought it down over his face. My immediate reaction was, I have just made a terrible mistake. His obvious relief meant that this was not a done deal, there was still some hesitancy about it. I think now that if I had said what I ought to have said, namely that there was no convincing evidence of an "apprehended insurrection," which was the legal rationale for imposing the act, Gérard Pelletier, who was a staunch civil libertarian, and obviously troubled about this, would have bolted as well. There were others, like Donald Macdonald and Don Jamieson, who also must have had their doubts. I am speculating here.

I don't think Trudeau could have pushed it through. What did it, I now think, was the combination of general hysteria outside, and his aura of control inside. At the time, I thought he was fully in command, but in retrospect, he seemed to be almost an observer, rather than a moving force. However, he seemed so damn certain that the course of action being pressed on him by Lalonde was right, that our common sense went out the window, and we gave him backing for what turned out to be a massive injustice — not merely the military occupation of Canadian cities, but the arrest and detention, without charge, of more than 400 Canadian citizens (or, to be exact, French Canadian citizens), who were held without bail. They were beyond the reach of habeas corpus, a right wrenched out of King John at Runnymede, in 1215.

The hysteria was both inflamed and endorsed by such statements as those from John Turner, the minister of justice, that if Canadians generally "knew what we knew," they would understand the need for drastic action. He said, "It is my hope that some day the intelligence upon which the government acted can be made public, because until that day comes, the people of Canada will not be able fully to appraise the course of action which has been taken by the government."

There was no secret knowledge that explained the imposition of War Measures. Everything we were told in cabinet came from the streets outside. Turner also argued that "under the present law, the prosecution of this type of violent, criminal conspiracy is rendered difficult, if not impossible, under the present provisions of the Criminal Code."

Pierre Laporte was found murdered on October 18, two days after the imposition of the War Measures Act. James Cross was found and freed on December 3 as a result of normal police surveillance, and his kidnappers flown out to Cuba. Laporte's kidnappers were arrested on December 28, again through the use of ordinary police measures.

Jean Marchand claimed that "these people have infiltrated every strategic place in the province of Quebec, every place where important decisions were taken…this is an organization which has thousands of guns, rifles, machine-guns, bombs, more than enough [dynamite] to blow up the core of downtown Montreal." Nonsense. None of the sudden, secret police raids turned up the guns, rifles, machine guns, bombs, or dynamite, although they did sweep up Pauline Julien, who sang separatist songs.

Gérard Pelletier wrote a whole book, *La Crise d'octobre,* which endeavoured, painfully, to explain why we had suspended the civil liberties of the nation because of two kidnappings. In it, he placed the number of FLQ terrorists at between forty and fifty, backed by 200 to

300 active sympathizers and 2,000 to 3,000 passive supporters, who supported separatism, but not violence. He did not explain how this number of people was going to shred civil order in the province.

When the War Measures Act was proclaimed on October 16, 1970, two reasons were given. The first was that there was an apprehended insurrection, the evidence for which Canadians were to take on faith. The second was that Quebec had asked for the imposition of the act, which was undoubtedly true, but might have been more frankly explained by announcing that the Quebec provincial police and the RCMP were agreed on the suspension of civil liberties, and everybody else went along.

We lost our nerve, and our common sense. George McIlraith got up in the House and solemnly told the nation, "A woman across the river from Ottawa had been kidnapped and the initials FLQ carved on her belly." You would think that might have sent reporters across the Ottawa River to check, but no, they just printed it. My daughter, Cathy, who was working as a school nurse, couldn't go to work because of the crisis; the Montreal school board for which she worked listed her under their "Quarantine Section."

Terry and I were assigned armed soldiers to protect us, as were most cabinet ministers, and there was a great deal of nonsense about this sort of thing. Robert Stanbury, the minister responsible for the newly created Information Canada propaganda machine, was outraged because he wasn't assigned soldiers; they had become a status symbol. He was duly assigned a couple of youngsters with guns to stand on his front lawn. They cross-questioned kids invited to a Halloween party at the Stanbury residence in the Glebe area of Ottawa. ("You say you're a witch, not a separatist? Prove it!")

In a bizarre twist, it became a criminal offence not merely to be a member of the FLQ, but to have ever belonged to that organization, a bit of retroactive legislation that could never have withstood a challenge under the Canadian Charter of Rights and Freedoms — happily, there was no such thing at the time.

It was Tommy Douglas of the NDP who stood in the House, day after day, and hammered the government for suspending civil liberties, and if you ask me today why I wasn't up there beside him I can only say, damned if I know. He showed political courage of the highest order.

## A BUDGET OF BUREAUCRATS

To understand why I did leave federal politics, I have to take you back to the first budget presented by the Trudeau administration, Edgar Benson's budget in 1968, which was my first real sense of how fully centralized the government was becoming. Benson, or rather his bureaucrats, had invented something new called a "social development tax," which in any way you interpret it in the English language means a tax on social development. When you put a tax on sales, it is called a sales tax, and it is not a tax to encourage sales; it is likely to have just the opposite effect. You put the tax on as a way to raise money. How could you call this a social development tax when what you were doing was taking away money?

The bureaucrats in the Department of Finance were convinced that inflation was just around the corner. They wanted to put a 3 per cent surtax on personal and corporate income to reduce incomes and, hence, spending. In accordance with fiscal agreements with the provinces, the federal government would have to share the increased revenue with the provinces, since this was a tax on incomes. Clearly, the Finance Department did not want to do this. By bastardizing the meaning of words and calling a surtax a social development tax, the department believed (and this turned out to be correct) that it could avoid its responsibilities under various tax arrangements with the provinces.

The tax receipts would come from the incomes of individuals and corporations, who would have less to spend. Since the provinces would not share in the returns, they would be unable to increase their spending. The threat of inflation was trumped up. In the ten years from 1963 to 1972, the consumer price index went up 11.7 per cent, an average of less than 1.2 per cent annually. It was, and was meant to be, a tightening and centralizing of the economy. Save for the actual statistics, I said all this at the cabinet meeting at which this was discussed.

I do not know if the prime minister knew or understood the significance of the details of the budget, or if members of the Priorities and Planning Committee had been informed. I do know that the proposal was not presented to cabinet until the morning of budget day, at the same time that it was being presented to journalists in the lock-up in the same building. Moreover, it had been flown a day earlier to all Bank of Canada offices in the ten provinces, to be distributed that evening when Edgar Benson gave his budget address. When Trudeau, who thought my position made a certain amount of sense, asked, "Is it too late to change some of this?" the answer was an emphatic yes.

That evening, Jean-Marc Poliquin of Radio-Canada called me at home. He said, "Eric, I know you are bound by cabinet solidarity, but I want to ask you a hypothetical question. Jean-Jacques Bertrand [then premier of Quebec] has declared that the budget cheated Quebec of $125 million in income taxes, with the introduction of a social development tax, which evaded the income tax agreements. If what he is saying were true, would the amount of $125 million be about right?"

I replied, "Yes, about right."

I happened to pass the prime minister in the Centre Block the next morning. He said, "Eric, I have had several calls from your colleagues about reports on the CBC last night."

I responded that I did not know if Premier Bertrand was right, but said that if he had been, the province would indeed have lost about $125 million. I realized that this was a specious statement. Trudeau said, "Please try to be more discreet next time."

The whole approach on this issue seemed to me very Orwellian and misleading, but of course I got nowhere. My cabinet colleagues thought they could sell a social development tax, and that was that. I wouldn't let up on it and Benson didn't really know what he was talking about; he had in effect been handed this by his bureaucrats, and his job was to get it through. The country was supposed to believe that we, the members of cabinet, had made these changes, when in fact they had been dictated by the mandarins in the Department of Finance and approved by the mandarins in the Prime Minister's Office (PMO). All we had to do was say: Ready, aye ready.

The background to this was that the Royal Commission on Taxation (or Carter Commission) had come down in 1967. Appointed in 1962, the commission had been delegated to look at the whole tax system for the first time in decades, to see what could be done to make it fair. The chair was a sixty-year-old Toronto tax accountant named Kenneth Carter. By the time he had been through ninety-nine public hearings, received 346 briefs, and spent five years cogitating furiously, he had become convinced, correctly in my view, that the tax system was inefficient, clumsy, expensive to administer, and retrogressive. Moreover, the poor paid taxes at a much higher rate than the rich, for the simple reason that unlike the rich, they could not conceal most of their income from the taxman. This, from Carter, who was a solid, true-blue Conservative.

Carter's solution was so dangerous because it was so simple — hostile commentators later reduced it to five words: "a buck is a buck." He proposed that every scrap of income, from capital gains to expenses to cover a business lunch, should be treated as income, and taxed at the same rate as other income. It was a formula to send chills down the spine of every martini-luncher and headwaiter in the land.

Benson's solution to the danger that the wealthy might have to pay more taxes was, in his first budget, simply to ignore Carter. Then, when he did begin to fiddle with the tax system, it was by making up this 3 per cent tax. But he wouldn't share that with the provinces; he was determined to keep it all for Ottawa. His bureaucrats may have proposed this, but Benson accepted it and put it through cabinet. When that happened, I began to understand how centralist he really was.

When I realized that the promises so boldly trotted out during the 1968 election — I had used the "just society" slogan in my own campaign — had been delivered for implementation to the tender mercies of the same bureaucracy that had created an unjust society, I went home and told Terry, "We may not be here very long."

### THE CARTER REPORT: ABANDONED ON A HILLSIDE

What happened to Kenneth Carter's monumental work, just to deal with that for a moment, was that committees were set up to study it to death; then there were reports, and more committees to study the reports, and new reports and more committees — until everybody eventually forgot what it was all about. The Carter report, which made sense in 1967 and makes even more sense now, was treated like one of those Oriental babies you read about; it was put out on a hillside, and left to perish alone and unmourned.

The difficulty I faced was that, as already mentioned, none of the economic portfolios in the Trudeau government was headed by anyone who knew anything about macroeconomics, with the exception of Jack Davis, minister of fisheries and forestry, which meant that policy was made by the same Finance Department bureaucrats who had produced the mess Carter was trying to straighten out. They brought their gems of wisdom, like the social development tax, to the minister, who puffed on his pipe and signed on the dotted line, and then, when someone raised an objection in cabinet, it was too late to do anything.

You would go to a meeting with seven cabinet ministers and a dozen or so advisers from the Department of Finance and Revenue Canada to discuss Carter, and be presented with a massive pile of documents covering all the topics to be discussed. You had never seen this material before in your life; you were not even given a chance to read it before the discussion opened, led of course by the mandarins who alone knew what was in the material. This went on every Wednesday evening until 11 p.m. or midnight, and then officials from Finance would go around and collect all the papers. I held on to some by simply refusing point-blank to hand them over when asked to do so. I was amazed that anyone could consider this process as an honest attempt to come to grips with tax reform. We were being led around by our noses. The fact is that while I blame the bureaucrats for the way they bulldozed and bamboozled us, we let them get away with it. What was missing was the political will to take control and say: No, by golly, you are not going to do this anymore.

Trudeau made much of the plans he had to reconstruct the civil service on new lines, but the really big changes he made were to move Robert Bryce, who had been deputy minister of finance, over to the PMO, as his economic adviser; Simon Reisman, who had been secretary of the Treasury Board, to deputy minister of finance; and Al Johnson, who had been economic adviser to the prime minister, to secretary of the Treasury Board.

This wasn't reorganization, it was musical chairs. The same people were still giving the same advice. Trudeau, on this subject at least, was all windup, and no pitch.

It got worse. In 1969, Benson produced his own White Paper on Tax Reform, which actually promised some changes, such as a capital gains tax (but in direct contradiction of Carter, only half the gain would be taken into income). Benson also proposed an end to the then current three-year tax holiday for new mining projects, and a measure to tie depletion allowances connected with oil exploration to spending on new exploration. If you wanted the tax break, you actually had to spend money for the purposes for which you said you needed the money.

These proposals brought forth one of the loudest, best-heeled lobbying campaigns in Canadian history. Dark, rumbling speeches came from the bowels of the Canadian Club, the Rotary Club, and other outposts of enlightenment. There were orchestrated phone calls to MPs; write-in letter campaigns to the newspapers; and the familiar cries of bank presidents, insurance executives, and other assorted moguls, who told us that these changes, if implemented, would lead to a stampede of all our best and brightest across the border to the United States. Does this sound familiar?

The Carter reforms were not officially dead until March 1971, when Benson said in a speech in Kingston, Ontario, that "the White Paper will never be legislated." But when we were dealing with the proposals in 1969, we believed that the government meant to fulfill its promises of reform. Then, when we received the *Summary of 1971 Tax Reform Legislation* in cabinet, I got a new shock. The budget contained two paragraphs that embodied a revolution in our taxation system, buried in the tortuous prose of the Finance Department:

> ### Interest on Money Borrowed to Buy Shares
> The present tax system does not permit a corporation to deduct interest on money borrowed to buy shares of other corporations because the dividends on these shares are normally tax-exempt. To encourage Canadian ownership and investment, the bill provides a full deduction for interest on money borrowed by a corporation to buy shares in any other corporation. The present system allows a deduction for individual taxpayers and this is retained.
>
> This deduction for interest provides a substantial incentive for Canadian corporations to invest in other corporations and permits them to compete on an even footing with foreign corporations. Assuming a tax rate of 50 per cent, the cost of borrowing money for share purchases will be cut in half.

This was an instrument for the creation of megacorporations, mergers, and concentration, and it has done more damage than any single budget change I can think of. For a giant corporation wanting to buy out a competitor, the cost of borrowing had been cut in half.

This proposal had come up in a meeting of the cabinet's Committee on Economic Policy, and I thought I had derailed it. In the spring of 1971, this committee had a heavily charged agenda, including consideration of a chapter of a new fair-competition bill, prepared by the minister of consumer and corporate affairs, Ron Basford. The "interest on money borrowed to buy shares" item did not appear on the agenda. Bud Drury, the committee chair, was simply handed a paper that Benson and Reisman wanted passed right away, with no documentation whatever.

I said, "What are you saying?"

I was told by one of the Finance officials standing by that "this was something external to tax reform, as an added incentive to investment to broaden the sphere of investment."

I said, "Wait a minute. This can be very damaging," and Bud Drury, who was chairing that meeting, said, "How so?"

I replied, "This very morning, I received from Sam Bronfman a copy of the fiftieth annual report of Seagram's. I flipped to the back of that report to look at the number under 'income before taxes.' Suppose it was about $100 million. Under this, he could end up not paying a cent in taxes."

Everybody just looked at me. They had no idea what I was talking about, although it was not very complicated. "Look," I said, "he makes $100 million; he goes out and borrows a billion dollars to buy up his competition, and pays 10 per cent per annum for the necessary loan. Ten per cent of one billion is $100 million; he writes the whole thing off against income, and the Canadian taxpayer finances half the cost, because he would otherwise be paying at a rate of 50 per cent."

That got a nod or two.

I went on, "At this very meeting, we are going to be asked to approve legislation which the minister for consumer and corporate affairs plans to bring in to block corporations from reducing competition. How can you square that with this?"

Simon Reisman, who is very quick, got it at once. He said, "We didn't think of that. Ben, maybe we should consider this."

Benson nodded. The item was removed from that day's agenda.

I relaxed and ceased to worry about it, and suddenly, here it was again, like the cat that came back, now as an official part of the *Summary of 1971 Tax Reform Legislation*.

And when I made my protest, I was told, as usual, that it was too late. Nothing could be done. And the only explanation I was ever given was that the Americans were doing it, so we had to do it, too.

The really galling thing about this was that when the budget was released, under the rubric of "tax reform," I was required to explain it to the French journalists in the budgetary lock-up, while Benson was explaining it to the English group. None of my colleagues felt they understood it well enough to answer questions, so I found myself explaining something with which I profoundly disagreed, without ever letting on that this was the case. That night, I got a telephone call from one of the really sharp French Canadian journalists, who said, "Eric, I noticed you never once used the word 'reform' in connection with this budget. Why was that?" The phrase I stuck to throughout was "les changements fiscaux" (the fiscal changes).

I said, "I have no comment on that."

## THE CASE OF THE FLYING DOLLAR

Part of what irritated me in Ottawa was the sheer boneheadedness of the advice we were being given by the mandarins — and that we were acting upon. Earlier on, I got so upset by this that I went, in late November 1969, to see Trudeau in his office. On October 27, the German government had floated the Deutschmark. We did nothing. As I was about to leave the prime minister's office after a discussion about the Post Office, I said, "Pierre, I know it's not my affair, but I want you to talk to the Bank of Canada and the Department of Finance."

He looked up, puzzled, and I went on. "The Germans freed the mark two days ago. The mark was undervalued at its fixed rate, and as a result there was too much buying by speculators who knew it had to go up." I explained that this pressure had been increasing daily, causing headaches for Germany's central bank, the Bundesbank.

"The mark is now increasing in value, since the float, and will probably slow down when it is worth about 8 to 10 per cent more. Germany will then fix the rate at the higher value. At this point, there will be only two monetary units undervalued, the yen and the Canadian dollar. The Japanese know how to defend themselves. We don't."

"What do you suggest?"

"We should allow the dollar to float upwards to meet the pressure from the American dollar."

He said, "I don't understand all this. This stuff is not my field."

I tried to keep the dismay out of my voice. "I thought you attended the London School of Economics?"

He shrugged. "I did; but you know what that sort of thing is about."

He simply would not do the work to grasp the argument himself, and I am sure that, with his intelligence, he could have become an expert in these matters. But he had not been interested.

He said, "Put it on the agenda for the next cabinet meeting."

"I can't. It can only be introduced by the Department of Finance, and they won't do it."

"Tell me more about it."

I said, "The people who are now making a killing on the mark will bring their money home and look around for another undervalued monetary unit. They will gamble on the dollar going off its fixed rate."

"Oh." He was absorbing it, now, and there was a knock on the door. An aide came in to say that Senator Martin was here for his appointment. Trudeau said to her, "I'm very sorry, but you'll have to reschedule him." So much for Martin. He turned to me. "Go on."

I said, "The speculators will come here because the Japanese know how to protect the yen, and we don't know how to protect the Canadian dollar. Any youngster working on the bond desk at Nesbitt, Thomson will see that he has more orders to buy the Canadian dollar coming up here and we'll have to accept American dollars and put them in the Exchange Fund to keep our dollar where it is. We'll be taking money out of the market to do that, and it is not sustainable. The American dollars will be isolated in the Exchange Fund; and the supply of Canadian dollars going down will force interest rates in Canada to go up."

He got it. He said, "Leave it with me, I'll take it up." What transpired after that Richard Gwyn learned from his sources.

When Trudeau suggested to Marc Lalonde, Simon Reisman, and Bob Bryce that perhaps we had better think of floating the Canadian dollar, Bryce immediately said, "We'd better think hard about this before we do anything."

That delayed it for a week. Then Louis Rasminsky, the governor of the Bank of Canada, was brought in, and he had all sorts of reasons why the policy we had been following was the right policy and should not be changed. So again, nothing happened.

Then in mid-January of 1970, Benson turned up in cabinet with a request for a loan of $300 million. When Finance wanted money, nobody ever questioned it, but I had been watching the cash position of the government and I knew it was quite strong. I said, "May I ask a question?"

Trudeau nodded assent.

I said, "Ben, what do we need the $300 million for? The last time I looked, we had a very strong cash position."

He pulled his pipe out of his mouth, looked at it, and answered, "For general purposes."

I said, "Perhaps it's more than that."

"No, that's all." He stuck his pipe back in his mouth.

"Could it be that there's a lot of American money coming up here to buy Canadian dollars?"

Then he blundered. He pulled his pipe out again and muttered, "Could be."

That got Trudeau mad. He said, "Mr. Benson, if a colleague asks a question, do your best to answer it." This was said very politely, but with a bite. When the prime minister called you Mister, you knew you were in trouble.

I said, "I think you had lots of money and if you need to borrow more, it must be to buy American dollars and put them in the Exchange Fund."

Benson stared straight ahead, but made no reply.

I went on, "This will put pressure on interest rates here; they will go up, and our business community will suffer."

Nothing changed. Trudeau obviously felt it would be going too far to intrude into Benson's portfolio, even though it must have been obvious to him that we were headed for trouble.

It came in May. Trudeau had been away to Japan and landed in Vancouver to be confronted with an exchange crisis. He had to fly straight on to Ottawa, landing at about 3 a.m. on a Saturday morning, and we were all summoned post-haste to an emergency meeting in his office.

Earlier that week, Robert Stanfield, the Conservative leader, had asked in the House if the government was giving consideration to floating the Canadian dollar. The answer was no — it had to be — but the fat was in the fire. American dollars were pouring in and we were having to suck them up, and interest rates were starting to rocket upwards. In three months, $709 million had vanished from our reserves.

I was the first to get to Trudeau's office, and he waved me in. "I'm glad you're here."

"What's it about? The dollar?"

"Yes."

I said, "When was the last time after I spoke to you that you heard anything from your officials about the flexible dollar?"

He said he wasn't sure, but he thought it was about six months later.

I said, "No, it wasn't. It was one billion, two hundred million dollars later."

When the others arrived, about nine or ten of the cabinet, he said, "Well, according to protocol, I have to ask your permission to bring in the officials." That was given, and in came a group of mandarins, headed by Rasminsky of the Bank of Canada.

He began to explain that this wasn't really a crisis, and that we could continue to go along with the dollar at 92.5¢ U.S., but "irresponsible questions" in the House were creating a problem. I often wondered afterwards if his real solution would have been to close down the House.

I said I didn't think much of this and away we went on monetary theory for about an hour, while everybody else grew bored and restless. Then Rasminsky said that the International Monetary Fund (IMF) had sent some people up here — including Pierre Paul Schweitzer, the head of the Fund — because they were worried that we would float the Canadian dollar.

Trudeau said, "What would be the problem?"

Rasminsky explained that if a small country like Canada felt it could devalue its currency, so would other nations, and the IMF was concerned that this would lead to "market instability" — another term for allowing the market to do its job and decide what currencies are really worth.

I lost my cool a little, and said, "Well, Prime Minister, I don't give a damn about what the IMF thinks. I care more about what is of benefit or harm to the Canadian economy, and if we keep on this way we will be looking at more borrowing, higher interest rates, and a sharp rise in inflation."

Rasminsky turned to me and said, very coolly, "Well, Mr. Minister, you may not care much about the IMF, but I can assure you it is a bulwark of many nations, and I care about it very much."

I backpedalled a little and said, "Well, there comes a time when Canada is paying too high a price to follow the IMF line."

Simon Reisman got into it, to back Rasminsky, and said, "Prime Minister, given that there are only ten of your colleagues here, perhaps we should put this off until the full cabinet meets on Thursday. What do you think, Ben?"

And the honourable minister of finance sucked on his pipe and said, "I think that would be a very good idea."

Rasminsky thought it would be a good idea, too, but by this time Trudeau was beginning to get the drift, and he said, "Eric?"

I said, "Prime Minister, you know I have strong opinions and you know I express them sometimes very extravagantly, but let me tell you what is going to happen if we don't take action now. You have had your staff call twenty-eight ministers or their executive assistants to come to this meeting, and you have just got off a plane from Osaka in Vancouver, and been told you had to take another plane to Ottawa at once to have this cabinet meeting. The press even now may be speculating on what can possibly be going on, now, in this room. They know you flew across the nation to arrive at 3 a.m., and they know Stanfield asked a very pointed question, and believe me, they are capable of putting two and two together."

He sat back in his seat and looked thoughtful.

Then he turned to Rasminsky and said, "How are we to answer questions about this? Aren't the media bound to say this meeting must have been about the exchange rate?"

And Rasminsky made a mistake. He said, very stiffly, "Now, Prime Minister, how could the press find out what we have been talking about? My officials are all sworn to secrecy, as are all your ministers."

I said, "If we don't settle this now, by Monday morning a billion dollars in U.S. funds will be crossing the desks of Ames and other dealers hunting for Canadian dollars."

Rasminsky didn't want to say "Nonsense," but he came close.

By this time, Trudeau had heard enough. He turned to Benson

and said, "Mr. Benson, how soon could you declare that we are floating the dollar?"

Ben didn't know.

Simon Reisman said, "We could make it by five o'clock this afternoon."

And we did, and the dollar floated, and the crisis ended.

What was so frustrating in all this was that Trudeau could be deci-
sive, crisp, and forceful when he was given both sides of an issue. But
most of the time he was hearing only the Bank of Canada and the
Department of Finance, where good economists being funnelled in at
one end ended up echoing the American line at the other end.

I had, of course, made more enemies in this exercise against the Bank
of Canada and the Department of Finance. Being right only made it
worse. Neither institution enjoyed being crossed.

The exchange crisis was the only time my advice was taken seriously
on economic matters, and I realized that this was partly because, as pre-
viously noted, one was not supposed to comment on the workings of
other departments. There was none of the free exchange of ideas, arguments, and opinions that characterized the Lesage government in Quebec. Trudeau had a mind that demanded order, not questions, and every
time I opened my mouth to comment on matters in the area where I had
some experience and expertise I made another enemy in cabinet.

**THE LAST STRAW**

The 1970 budget, which was delayed because of the October Crisis, was
the last straw. It included a provision for depreciation at the rate of 115
per cent for new plant and equipment purchases. If you spent $100 mil-
lion, you were entitled to deduct from earnings not $100 million, but
$115 million in depreciation. When is a cost greater than the real cost?
When the Department of Finance says so.

Take, for example, a manufacturer who decides to produce respira-
tors. Suppose the lowest possible cost of manufacturing involves an
investment of $2 million and the employment of forty-eight workers.
The government gives the manufacturer an incentive (depreciation, tax
reduction, subsidies, whatever) to use more capital. This enables the
workforce to be reduced by eleven people. I have done it. Government
policy favours capital, which is in short supply, over labour, which we

have in surplus. People see the thirty-seven jobs that are created, but they have no way of seeing that their government has paid out their tax money to make other jobs disappear. That is the inevitable result of high depreciation allowances.

What is more, the tax system discriminates in favour of people who have the money to build plant and equipment in a hurry — the Americans. Canadian sources do not have the time to gear up, so the new assets are bought from American suppliers. What was so maddening about the 1970 proposal was that, like all of these crash programs designed to make employers invest more, and so promote job growth, it was bound to be self-defeating. The money would go into plant, not people; jobs would shrink, not grow.

There were other giveaways for corporations in the budget, including extended tax exemptions for the oil, gas, and mining concerns, and allowing corporations to pad their costs by deducting 150 per cent of the amounts spent on "research."

Because we were still in the midst of the turmoil of the War Measures Act when I first got a look at these proposals in December 1970, I felt I could not make my position public. But I also felt, as Tom Kent put it in the epigraph at the top of this chapter, "I could not live with a government whose economic policies were inducing unemployment."

I went home and brooded about it. I contacted a number of economists and, over the next three months, prepared a detailed paper on the shortcomings, as I saw them, of the approach that was then being taken. I outlined seven "structural distortions" that result from government subsidies for the employment of capital. I also prepared a series of charts designed to show how the tax system was being used to finance the takeover of the Canadian economy by Americans.

If foreign ownership dominates the mining and petroleum industries, our tax system has clearly invited this concentration. We have not only extended a warm invitation to foreign capital, but we have told it where to go. If you want to invest in the service industries, we say, you will have to pay taxes on 87 per cent or 90 per cent of your profits. On the other hand, in metal mining you will have to pay on only 13 per cent, and in petroleum on only 5.7 per cent.

The invitation says in effect, "Come and gut us."

## MY LAST STAND WITH TRUDEAU

These matters were very much in my mind when Irving Brecher, a senior economist at McGill, telephoned to say that he was in charge of the upcoming June meeting of the Canadian Economics Association at Memorial University in St. John's, Newfoundland. He said that the president of the association, Professor John Graham of Dalhousie University, had put forward my name as the main speaker at the formal luncheon. I jumped at the invitation as a chance to make my views public. This resulted in a speech that John McDougall, an associate professor of political science at Western, later called "the most important paper" of my life. He added, "Kierans was never to hold public office again, and in that sense his days as a political actor were over. However, the address was actually the beginning of a new career, one of holding the country's other political actors to account." *

It was, in fact, the paper I had been working on for three months; it contained many of the views I have already set down here, along with others I will be coming to shortly. I could not make these views public while still a member of the Trudeau cabinet, and I felt I owed it to the prime minister to let him know how I felt.

I took my arguments to Trudeau in a private meeting over lunch at 24 Sussex Drive on April 27, 1971. He listened to me very gravely, with full attention, and interrupted me from time to time to ask if I could not soften my views enough to allow me to remain within the cabinet; the answer was no. Then I told him that if I floated these opinions out to the public, especially those dealing with the tax treatment of the petroleum industry, he would not win a single seat in Alberta in the next election. (Actually, he didn't anyway, as it turned out; but at this time he held five.) That changed the climate of our discussion at once, and it was clear that my parliamentary career was over. I went home and wrote my letter of resignation.

That night, I telephoned my mother, who was then eighty-six, to say that I was resigning.

"Are you doing the right thing, Eric?" she asked.

---

* John N. McDougall, *The Politics and Economics of Eric Kierans* (Montreal and Kingston: McGill-Queen's University Press, 1993), 157.

"Yes, dear, I am."

There was a pause, and then, "Can you get another job?"

## THE POWER OF THE PMO

Looking back now, I can see that I must have been a constant irritant to some of my colleagues in cabinet; but this was at least in part because I believed, based on my Quebec experience, in two things that did not seem to obtain in Ottawa. The first was the right and duty of any minister to voice his or her views on any subject under discussion. The second was the notion we all learned in school that ministers have a responsibility to fulfill; and if they don't or can't fulfill it for any reason — from incompetence to fundamental disagreement with a government policy — they are obligated to resign. Cabinet resignations on matters of principle seem to have gone out the window, and one reason for this, I suspect, is that in so many cases the ministers do not, in fact, bear responsibility. It has been taken away from them, housed in the bureaucracy, or in the splendours of the Prime Minister's Office.

Canada today is run by the PMO and PCO, whose mandarins instruct the elected members as to what they should do and say, and what opinions they must support. The notion that the prime minister is *primus inter pares* — first among equals — which appears in every textbook on political science, has become a lame joke. The prime minister has no equals, nor any who can remotely aspire to be equal except by taking over the job. The position is more like a president than a prime minister, but within a system not designed for such overwhelming centralized control, and in a regionalized nation where such control is not merely awkward, but dangerous to the public weal.

This shift in control was well underway, but not complete, when I left. At one point Marc Lalonde, the grand vizier of the PMO, who had not yet been elected to anything, decided to instigate a series of regular meetings among the ministerial aides — the special and executive assistants — in order to "talk things over." Or to put it another way, so that the PMO would have an entree into every ministry at the political level. Richard Gwyn mentioned this to me, and I hardly knew what to say. I certainly couldn't prevent his attending, an action that he might well have resented, but the whole idea made me angry. I simply told him that it would not bother me if he did not attend. I gathered later that other ministers were somewhat blunter on the subject, and the project soon faded away.

It turned out that it would have been a waste, anyway. Before long, the PMO did not need to consult the aides to ensure co-operation; it simply issued orders.

The growth of power at the centre has been incremental, and parallels the increasing centralization of policy direction in Ottawa. As the federal power grew, so did the heart of that power. In Pearson's day — and I am not a particular fan of the man — ministers still held considerable independent clout; today, with the exception of the minister of finance, they are more like the secretaries in a U.S. cabinet than Canadian ministers of the past, who used to represent their regions, their constituencies, and their own political principles, rather than simply fronting for the administration and the bureaucracy. When you hear a cabinet minister today dodging personal responsibility for some horrific blunder on the grounds that it was "an administrative error," about which he or she had no knowledge, the sad thing is that it is probably true.

Ministers *don't* know what is going on half the time. (When Human Resources Development Canada Minister Jane Stewart was castigated by the auditor general because her department had spent more than a billion dollars without adequate controls, her explanation was that this was a huge program, and there were bound to be mix-ups, and of course she wouldn't resign just because money couldn't be accounted for.) And ministers don't formulate policy. They have shifted the burden over to the PMO, the PCO, the Department of Finance, and the Bank of Canada, with results that are bound to prove disastrous to us all.

## Ten

———•◦•———

# A NEW CAREER

*Interviews with these government insiders shed some interesting light on an otherwise anomalous feature of the whole story of the Kierans Report. Despite the report's apparently heavy impact on other provincial and federal policies during the 1970s, the government in Manitoba proved very reluctant to pick up on its main recommendations or, in Mark Eliesen's less delicate description, "ran from it like Napoleon from Moscow."*

— JOHN N. MCDOUGALL, *THE POLITICS AND ECONOMICS OF ERIC KIERANS*, 1993

I WAS STILL A MEMBER of Parliament after my resignation from cabinet, and a good deal of pressure came on me, especially from some of my French Canadian colleagues, not to vote against the legislation that was introduced to embody the so-called reforms I had been attacking. This was, officially, Bill C-59, An Act to Amend the Income Tax Act. Be absent, be sick, be anything but a negative vote, was the way it was put to me, but I didn't feel that was right. Accordingly, I spoke against the measure, and Trudeau, with what I thought was a good deal of *politesse*, came into the chamber to hear at least the first part of my speech. I guess when he realized he had heard this before over lunch, he decided that was enough, and he nodded to me, got up, and left the floor.

In due course, I stood in my place to vote against the budget.

### THE CALL TO McGILL

My resignation hit the newspapers the next day, and I soon got a call from my old friend Jack Weldon, at McGill, who wanted to know if I was coming back. I still had tenure as a professor there. I said, "Oh, I don't think so; I have some commercial things I want to concentrate on."

I still owned Canadian Adhesives, although I wasn't paying much attention to it, and it seemed to me I should be exploring the possibilities in that direction, rather than going back to doing something I had already done before.

In July, I received an invitation from Walter Gordon to join the Committee for an Independent Canada (CIC), a nationalist organization that had been formed in 1970 by Walter, Peter Newman, and Abe Rotstein, an economist at the University of Toronto. I was never much of a joiner, so I put Walter off, but I did agree to make a couple of speeches for the CIC, and in due course, I did so.

Then I got another call, this time from Howard Ross, dean of the Faculty of Management at McGill, and he asked me to come to talk to him and some colleagues about returning to the university. Howard wanted me to give four lectures at the university, open to all students and faculty, during the 1971–72 academic year, when I would be filling out my term as an MP. His motive, he told me frankly, was to have me attached to the faculty and then to have me succeed him as dean in September 1972. I agreed to the lectures, but told him that my preference was to rejoin the Department of Economics. I agreed to return there after my tour as an MP ended, in the fall of 1972.

I didn't run in the October 1972 federal election, but I did play a small part in it. I wrote the foreword to a book called *Louder Voices: The Corporate Welfare Bums,* which was put together by federal NDP leader David Lewis. The book carried the attack on tax giveaways that I had enunciated, in vain, in cabinet. John Turner, who replaced Edgar Benson in Finance, had brought in a budget in May containing even more and fatter corporate handouts, so I felt no compunction about writing in support of David's views. Turner had not come up with all these giveaways, I was certain; he was merely, once more, approving the plans and policies handed up from the same mandarins who ruled the nation from behind the scenes.

In my foreword, I sketched the history of concessions made to business through the tax structure, and wondered what would happen to an individual taxpayer who tried to inflate his or her charitable donations by 15 or 33 per cent, as businesses were allowed, and encouraged, to do, on particular expenditures. I referred to Kenneth Carter's thesis that "a cost is a cost," and noted that "a cost is not a cost when it is padded."

This foreword naturally angered any of the establishment Liberals who were not already furious with me, and led to speculation that I was, in fact, not a Liberal but an NDPer. (Max Saltsman, the colourful NDP member for Waterloo, encouraged this view with a crack in the House of Commons while I was still a member. When he rose to speak on a piece of legislation dealing, in a very timid way, with foreign takeovers of Canadian firms, Saltsman was asked how many speakers the NDP was planning to put forward on the measure. He replied, "Three. Four if you count Eric Kierans.")

I was asked directly on television, on the program *Question Period,* "Why do you remain a Liberal?" My questioner was George Bain, a very shrewd observer, and I replied, "Well, you tell me where to go. It's not quite clear if the other parties have answers either. No, I think basically I feel that the Liberal party is probably the party that can institute the changes. But what they've really got to do is go to work on what we might call the Establishment around here."

It didn't matter much which party was elected, if the shots were all being called by the same offstage bureaucrats. And I had not seen anything — still have not seen anything — to suggest that the NDP, if it formed the government in Ottawa, would be any more able to cope with the mandarins than the Conservatives or Liberals had been able. Diefenbaker, who was famous for his attacks on the mandarins, was absolutely right.

I voted NDP in the 1972 election, and I wrote a letter to the prime minister to tell him why, as a voter in his Montreal riding of Mount Royal, I was doing so. "If I were to vote for you, it would mean that I accept and approve courses of action which I firmly believe will worsen our present problems."

I released the letter to the press.

## MANITOBA BOUND

Terry and I were having a rather quiet time of it — I was merely finishing off my term as an MP, running a business, and commenting on politics and economics (not much to do compared with a cabinet post) — when I heard from Jack Weldon again. He had taken a leave of absence to go out to Winnipeg as head of the Planning Secretariat in the Manitoba NDP government of Ed Schreyer. The Secretariat was something of a new wrinkle: a group of bright, mostly young, people brought in to stir things up and get around the solid phalanx of bureaucracy that always comes to bedevil any government. Jack wanted me to work on a report on the Manitoba mining industry, which he suspected was getting away with murder, although of course he would never have put it that way in public.

I was intrigued. I had been writing about taxation policy, resources policy, and the mining industry for some time — most recently, in connection with the Mackenzie Valley Pipeline, as we saw in chapter 8. Here was an opportunity to take a close look at the practices of such an industry, and I could not resist. The result was a contract that saw me flying out to Winnipeg every week, working my head off, then flying home to catch up on all my other duties. I was paid $150 a day, plus expenses.

The key personality and top thinker in Schreyer's cabinet was certainly not the premier himself. An amiable soul, he was smart enough, but inclined to accept the advice of others whenever the alternative that presented itself was actually to do a lot of hard, slogging work. The best mind in his entourage (Jack was just a visitor, as everyone knew) was Mark Eliesen, a slender, dark, fiercely hard-working individual who went on to become chair of Ontario Hydro (when that position was within the gift of an NDP government under Bob Rae; then Eliesen flitted to the NDP government in British Columbia).

Although I was to report to the premier, and was hired by the secretary for the Planning and Priorities Committee of cabinet, my "Report on Natural Resources Policy in Manitoba" was aimed, in the end, at Mark and Jack. That report, tabled in the legislature on March 2, 1973 — I was back at McGill, by this time — was highly critical of the mining industry in the province.

I noted that although the resources employed were the property of the people of Manitoba, these citizens received very little benefit from their ownership position. Federal economic policies — especially the tax policies I had already criticized in the federal cabinet — and the domination of the industry by a handful of giant, multinational firms, led by Inco, combined to remove most of the benefits. Some of those benefits were sent into the pockets of those firms' shareholders, but by far the greater percentage was retained by the corporations themselves.

The nub of my argument reached back to David Ricardo, and the theory of economic rent. In Ricardo's time, at the beginning of the nineteenth century, most of the best farmland had been enclosed by landlords, with the former tenants simply driven off. Ricardo developed the theory of economic rent to describe payment for the use of land and other natural resources, which are in fixed supply. It is the limited supply of resources that makes these payments different from other cost inputs, such as wages, interest, profits, or, indeed, rents paid to a landlord. Economic rents are unearned. Ricardo made this into a virtue.

In the case of resources, the fixed supply belongs to the people of the province, not the mining industry. The people of Manitoba were the landlords, and the government was in the same position as an agent for the landlord. But successive governments had done far more to satisfy the claims of the tenants, that is, the mining companies, than the landlords. The mining giants were paying very low taxes. Between 1965 and 1969, Canadian mining companies generated $2.5 billion in profits; of this, 85.3 per cent was divided between shareholders and retained earnings. The three largest mining companies in Manitoba were paying provincial taxes at the rate of 8 per cent. The value of the metals produced by these three companies came to $676.1 million, and the book profits of the companies to $192 million. Put another way, for every dollar of metal produced from Manitoba resources, the people of Manitoba, the owners, received 2.3¢, and the mining companies 26.1¢. I argued:

> The annual sale of Manitoba resources is composed of two elements, the costs of production and the surplus. If the surpluses were to remain in Manitoba to be invested in whatever sector would yield greater benefits to the people and the economy, the value of the depleted resources would remain. This is what would happen if the resources were developed by crown corporations. When the surpluses are withdrawn to be invested elsewhere, there is a net consumption of Manitoba resources. Manitoba is poorer although some corporations will be richer. The natural wealth of Manitoba has been converted to their advantage.

I wrote that obviously the province should be getting most of this money to spend on improving its economic base, and developing better social and educational services. The government should stop leasing mineral lands to the private sector and pass a law to ban the transfer of leases; any leases already transferred would revert, when they expired, to the Crown. Manitoba Mineral Resources Limited, a Crown corporation, should be established to create and develop mines in the province. I said that the challenge facing Manitobans was to keep the surpluses generated by this industry and "make them work at home," rather than having them shipped, as most of them were, across the border, or to the east.

I noted that the problem was not unique to Manitoba. The concentration of corporations was nationwide: "It is not wildly imaginative to suggest that the day may not be far distant when Canadian resources will be controlled, not by the ten provinces, but by fewer than ten giant resource corporations." I believe that day is much closer now than it was when I wrote those words.

I added: "Thus the provinces are faced with the challenge laid down by the giants if they wish further development, or of deciding to go forward themselves through the medium of a giant corporation."

To soften the inevitable response that I was just another state socialist, I included what I thought was a key paragraph that was decidedly liberal, and nineteenth-century liberal, at that:

> A government is above all responsible to the people for using all their resources efficiently and wisely in accordance with the proprieties the people have set. If their credit and capital are squandered, if their labour is not employed and if their resources do not yield the highest possible returns, the government must answer. It is not a question of capitalism or socialism. It is simply searching for the better way. In any event, one cannot nationalize what one already owns and it is clear that the province owns its own resources. What must be determined is the manner in which one can gain the highest return from that wealth, both now and in the future. This is not a matter of questioning the rights or sanctity of private property. The issue of proprietorship has long been settled. It is public.

## THE PREMIER SIDESTEPS

Poor Premier Schreyer. When I handed in my report, he put on a brave smile, but I might just as well have handed him a live coal. The mining companies, needless to say, went into a tantrum. The *Northern Miner* newspaper, bible of the industry, claimed: "[Kierans's] socialistic views led to his resignation from Pierre Elliott Trudeau's Cabinet." This would have come as quite a surprise to Pierre, if he were ever to have read the report. The Manitoba Mining Association upped the ante; I wasn't a socialist, but the author of "a communist document." And the president of Sherritt Gordon Mines lamented that "our traditional way of life is being demeaned and denied," although it was not clear by this whether he meant the tradition of expense-account lunches or the tradition of not paying taxes.

The Mining Association of Canada launched an expensive ad campaign, featuring full-page newspaper ads headed:

Does Anybody Out There Give A Damn If the Mining Industry
is Being Taxed to Death?

Sidney Green, the Manitoba minister of mines, a feisty lawyer who had run against Schreyer for the leadership of the Manitoba NDP in 1969, supported much of what I had to say, and in the end did bring in legislation to establish a government-owned corporation to explore and develop new mining properties. But he backed away from the far more important proposal: to eventually take over the existing properties by refusing to allow them to be transferred within the private sector, or to tax them appropriately.

Jack Weldon liked the report, and so did Mark Eliesen. However, the timing was wrong; the NDP was heading into an election, and Premier Schreyer was intent on proving to the public that the party was not responding to the demands of its radical Waffle group.* After praising my report as an "invaluable contribution," Schreyer kicked it over to a task force for study, or to put it another way, put the baby out on the hillside to see how it would fare. My copy of the press release announcing this development contains my handwritten note: "Kiss of Death."

Still, I believe the report had an impact. This was a time when people were becoming increasingly concerned about the domination of the

---

* In 1969, a caucus of NDP members organized Waffle — a purposely ironic name — to promote a socialist and nationalist agenda. Its demands included the replacement of U.S. private ownership with Canadian public ownership, the right of Quebec to self-determination, and the establishment of an independent Canadian labour movement.

economy by a few giant firms (a concern that seems today to have disappeared, washed away by the notion that the bigger the better, when it comes to corporate size), and some policy changes did, grudgingly and slowly, follow. The only real benefit from my work I claim today, however, is that it has helped to bolster the argument that the resources of this rich land belong to the people, not to the corporations, and that the people are entitled to a far better return on their assets than they are now receiving.

When in 1974 I asked Premier Schreyer why the report had been set aside, he replied that his officials had stated that the benefits to Manitoba had been exaggerated and doubtful. I marched into the office of the deputy minister of finance, and asked him where I had made the mistake. He replied that I had forgotten to deduct the equalization payments that Manitoba would lose. In other words, if Manitoba made $30 million in profits from the mining firms, they would lose $15 million from the federal government in these transfers. The Manitoba government refused to tax the mining industry modestly ($30 million), because it would lose half the amount in transfers. But of course the Canadian taxpayer would also have saved $15 million in taxes. It was a bizarre argument.

This assignment led to another, after Schreyer's re-election in 1973. I was asked to look at the development of his province's hydroelectric power. This time, I was to report directly to the premier, and not to release the information to anyone else — an arrangement I would never again accept. My report was in the form of a letter to Premier Schreyer; I have no idea whether he even read it.

The real problem facing Manitoba at this time was that the province was relying entirely on the rivers of Manitoba for electricity, rather than developing other sources. Manitoba Hydro was calling all the shots, and they had a natural affinity to the big American cities to the south, which used a lot of power in the summer for air conditioning, while Manitoba used it mainly in the winter for heating. Thus, the Canadian public corporation and the American private one had a mutual interest in sharing development. The upshot was that Manitoba's policies seemed to me to be designed more to meet the demands for export of power priced at virtual cost — with all that that implied in huge engineering projects like the Nelson River Diversion — rather than to develop either more modest resources or conservation policies that would preserve the resources. And other options were being overlooked, such as exchanging hydro power for oil with Saskatchewan and co-operating with northeastern Ontario.

The utility wanted to build generating facilities on the Lower Nelson, at huge expense, to say nothing of the environmental consequences, in the hopes of selling the product south of the border. I very much doubted whether it had the financial capability to carry this out; the project would exhaust the province's credit. I wrote:

> If Manitoba cannot invest in "human conditions" — housing, education, health, welfare, pensions, resource development and the elimination of poverty — because Hydro dams have exhausted the credit of the people, it will not be sufficient to *damn* the lenders of the East or New York. People can and will rightly question the integrity of a government, which promises greater equality and pursues profitless grandeur.

I also questioned the integrity of the Manitoba Hydro reports to the utility board. Some years later, the board reached the same conclusions.

Whether because of my report or other factors, the series of dams contemplated for the Lower Nelson were put on hold.

## RENÉ SAYS NO TO PARIZEAU

In the middle of all this, I received a telephone call from René Lévesque, who wanted to talk to me about his own career. This was in late 1973, after he had been defeated twice in attempts to gain the premiership. In the second election, on October 29, 1973, the Parti Québécois (PQ), although it won 30 per cent of the vote, won only 6 seats out of 110, while Robert Bourassa's Liberals won 102 seats based on 52 per cent of the vote. There were the usual cries of dissatisfaction with the party leader, and René took them very much to heart, especially the claims that he was too soft in his approach to separatism. We ran through a list of those who might replace him if he stepped down, of both those elected and outsiders. He was rather in favour of trying to promote someone like Pierre Marois, a brilliant young lawyer who had made a fine reputation as a legal-aid attorney; but Marois had been defeated in the last provincial election, and had decided that his family responsibilities should finally take precedence.

I said, "How about Jacques Parizeau?"

"No." Just like that. No explanation, just a flat refusal.

He told me that if he could find a suitable replacement, he intended to go back into journalism, and talked about writing for *Le Journal de Montréal* to support himself. When I got back home I kept mulling it over, and called Frank Walker, then the editor of the *Montreal Star,* but he did not seem notably enthusiastic about hiring René. In the end, René stayed in the leadership, and brought the PQ to its stunning victory in November 1976.

## BACK TO MCGILL — AND ACADEMIC TUSSLES

My return to the academic world and McGill in fall 1972 was marked by a headline in the *McGill News* that read, "Eric Kierans, Volatile Economist, Returns to McGill," and by a number of complaints conveyed to the university's fundraisers, especially by Noranda Mines, a long-time and generous supporter of the Engineering faculty.

Despite this somewhat uneven welcome, my second tour of duty at the university was a lot of fun. I had more leisure this time, since I wasn't in charge of a school. Therefore, I could do a lot of studying; engage, naturally, in some of the infighting that is as much a part of university life as football rallies; look after my own business interests; and make my voice heard as best I could in economic and political debate.

I was assigned an office in the Stephen Leacock Building, not far from my old haunts in Purvis Hall, and I taught undergraduate courses and graduate seminars while running the graduate program in Economics. Cyril James had retired by this time, and we had a new principal, Robert Bell, but that did not mean that peace had settled on the campus. In our own corner of the lot, there was a distinct split in the Economics Department between left-wingers — like Jack Weldon and a smart, bustling young economist named Tom Naylor — and right-wingers like Irving Brecher, who had been on a leave to work for the Economic Council of Canada, and who had been very close to Simon Reisman for years.

Irving did not appreciate my criticism of Reisman in the foreword to Tom Naylor's brilliant two-volume *History of Canadian Business,* which was published in 1975. Reisman had bailed out of the official bureaucracy, where his latest role had been deputy minister of finance, to set up a consulting firm with Jim Grandy, who had recently stepped down from a similar role in the Department of Industry, Trade and Commerce. I objected, writing

> Two of the most powerful bureaucrats, laden with honours for their public service and the most generous pension arrangements granted by an unwitting public, take an early retirement, settle in on the tenth floor of the newest Ottawa skyscraper and prepare to guide the oligopolies that can afford them through the labyrinth of the federal bureaucracy.

Irving Brecher was a strong supporter of the government's scandalous handouts to business, and was supported on the right wing of the Economics Department by Antal Deutsch and Tom Velk, the latter an expert on banking who had worked for some years in the U.S. Federal Reserve system. The department's chair was Tom Asimakopulos, who was a close friend and associate of Jack Weldon's.

Our discussions were lively, to say the least, but were conducted as arguments, not wars.

## KIERANS FOR NDP LEADER?

While I was enjoying academic life again, along came an invitation, from Sid Green, for me to run for the federal leadership of the NDP. I have no idea what was in the back of his mind; I was not a member of the party, not a supporter of state socialism (the party was working its way out of adherence to the notion that the principal means of production should be in the hands of the state, but it was still ambivalent on this in 1975), and had absolutely no constituency within the party. Possibly what was going on was that Ed Broadbent, then the MP for Oshawa and a popular choice for the party leadership, was suddenly playing hard to get. Perhaps Broadbent needed a reminder that he was not involved in a coronation, but a leadership contest. David Lewis had been defeated in the 1974 election, and the job was open. Sid sprang this on me when we were driving down the middle of Portage Avenue one day in 1975, and I'm glad he was driving; I might have run the car into a lamppost.

I asked Jack Weldon to do some unofficial snooping around for me, and he came back to report that Broadbent had the job locked up and would go for it. It was also clear that two of the men who seemed to be most intent on having me run were Sid Green and Jeremy Ackerman, the party leader in Nova Scotia who subsequently became adviser to the Conservative provincial government. They were both party mavericks, and were using my name to stir up interest in their leadership convention. I simply said no.

When the Parti Québécois suddenly vaulted into power in 1976, to the astonishment of almost everyone, including and especially party leader René Lévesque, many of my colleagues at McGill felt under siege. As a symbol of Anglo arrogance and power, the university had been under attack by separatists for some time, and there was a nasty confrontation in 1969, when 10,000 young people marched on the institution, demanding that it be turned into a French university. I had more confidence than they did in René's common sense, and argued that if we made French students more comfortable in the university, we would come to no harm, and might even learn something.

I also began to bring in outside speakers who had something to say, not merely to the Economics students, but to the university and the community in general. One of these was Milton Friedman of the University of Chicago, with many of whose monetarist theories I disagreed entirely, but who was certainly a major figure in our age, and a Nobel Memorial Prize winner. Another, for whom I had much more personal admiration, was Emmett Hall, the distinguished jurist and author of the report of the Royal Commission on Health Services — a report laid before the Diefenbaker government in 1964 and studiously ignored, but which became the rationale behind universal health care soon after. Harry Johnson, a Canadian who held dual professorships at the University of Chicago and the London School of Economics, came whenever I asked.

René and I were still in touch, by telephone, and luncheons, and I was pleased to be invited to serve on the boards of both the provincially owned steel company Sidbec and the Caisse de dépôt et placement, although these appointments only heightened the suspicion of some of my academic colleagues that I was not quite a fully redeemed academic.

One day, I got a telephone call from René to seek my advice on an economic matter. "If we win this thing," he said, meaning if the province was able to separate entirely from Canada, "Parizeau tells me we have to have our own currency. We can't use the Canadian dollar. Is that right?"

"Certainly," I replied. "If you don't control your own currency, you cannot control your own economy. Parizeau is simply telling you what any economist would say."

"Hell!" said René, and slammed down the phone.

I was intrigued when, after he himself became premier, Parizeau suddenly discovered that the rules didn't apply anymore. Quebecers, a basically conservative people who would have recoiled in horror at the thought, and expense, of floating their own currency, could use the Canadian dollar after all. Well, they can, of course; the thing is physically possible. But they would find it almost impossible to maintain an independent economic policy based on the loonie.

## THE SUN LIFE AFFAIR

The feelings of uncertainty and concern were very much intensified when, in January 1978, the president of the Sun Life Insurance Company, Thomas Galt, announced publicly and noisily that he was moving the entire head office down Highway 401 to Toronto, in protest against Bill 101, the legislation designed to place more emphasis on French in the province. Galt huffed that since French was to become by law the dominant language here, "We can no longer envisage our ability to recruit, or retain in Montreal from outside Quebec, sufficient people with the necessary qualifications and competence in English to transact the daily business of the company."

The obvious solution to this dilemma — to begin to instruct the staff in French, and to hire more French Canadians — seemed to escape Galt. I had a somewhat jaundiced view of Sun Life anyway, since the president had told me, when I was still the Minister of Health in Quebec, that any public pension plan was nothing more than "a giant step towards socialism." This latest outburst sent me to my typewriter to fire off a letter that appeared in the Montreal *Gazette* on February 10, 1978.

I used the occasion to comment on the climate of confrontation that had been created by the seizure of control over the national economy by the federal government during the Second World War, and went on to point out that Quebec was only one of the provinces engaged in the struggle to restore some sort of balance. Bill 101 had to be seen in that context as part of the province's assertion of its own need and capacity to govern itself within the federation, on the basis of an understanding of its own rights set down when the original arrangement of Confederation occurred in 1867. I argued that the concentration of power in Ottawa that had been imposed on Quebec in 1945 was at an end, and we ought to recognize this fact.

However, in Ottawa, policy was being set to suit the needs and demands of multinational corporations, which had now evolved into "cosmocorps." These world-striders were, I wrote, "the instrument by which Canada has gained a satellite status...We are dependent on the very giants we have created. The cosmocorps can go anywhere and do anything while the federal politicians and bureaucrats who helped make them great can only sit at home and fume."

In these circumstances, it was not remarkable that the Quebec government felt it had to act to protect its own people, because it was obvious that Ottawa never would.

As to Sun Life:

> The point about the whole affair is that the Sun Life has to pull out of Quebec. It has no choice, for it has become an anachronism, a completely English-speaking operation in a French-speaking community which it has never recognized. *Maîtres-chez-nous* was supposed to go away.

This brought a public response from my McGill colleague Irving Brecher, in which he called my argument "wrong-headed and dangerous," because it dared to question the dominance of the multinational corporation, which was "here to stay, whether Professor Kierans likes it or not."

This argument by trained economists on behalf of large corporations has always enchanted me. Might as well say poison ivy is here to stay, so we ought not to try to do anything about it. It is part of the notion, which history, experience, and common sense deny, that economics is something apart from politics, and that it is wrong for politics to try to interfere with such economic instruments as the cosmocorps on the trifling grounds that they threaten to usurp the civil state.

This general argument got imported into an academic tussle at McGill that went on, believe it or not, for ten years. If traditional procedures are likely to prove unfavourable, ignore them. It is wonderful to have time to spare. The issue became involved in the wish — which became a demand — of Antal Deutsch, an associate professor, to be named as a full professor. The distinction is not merely a matter of prestige; money is attached.

Before his application could even be considered, Deutsch asked the dean of arts to have a special committee appointed to consider his case, bypassing entirely the regular procedures in the Department of Economics. In short, the people who had worked with the candidate and knew something of his abilities were not to have any say in the matter. The normal way to handle this sort of thing would have been for him to make his application to the department, and the senior professors attached to the department would decide whether or not to pass it on to the administration with a favourable recommendation. However, Deutsch wouldn't have that; he wanted his form to fly on by his colleagues. Moreover, Jack Weldon and department chair Tom Asimakopulos were to "recuse" themselves from any dealings in the matter, because Deutsch had had "sharp disagreements" with them in the past. (I had to look "recuse" up in the dictionary; I had never seen it before. It means to excuse oneself because of a possible conflict of interest or lack of impartiality.)

Apparently, in the applicant's view, only dull disagreements were allowable. The nub of his thesis was that Jack and Tom were leftists, which made them suspect. I thought that if anybody should be recused from dealing with Deutsch, it ought to be me. I had had many dealings with him in my role as chair of the graduate committee. On the lists of Ph.D. candidates, I had noticed that one candidate under his supervision had been at it for ten years. I would probably have voted against Deutsch, but he said nothing about me; he wanted Jack and Tom off his case.

It wound up in one of those turf wars, with Deutsch refusing to appear before any committee that contained the other two, and me (Chairman of the Graduate Committee) insisting that there would be no meeting without them. My basic attitude was that Deutsch should back off until his application had been dealt with in the normal way; if he was refused, he could then appeal to the administration, which was why the system was set up that way.

No such luck. The matter was bounced to the university senate, which gave it to a professor of mathematics to arbitrate, but he died before he could come to any conclusion. So then it went to two other academics with no economics background, who were to decide whether or not Deutsch was a sound economist. This caused me to lose my cool and write a very strong letter to Principal Bell, attacking the notion that you could send in outsiders to interfere with an academic department on a matter that the department itself had not even been allowed to consider.

This got me into trouble with the senate, because of the intemperate language I used in my letter. The outcome was that the senate, affronted on behalf of the administration, rebuked me, along with Tom and Jack, and appointed a committee to look into Deutsch's claim; he was duly made a full professor. It did not end there. Jack asked the Canadian Association of University Teachers (CAUT) to look into the matter, and in 1987, nine years after the Deutsch affair began, the CAUT came back with a report that said, in effect, that the administration had blundered, and that the senate reprimand was dead wrong.

By this time, I was long gone from McGill. It was normal, in the world of academe, for a university to offer a three-year extension to professors when they reach the age of sixty-five, but no such thing happened in my case. Jack wanted me to keep up the fight, and make an extension of my appointment part of it, but by now I was weary of what seemed to me a lot of petty nonsense, and I declined. Jack was also disappointed because I wouldn't back his choice for a new department chair. I told him that I thought the left wing had had its way long enough; it was time to turn the chair over to someone else. He never quarrelled with me, but he was obviously upset.

While at McGill, I was, as ever, running Canadian Adhesives, although more and more leaving it to its own manager, Graeme Hayward; and to Alan Love, whom I had named president. They had taken the firm from a rather slapdash outfit with fifteen permanent employees to a modern manufacturing company — with thirty-five permanent and, on average, thirty-five temporary employees turning out glue, caulking, and sealants. And making steady profits for all of us.

I was also, as mentioned above, serving on the boards of two of the key provincial concerns, the steel company Sidbec and the Caisse. I had not been on the Sidbec board long before I realized why I had been sent in there. The management side of the company was in a dreadful mess, mainly because the chief executive officer was trying to serve as both president and chair, that is, to combine the functions of CEO and chief operating officer. This nearly always leads to trouble, and it was obvious that unless something was done, the firm was headed for disaster.

I phoned René, and he said, "Do what you have to do."

What I had to do was to mount a campaign on the board, which was not hard to do since Sidbec was performing very poorly. At the very next meeting of the board, the chair complained of overload and I immediately suggested that the two positions be separated. He complained to the premier, threatening to resign if my suggestion was followed. René simply accepted his resignation.

## CONTROVERSY AT THE CAISSE

It was not so easy to deal with the problems at the Caisse. You will recall that this body was set up to deal with the huge pool of investments used to fund the Quebec Pension Plan. One of the key points made by Jean Lesage when this institution was established was that it should be run on normal financial lines; it was not some sort of piggy bank for the provincial government. Its first duty was to ensure that the savings of the people of Quebec were always there to meet the needs of its pensioners.

I had been placed on the board officially by Jacques Parizeau, who was then minister of finance in Lévesque's government, but I had good reason to believe that it was René who wanted me in there. My first year on the board went along well enough. I objected from time to time when it seemed to me that loans were going out without sufficient collateral, but these were not major concerns. Then a request — actually, it was more of a demand — came to us from Parizeau that the province wanted to be able to borrow money from the Caisse at a rate lower than the lowest market rate then available in Canada. There is a crucial distinction between the "lowest market rate" — a perfectly reasonable rate at which to advance funds to the province, since there was no risk attached — and the lowest rate available anywhere. In 1980, which is when this came up, that lowest available rate happened to be the rate at which Premier Peter Lougheed of Alberta was lending out money from the Alberta Heritage Fund.

There was another problem. The Caisse was surrounded by all kinds of safeguards, including one which said that it could not advance a loan that would amount to more than 30 per cent of the amount involved, to any one borrower. If a borrower needed $300 million, the Caisse could put up $90 million, but not a penny more. Watching Parizeau's 1980 budget speech on television, I jumped about a foot in the air when he suddenly said that Quebec would need a good deal of capital over the next year, and he intended to borrow up to 40 per cent of that from the Caisse. Well, he couldn't; not if we were to keep the original agreement.

You had Parizeau saying, in effect: I should be able to get as much as I need from the Caisse, and at least as cheaply as from Alberta. And me saying: Well, no; the fact that the Alberta Heritage Fund is willing to lend money at subsidized rates does not mean that the Caisse should do so. Our job is to ensure the people of Quebec get the best available return on their money, and that the fund itself is safeguarded.

The dispute came to a head, unfortunately, in the middle of the first referendum battle. And a lot of people, headed by René, thought that I was either deliberately intent on embarrassing the separatists by taking this stand, or wilfully blind to what is always called "the optics" of a situation — one where an Anglo appeared to be defending the provincial purse against the ravages of a greedy government. I was not, however, the only one who took this stand.

The head of the Régie de rentes (the Quebec pension plan) pointed out to the board that if we allowed the government to borrow from the pool at subsidized rates, there would be that much less to be distributed to the pensioners of the province.

Much more significantly, Marcel Casavan, the president of the Caisse, had resigned early in 1980 over this specific issue, when Parizeau's deputy ordered him to lend money at below-market rates. Then, at a meeting of the board in Quebec City on March 17, after I had to leave for another appointment, a resolution was pushed through to change the basis on which loans could be made. I was furious when I found out what had happened, and I brought up the issue at a board meeting on April 21, 1980, where my motion was voted down.

To this point, the public had no idea what was going on, so it seemed to me my duty to resign, and to make public my reasons for leaving, which I did by sending a copy of my letter of resignation to *La Presse*.

There was quite a storm. This happened just two weeks before the referendum vote on sovereignty-association; whether it affected the outcome, I very much doubt, but certainly René felt it was designed to do so. Jean Dufresne, a reporter at *Le Devoir,* who had his own open-line television show, invited me to come on and answer questions from an outraged public, which I did. Actually, only about half the callers were hostile. Most of them wondered why, if I had to make this stand, I couldn't have done it earlier. Well, it hadn't happened earlier. I wasn't the one who determined the timing; the government did that, and for me to wait until after the referendum would have been a clear dereliction of my duty as a director of the Caisse. As a matter of fact, I was a Caisse director appointed to represent the interests of the pensioners, not the borrowers.

René claimed that I had been at the meeting in March when the decision to change policy was made, and that I must have fallen asleep. (Our exchange of letters appears in the appendix.) So I had the minutes produced to prove, first, that the item had never been on the agenda, and was added during the meeting, after I had left; and second, that I was not there to vote on it. It didn't ease the pain much for René, especially when the PQ lost the referendum.

I had no regret whatsoever about the action I took in connection with the Caisse, but at the end of the day it was clear that I was wearing out my welcome with the government of Quebec.

## MINDING MY OWN BUSINESS

When my contract at McGill came to an end, I spent a year at the École des Hautes Études Commerciales, the management school for the Université de Montréal, and spoke on the role of the multinational corporation. But it was the wrong audience for me. Instead of being angered or offended by the takeover of the economy by a smaller and smaller group of greedy adventurers, they just wanted to know where to sign up.*

The next year, 1981, was a tough one for Canadian Adhesives, and I had to devote more and more time to it. The nation was in the grip of a long, bitter recession, and it quite drastically affected the building

---

* The MBA students at the Hautes Études Commerciales had caught up with the corporate revolution.

industry, where I had most of my sales. I decided to spend more time at the company. The key employees, who had been running the company, were, not surprisingly, a little miffed when I began to turn up every day shortly after 6:30 a.m. and pry into what they had come to think of as *their* business.

Then one day in 1982, clear out of the blue, Terry got a call from John Graham, my old friend from the Canadian Economics Association, now a senior academic at Dalhousie University. He said, "How would you and Eric like to move down here?"

"We'd love it," said Terry, just like that.

# Eleven

—·◆·—

# HALIFAX

*When they founded the town of Halifax in 1749 His
Majesty's Board of Trade and Plantations decided to name it
in honour of their president, George Dunk. He happened to
be Earl of Halifax and they chose the title rather than the
family name. Haligonians are duly grateful.*

— THOMAS RADDALL, *CENTURY*, 1967

The DECISION TO GO BACK to Halifax was not a whim, but in fact something Terry and I had talked about many times over the years; it was our first home after marriage, and we had made it a habit to go down to the east coast on holidays once every two years or so. The other summers, we usually spent at Tadoussac, in Quebec. We had promised ourselves that one day we would move to the Nova Scotia capital when we retired. What triggered the decision was the personal call from John Graham to tell Terry that Dalhousie would offer me a part-time professorship if we would make the move.

We decided that if we were going to move to Halifax, we might as well do it right, so we put the house on Queen Mary Road in Montreal on the market, and set about to build a new one in Halifax. This turned out to be very complicated, while living in Montreal. We found the lot we wanted, on the Northwest Arm, just off the mouth of Halifax Harbour. Obtaining the lot involved a number of legal complications, which is apparently the case almost any time you buy property in Nova Scotia; but in the end, we had what we wanted. We lived for a time in two places — our house in Montreal, and our summer home near Chester, Nova Scotia.

Bruce Oland, the genial scion of the Nova Scotia brewing family, took a sort of paternal interest in us, and one day after mass he yelled across at me, "I hear you've bought some property; who's your contractor?" I said that I would get quotations from at least three, and Bruce said, "Get all the quotations you want, but use Peter Corkum." This turned out to be very good advice. Peter Corkum was a contractor of solid ability and absolute integrity, and he built us a wonderful house looking across the Arm, where in the evening we could see the fleets of yachts sailing from the Royal Nova Scotia Yacht Club and the Armdale Yacht Club. I had a fine den; Terry had a room with perfect light, where she could sculpt and paint. Terry designed a sunken living room, which was very reminiscent of the one we had in Hampstead, and it looked even more gracious. Being on the Atlantic Ocean and looking out to sea helped.

We were learning rapidly that Halifax is not like other places. I went to the Royal Bank, with which I had been dealing in a major way in Montreal for about half a century, and asked for a temporary loan to build the house, with interest set at the bank's prime rate. The Montreal branch had passed on the terms that they had always granted me, and the young man with whom I was dealing seemed amenable to this. But he suddenly got up and disappeared into the next cubicle. Since the walls didn't go up to the ceiling, I could hear his dilemma. He was asking his boss how to fill out the form for a loan at prime; he had never seen such a thing before in his two years at the post.

"Put down prime plus zero, you fool," he was told.

This seemed to me perfectly symptomatic of the way Maritimers are treated by the big banks; they don't get the chance to make a loan at the rate commonly used for sound creditors everywhere in central Canada.

My teaching chores were not onerous, but as always they were interesting. I found the Nova Scotia students much less inclined to challenge or question anything I said than the students I had been used to at McGill. I soon learned that this was not because they were any less intelligent or informed; it seemed to be a matter of Maritime politeness, or deference, call it what you will. I would have given anything to have someone say, as they so often did at McGill, "Prove it." The only student I had at Dalhousie who asked pointed and persistent questions was an army major who was taking a course in economics as a sideline to his training, and who obviously found that it opened new vistas for him.

## I THINK, THEREFORE I THINK-TANK

One day when my son, Tom, came down to visit us, he introduced me to a man named Louis Vagianos, who was the research director of the Institute for Research on Public Policy (IRPP). Tom was on the board of the IRPP, it turned out, and I was intrigued to learn that this think-tank had been set up with an endowment fund of about $23 million in 1972. The institution was created "to facilitate informed public debate on issues of major public interest." This it did by staging conferences, financing papers, and running its own research programs. The federal government and every provincial government except Quebec had contributed to its establishment (which makes it rather ironic that the IRPP is now operated entirely out of Quebec).

At this time, the IRPP had its main office in Halifax, and its most interesting venture there was to produce a magazine called *Policy Options,* which was founded by Tom Kent, and edited by Tom and his wife, Phyllida. It was later edited by Walter Stewart, until the Halifax operation was closed right down and everything moved to Montreal in 1993. Louis Vagianos, among his other duties, served as managing editor, and it was not long before I was turning out articles on economic and political subjects for *Policy Options.*

The IRPP offered me a post as resident fellow in Halifax, which I was delighted to accept, since it gave me a cluttered office on the third floor of one of the old houses that the university owned — and provided free to the IRPP. The post also provided secretarial help by some of the brightest and most engaging women I have ever worked with. I settled down to a routine of thinking, writing, walking — three times a week, I walked about six kilometres around Halifax, a lovely city for the purpose — and, of course, arguing. I also got into the habit of commuting back to Montreal at least once every two weeks, to see my mother, and to keep an eye on Canadian Adhesives, which was now my major source of both income and investment. Troubles were building up there, and I would soon have to deal with them.

Then, of course, there was *Morningside.*

## WE ARE ALL HERETICS

I was first approached about appearing as a regular panellist in late 1982, and I cannot remember whether the subject was raised by Peter Gzowski, the host, or by Sue Bishop, the producer. I had made a couple of appearances on the program during its periodic visits to Montreal. I would go down to the studio on Dorchester Boulevard and chat with Peter about some political or economic development. Like everyone else in Canada, I found him an engaging and intelligent interviewer, and I jumped at the chance to do a regular stint from Halifax, with Dalton Camp and Stephen Lewis.

The rationale was that this was a political panel — with Dalton representing a Conservative point of view, Stephen an NDP approach, and me a Liberal outlook — which turned out to be a bit of a joke. I knew Stephen and Dalton as political figures only, but we became on-air friends very quickly. Among other things, we were seldom in the same city at the same time; I think the only time we were in the same studio together was for a joint picture of the panel.

Every Monday afternoon, one of the line producers, usually Harry Schachter, would phone to suggest topics for the show on Tuesday morning. Officially, we were the "political panel," but this was usually shortened to KCL, an abbreviation made up from our surnames. I would usually accept Harry's topics, which had come out of an editorial meeting in Toronto earlier that day; occasionally I would demur (I once said I thought it was a very bad idea to talk about racism on this kind of panel, but we went ahead anyway; I was right — it is a subject that cannot be covered in twenty-two minutes); and occasionally I would suggest another topic. Then I would do some homework to be ready for the twenty-two-minute session the next day, where Peter would serve as master of ceremonies, and referee a free-ranging discussion of current affairs.

I would go down to the CBC studios on Sackville Street, just behind Citadel Hill, either on foot or by car. I would be settled into a studio, given a cup of coffee — which I seldom got around to drinking — and a headset, and away we would go. The show was live from Halifax, delayed by an hour elsewhere in the country. I was paid a fee of $150 an appearance.

At first, the show was pretty rocky; all three of us tended to be time-stealers, and we had usually prepared lines that we wanted to throw into the discussion. Gradually, however, Peter worked us into a semblance of order, with a technique somewhere between that of a lion tamer and a

Grade 6 teacher. We respected him, and he taught us what I think is the most important lesson in these matters: to listen to each other. We very quickly discovered that each panellist nearly always had something interesting and relevant to say, so that instead of contesting every point we sort of bounced off each other. Peter's questions were always curious rather than aggressive; he stood in place of the audience, rather than someone trying to show how clever he was. The result was that we improved as we went along, and learned to add something to what the other panellists said.

The show broke all the rules, and it was wonderful. We were three non-young white males, violating every politically correct dictate in the land and laying down the law on everything from how the Tory government behaved — badly, we usually thought — to whether it was permissible for Liberal senators to use deliberate stalling tactics to hold up the GST. The issue of the senators was one of the occasions when we all agreed (this was not as rare as you might think, given our different political backgrounds). Stephen, a bitter opponent of the GST, nevertheless said he wouldn't blame Prime Minister Brian Mulroney if he packed the Senate to get through a measure that had been approved by the House of Commons. Dalton later noted that the main thing the three us had in common was that we were all heretics, as far as our supposed parties were concerned.

The first run of the panel went from January 4, 1983, to mid-September 1984, when Stephen was named ambassador to the United Nations by Mulroney (to the astonishment of almost everyone, including both Dalton and myself). He was replaced by Dave Barrett, the former NDP premier of British Columbia. I liked Barrett, but he was much more partisan than Stephen had been, and the chemistry between the three of us was never the same. We limped along, more or less, until Dalton was appointed as an adviser to Mulroney; the panel was dropped in September 1986.

However, Stephen's appointment came to an end in 1989, and Dalton was not only out of the Mulroney government but becoming an increasingly skeptical observer of that government, so KCL was revived in September 1989 and ran, with some interruptions, until March 22, 1993. We had one reunion appearance on October 24, 1995, to discuss the dismal federal performance in that year's referendum on Quebec.

For the purposes of this book, the CBC was kind enough to send some background material on the program, and with this was the note on me from the "Contact File," which is the first place producers go when they want to know something about an outsider. I must say I got a kick out of Eric Kierans as seen through the eyes of the CBC:

> COMMENTS: QUIT DURING TRUDEAU ERA & VERY CRITICAL OF TRUDEAU ECONOMIC POLICIES. GOOD TALKER. IMPATIENT WITH UNPREPARED PRE-INTER-VIEWERS (KNOW WHAT YOU WANT FROM HIM BEFORE YOU CALL HIM) / ECONOMIST.

Looking through the file, I am astounded by the range of topics we covered, everything from hot political topics, such as Trudeau's resignation and Brian Mulroney's ascent, to social issues, such as the right-to-die debate, capital punishment, and my suggestion that we hold a national referendum on the question: Should we move the national capital to Winnipeg? I was in favour, but Dalton wondered, "What will we do with Ottawa?"

I knew we were a success when I got a call one day from Peter to tell me that Senator Keith Davey had been on the phone demanding that I be taken off the panel, because I was no Liberal. Earlier, the Tories had protested against Camp, and the NDP against Stephen.

"That makes it complete," said Peter. "I guess from here on in we can do no wrong."

Dalton, writing about the panel in the foreword to Peter's book *The Morningside Years,* noted:

> I suspect the popularity of *Morningside*'s weekly panel of political commentators — principally Eric Kierans, Stephen Lewis and me — was a pain in the ass to many. The troika offended the CBC's gender requirements and more — we were all white males over forty. All of us were, from time to time, rebuked by partisan members for not standing up for our presumed parties. The Liberals filed a formal complaint about the continued reluctance of Kierans to uphold Liberalism, and, according to Gzowski, people complained wherever he travelled about my inadequacies as a spokesperson for the proper Conservative view, nor did Lewis escape charges of lacking socialist fervour...

...As we went along, we came to like one another, and the mutual affection, and mutual respect, showed. *Morningside*'s listeners enjoyed KCL for the civil tongue the panel kept in its head, or cheek, which effectively demonstrated what most Canadians believe, which is that politics can be argued with sincerity and passion but without heat and still shed light on the subject.

One subject on which I held forth with a passion that surprised the others was the pope's support for Croatia during the breakup of Yugoslavia. I knew quite a lot about eastern Europe, because my daughter-in-law, Inta, Tom's former wife, was Latvian, and I followed the fate of her nation when the Russians marched in and took everything. Her father, a wealthy brick manufacturer in Riga, was forced to flee to Canada, and we often talked about the convoluted politics of the region. When the pope backed Croatia, I said that all you had to know was that history was repeating itself. Chancellor Helmut Kohl of Germany was taking a similar position, and as in the Second World War we were facing an alliance of Catholics, Germans, and Croatians against the Serbs. We were inviting another holocaust. Few people remembered that earlier tragedy in which Croatians and Germans massacred tens of thousands of Serbs.

On *Morningside,* I called the pope's behaviour "reprehensible," and I think the other guys were surprised not so much by such strong language from a strong Catholic as by the fact that I knew what I was talking about.

I got some notion of the power of the program itself in an incident involving Alexandra McCurdy, a ceramist whom Terry had met through sculpture classes. She had approached Terry to ask, "Do you think Eric could get me on *Morningside*?" When Terry told me how good her work was, I agreed to make the call, and to my astonishment the producers took it up at once, and within a month she was on the show, talking about her work. Now, the listeners couldn't see her art; they could only hear Peter's enthusiasm, and it was enough. Her career took off.

We received a lot of mail, inevitably, and we were always pleased to hear from listeners, although I quickly noticed that the letters tended to follow a format; they would start out with praise for the program, and expand to the writer's own views on whatever topic was under discussion. The proportion of praise to self-expression was about one to ten, which always tickled me, although the letters were very often of exceptional quality.

Many times when we were doing the show, the thought occurred to me that there is nothing quite like this anywhere else in the world, and I don't just mean *Morningside,* I mean the whole CBC as a national institution aimed at binding together a diverse, quarrelsome, and regional nation by intelligent interchange. This was happening at the very time that successive governments, first Conservative, then Liberal, were cutting the heart out of the CBC budget and destroying the service they themselves had created.

As we went into our third and fourth years of what might be called our reincarnation, I thought the topics we were covering began to fall off to the trivial. I had, and have, a feeling that there was a philosophy inside the CBC that this sort of thing is good for only about five years, and then you need to move on. Harry Schachter telephoned one day in mid-1992 to ask if I would be interested in another panel with four people — five with Peter — and I said I didn't think I could make a real contribution with so many disparate voices. They were starting to run a panel on Friday mornings with five contributors who were apparently more acceptable to the political party brass, and most of the best current issues were being discussed there. I know nothing about the internal politics of the CBC, so I didn't know whether they were tired of the heat from the political parties because we wouldn't parrot the proper views, or just thought the panel had served its time. (Harry Schachter recently confirmed to Walter Stewart that it was the latter.)

When I said I thought it was time to pull out, I got a very emotional call from Peter, which was flattering, but not persuasive, and KCL did not come back on the air when the 1993 season began.

I missed it, still do, and I am eternally glad I got to do it.

## THE MASSEY LECTURES

The *Morningside* job led to a number of other invitations to comment, and I appeared on CBC television's *The Journal,* wrote newspaper pieces, and was flattered to be asked to deliver the Massey Lectures on the CBC radio. As mentioned earlier, these were the lectures that, when they were reproduced in book form, I dedicated: "To Walter Gordon who foresaw most of this long before the rest of us."

The lectures were broadcast on the radio program *Ideas* and carried an analysis, a highly critical analysis, of Reaganomics both as a form of economics — essentially, social Darwinism — and as a form of world politics. Reagan, a man of numbing simplicity, had divided the world into two blocs, the Good Guys and the Evil Empire, and the happy coincidence of this approach was that America, as the gunslinger for the good guys, was taking over more and more of the management of affairs. The global corporation was the inevitable outcome and beneficiary of this approach. I said:

> Hyping the unthinkable, the threat of nuclear holocaust, has brought great dividends to the rhetorician of the White House. He cannot lose. When the nuclear tensions lessen, as indeed that insanity must, the United States will have regained undisputed economic leadership of the West, and this is what this exercise is all about.

Rereading those words today, it is very cold comfort indeed to reflect that they were all too accurate a summation. I linked these developments with the emergence of the global corporation, and the damage it leaves in its wake:

> The global corporation sells mass-production techniques, even in their branch-plant version. To be profitable, however, mass production requires mass consumption — that is, the homogenization of the tastes, needs, values and priorities of all the nations within which the firm and its subsidiaries operate. In the name of technical efficiency, we erase the differences among persons, the style and art of their living. People of different cultures and nations in various stages of development are made, through enormous selling and advertising pressures, to want the same things...
>
> ...The freedom of the individual to choose, to maintain his own preferences, and to search for his own satisfaction, is reduced...
>
> ...Corporations have become an end in themselves, when they were never meant to be more than efficient means of grouping the factors of production, land and labour with the support and thrust of capital saved, to expand the output of goods and services and thus establish a higher standard of living for the whole community...
>
> ...When forms of business organization were personal — partnerships or proprietorships — there was no problem about defining business ethics. Business ethics were personal ethics, and the

ethics of the person may be described by the one word — "sharing"...

...To command a corporation to love would be madness. Commanding a corporation to love would be asking it to distribute its wealth, to commit suicide. On the other hand, the corporation...can and must be forced to conduct itself so that its activities correspond with the aims of the community, with the state itself as the seat of power and elected spokesman of the people.

These lectures led some commentators to suggest that I had emerged as a nationalist, and a left-wing nationalist at that — a far cry from the days when I was the head of a stock exchange. Well, I certainly had become more of a nationalist, with the American example and its style of bullying in front of me, and the advantages of the Canadian approach apparent. However, I don't think the Massey Lectures represented so much a departure as a restatement of the notions of community and personal responsibility I had learned in Saint-Henri, applied to the grotesque phenomenon of global corporatism. I don't know whether that is left wing or not, and frankly I don't care.

## CANADIAN ADHESIVES COMES UNSTUCK

In the middle of teaching, researching, and talking, I suddenly had to deal with Canadian Adhesives. On one of my trips to Montreal, I went to see the vice-president of manufacturing, who happened to be in hospital, and he suggested that I should "pay more attention to things at the plant." He added, "We're having some problems with quality."

Back in Nova Scotia, I went around to a major Canadian Tire store in Bridgewater, and asked the manager about this. He told me they had had a number of recent shipments of caulking whose tubes began to leak, making them unsaleable. I phoned Graeme Hayward, who was running the business for me, and he said the Canadian Tire employees must have left the tubes out where the sun could get at them. I didn't think much of this as an explanation, especially when we did a quality check, which resulted in having to dump $400,000 worth of product.

When I received a sudden demand from Graeme to buy up about $340,000 in shares allocated to him at reduced prices, I realized that we were headed for serious trouble. He no doubt felt that he had been running the firm, and suddenly I was coming in over his shoulders to call the shots, and he resented it. The fact that I needed to take action only made it worse. A parting of the ways was inevitable. I promoted two men, who quickly set about straightening things up, and at the same time put out the word that I wanted to sell Canadian Adhesives.

The actual sale turned out to be incredibly complicated and dragged on for months. Canadian firms were not at all interested in buying the company at prices matching those being offered from abroad; I got a very attractive offer from a company called Henkel, in Germany, one of the largest privately held firms in the world. The deal was handled through its subsidiary in Milwaukee; cleared through the Foreign Investment Review Agency; sorted out through Richard Lewin, a really excellent young lawyer with Heenan Blaikie in Montreal; and seemed to be all settled — when it suddenly came unstuck. To this day I do not know exactly what happened; the Henkel offer was suddenly and mysteriously withdrawn.

Another firm, Rexnord Chemical Products Inc., of Milwaukee, had also bid on the sale, so I called my contact there, and he was on the plane the next day. I sold Canadian Adhesives in late 1984 for $7.2 million net, when everything was figured in. Naturally, I was criticized for selling out to an American company, but I didn't find the circumstance ironic; I found it humiliating. What it came down to in the end was that I could have sold the company in Canada for about $3.8 million or to Rexnord for $7.2 million. The difference was just too great. Any agent could have paid me the first sum, and then turned around and resold to collect the second.

Just to finish this part of the tale, Rexnord was later sold to a German company; Canadian Adhesives was sold back and forth several times and wound up with Henkel, who paid a good deal more for it than they offered me.

### THE FREE-TRADE DEBATE

This was all going on while I was still doing the *Morningside* stint, but happily it never became public. One of the topics that became hotter and hotter as the panel wound on was the Free Trade Agreement (FTA) with the United States, the centrepiece of the first Mulroney term. We were all of us, in various degrees and for various reasons, dead opposed. This obviously struck some listeners as odd, in the case of both Dalton Camp and myself. Dalton, after all, was a Tory, even if a Red Tory, and I was an economist. Economists are, almost by definition, in favour of free trade. And so I was, and am. My objection was that this agreement, and the follow-on deal, the North American Free Trade Agreement (NAFTA), which expanded the arrangement to take in Mexico, did not represent free trade but a regional trade bloc. Moreover, the inclusion of Mexico yoked us to a corrupt and oppressive regime, which we were to treat as an equal, and which clearly opposed open markets. (No one seemed to think it odd, from that day to this, that Mexico was bound by the rules of NAFTA to open trade with her North American partners, but that one of her major exports, petroleum, was traded only within the cartel conditions imposed by the Organization of Petroleum Exporting Countries [OPEC].)

Free trade in economic terms implies a lowering of tariffs to permit competition from abroad, not the erecting of barriers around a sectoral trading arrangement, and not a contract between one giant economy and hapless neighbours whose resources, by the arrangement, become readily available for the giant's grinding mills.

I vented my views on the FTA in the pages of IRPP's *Policy Options,* on the radio, and in debates which were staged, from time to time, to air the subject. Donald Macdonald, my colleague in the Trudeau cabinet, managed to twist himself into ardent advocacy of the FTA after his stint as the chair of the Royal Commission on Economic Union and Development Prospects for Canada, which reported in 1985. He criss-crossed the country, plugging the deal, and we debated it, publicly and privately.

The Purchasing Agents Association of Canada was holding its annual meeting in Halifax and had set up a debate on NAFTA. My debating partner was Frank Stronach, the extraordinary entrepreneur, founder and major shareholder of Magna International Inc.; our opponents were Donald Macdonald and John Risley, a leading Atlantic provinces entrepreneur. At one point, Risley worked himself up to such a pitch that he wanted Frank to step behind the curtain and "settle this right here and now." Cooler heads prevailed. It would not have been a smart move on Risley's part; Frank is quite a formidable man. This meeting was chaired by Mike Duffy, the CTV broadcaster, who came up to me with some glee and wanted to know how much I was getting for my part in the panel.

"Nothing," I told him.

"Boy," he said, "I'm getting $2,000!"

## WRONG END OF THE RAINBOW

The intellectual ferment set off by all this activity led to the writing of *Wrong End of the Rainbow: The Collapse of Free Enterprise in Canada,* with Walter Stewart. We worked on it over the winter of 1986 and the following spring; it was published in 1988. It began with the words "Something has gone seriously wrong with the workings of Canadian capitalism," and summarized my views on the development of the corporation from a useful way of organizing capital to perform all sorts of tasks — from running water systems to manufacturing locomotives — into an international, immortal behemoth, devoid of responsibility, restraint, or regard for the community from which it had emerged. The book was an expansion, in a way, of the argument set forth in the Massey Lectures.

The notion that the cosmocorps were non-political entities was absurd, and we were able to trace the steps by which they became very largely an American, or American-controlled, machine for creating wealth and gratifying greed. The FTA in turn was the logical expression of this development, a way to buckle Canadian resources into the American machine. We wrote:

> Our business community is in favour of joining the United States for the simple and obvious reason that it isn't our business community any more, it is theirs. When the president of Iron Ore of Canada, an American subsidiary, becomes prime minister of Canada, it is not remarkable that he favours greater American ties. The "free trade" argument has had no more vociferous exponent than that branch-plant president, Brian Mulroney, but that is not a surprise. Anything else would be a surprise.
>
> Nor is it surprising that the heads of our giant corporations — pardon, their giant corporations — favour such a deal. Canada, for most of these people, is just another extension of the American market. The fact that foreign-controlled firms import four times more in parts and components than do Canadian firms, do less research than Canadian firms, export less than Canadian firms —

all these matters, which are translated into jobs, represent nothing to the visiting tycoon — other than the proper working out of globalism, and the triumph of the world corporation.

To the chief executive of one of these companies, there is only one question worth debating: which arrangement will return the maximum profit to home office? And there is only one answer: a North American sectoral common market, whether it is called free trade or anything else.

## RENÉ

I was just getting into the research for *Wrong End of the Rainbow* when René Lévesque turned up in Halifax. His memoirs had just been published, and he was in the Nova Scotia capital on a book-promotion tour. When he called, I said, "Wait right there, I'm coming to get you," and drove off to pick him up at the Sheraton, the same hotel where the free-trade debate put on by the Purchasing Agents Association had taken place. As I drew up in front of the hotel, I could see him through the glass doors, sauntering through the lobby towards me, and no one seemed to recognize him at all, which was apparently a relief.

I took him home and we talked and talked about everything under the sun. Not so much politics as the talk of old political friends. He told me that one of his problems was that in Quebec, he was always on show, always expected to live up to a reputation that he had never courted, and could never fulfill, especially among the young PQers.

We wandered out onto the terrace looking down on the Northwest Arm and stood there in companionable silence for a while. Then he turned to me and said, "You know, it's funny."

"What's funny?"

"We start out in that chaos in Quebec and you wind up in a place like this" — he rolled his eyes — "and where do I wind up? Nun's Island." He had a condominium, and a very nice one, on the island off Montreal.

After a while, I wondered whether he shouldn't be heading off for the speaking engagement I knew he had that night. But he and Terry had many tales of the old days to share, and finally we delivered him to the Sheraton, and the Halifax Board of Trade, one hour late.

That was the last time I saw him. When he died suddenly of a heart attack, on November 1, 1987, Terry and I were over in Edinburgh, on a vacation. The CBC caught me by telephone in the hotel room, and they wanted me to make some sort of comment on René's life. I felt as if the bottom had dropped out of everything, as if someone had just hit me, very hard, in the stomach. I muttered, "Sorry, I can't talk," and hung up the phone.

What I should have said was that if there were only one other man in the world, I would want that man to be René Lévesque.

## Twelve

# CONSTITUTIONAL WARS

*Why build these cities glorious*
*If Man unbuilded goes?*
*In rain we build the world, unless*
*The builder also grows.*

— EDWIN MARKHAM, *MAN-MAKING*

WHEN HE WAS ELECTED in 1984, Prime Minister Mulroney set out as a top priority the achievement of a constitutional reconciliation with Quebec. This seemed a laudable goal; many of us were distressed when Quebec was left out of the 1982 constitutional agreement. Premier Bourassa had set forth a series of conditions that had to be met before his province would sign on to any constitutional change. These included direct provincial involvement in the selection of the justices of the Supreme Court of Canada; constraints on Ottawa spending powers that intruded into provincial jurisdictions; increased powers over immigration to the province; a revised amending formula for the Constitution, which would give a veto to each of the four regions of Canada; and, simplest and yet hardest, apparently, recognition in the preamble of the Constitution that Quebec is a "distinct society."

The debate went on, with most of the nation tuned out, for three years. The media were convinced that such changes could never be agreed to, and rumbled with the mutterings of many commentators that, once again, Quebec was making a grab for power. Astoundingly, however, in April 1987 after an eleven-hour session at Meech Lake, outside Ottawa, at which Mulroney preached, beseeched, cajoled, and cudgelled, the deal was struck. A committee was formed to prepare a text for another meeting in June, and an all-night session held in the Langevin

Block on Parliament Hill produced a text acceptable to the leaders of the ten provinces and the federal government at 5 a.m. on June 4. However, it still had to be ratified by each of the eleven governments by June 30, 1990, or the whole deal was off.

The National Assembly in Quebec quickly ratified the accord, putting pressure on the federal government to take similarly swift action. Prime Minister Mulroney established a special joint parliamentary committee to begin the process at the federal level, and it began its work on August 4.

I appeared before this committee on August 27, the same day that former prime minister Trudeau appeared. He launched into a scornful attack on Meech Lake, based on his obsession with the notion that any diminution of the federal powers would lead to chaos, balkanization, and outbursts of nationalism. As usual, no one stood in any doubt of his views when he was done.

However, it seemed to me that his interpretation of Canadian history was not merely wrong, but not supported by the record of history. Lord knows there were things wrong with what came to be called the Meech Lake Accord. It said nothing about Senate reform; nothing about Aboriginal rights; nothing about equity between the sexes. Just the same, it took a long stride back towards the kind of Canada we had before the huge accretion of power to Ottawa via the loan of provincial powers at the beginning of the Second World War — a loan that was never returned. The bulk of the opposition to Meech Lake appeared to be based on the refusal to recognize Quebec as a distinct society. Quebec *is* a distinct society; anyone can see that. In a way, every one of the provinces is distinct; travellers certainly know whether they are in Newfoundland or Alberta pretty quickly. But Quebec's distinction is based, obviously, clearly, unmistakably, on the language of 80 per cent of her people, and why the recognition of that fact should prove a barrier is beyond me.

## A DISTINCT SOCIETY THAT BEGAN IN 1774

Since the Quebec Act of 1774, Quebec has always been recognized as fully distinct in language, culture, and civil law, in a way that applies to no other province. Moreover, even a superficial reading of history will show that Quebec is no mere fragment of our nation; it lies at the very heart of Canada. Indeed, Canadian history begins in and with Quebec. The Quebec Act made it clear that Canada would be a nation of two distinct cultures and languages, for reasons rooted in common sense and historical need. Britain's victories in 1759 and 1760 left the new rulers of this country with a nightmare: the administration of half of North America, a land that was largely unknown, except that it was bound to be full of hostility and resentment.

Imposing British institutions and customs on the new subjects of the Crown was impossible. Indeed, resistance to British authority in the American provinces to the south was already spreading rapidly and becoming more open and more dangerous every day. London needed friends, allies, not more enemies. Somehow, Quebec had to be persuaded to remain neutral.

Accordingly, the British government made it clear that there would be no policy of forced assimilation directed against the French-speaking community of Quebec, and the Quebec Act of 1774 encoded this view. To the new British (French) colony, this act granted freedom of worship, respect for established traditions, and the retention of French Canadian civil law. The act has often been described as one of "unparalleled generosity" for its time; it was also one of considerable political astuteness, for it did exactly what it was designed to do. When the fractious new Americans kicked over the traces and entered into their war for independence, their calls on Quebec for sympathy and support drew nothing but a Gallic shrug, and the invasion of Canada turned into a bitter defeat.

The French of Canada saw nothing in the American experiment that would guarantee their language and religious rights, as the Quebec Act did. Language contains all that has meaning and value to a people — their culture and traditions, their distinctions, their identity — and the clear aim of this legislation was to preserve these for Britain's fractious new citizens. Thus, the tough nationalism of 65,000 Canadians, abandoned by a France that never understood what it had lost in North America, remained firmly fixed in place.

However, the official language policy of the Quebec Act was too much for the Loyalists who came pouring over the border at the end of the American Revolution and flooded into western Quebec. They immediately began clamouring for the customs of English common law, and greater recognition of English political and constitutional practice. They, too, understood that their traditions and culture had to be secured in their own language.

The British parliament responded to these demands by passing the Constitutional Act of 1791, which divided Quebec into the provinces of Upper and Lower Canada. Upper Canada was to live under English common law, while Lower Canada kept its language, French civil law, and customs and traditions. A side effect of the American Revolution was that Quebec, the successor state to La Nouvelle France, would become a duality. Canadians have lived this duality ever since.

Thomas Jefferson was fond of proclaiming that each generation should be responsible for its own constitution. Canadians in both Upper and Lower Canada took Jefferson to heart. Both provinces were soon on the road to rebellion, and for substantially the same reason. The assemblies were elected bodies, but the real power lay with the governors and their appointed executive councils.

The inevitable outbreaks of William Lyon Mackenzie in Upper Canada and Louis-Joseph Papineau in Lower Canada were easily put down, but the furore forced the British government to take notice. John George Lambton, better known to Canadians as the earl of Durham, was named governor-in-chief of the two Canadas.

## LORD DURHAM'S BLUNDER

Lord Durham recommended a legislative union of the two provinces, arguing that a federation of colonies would be weak and unruly. British to the core, he argued that Lower Canada should be made English, that the English "race" must ultimately prevail, and that an English majority was inevitable and would eventually obliterate the French. While he clearly recognized that Lower Canada was distinct, he did not count this as a benefit, and spoke of "two nations warring in the bosom of a single state." His solution was to wipe out one of those nations, and that recommendation led to the Act of Union of 1840, which created a unitary state called Canada, in 1841.

It never got off the ground; the consolidation of Upper and Lower Canada occurred in name only. Fundamental social, cultural, and language difficulties required separate statutes for Canada East and Canada West (French Canada and English Canada), and the division of many cabinet portfolios into two, so that we had the Attorney General West, Attorney General East, and Solicitor General West, Solicitor General East, and so forth. Ministries were two-headed as well: Macdonald-Cartier, Morin-MacNab, etc. Double majorities were required to pass most important legislation, and these became increasingly difficult to obtain. The fractured union was grinding to a halt. By the early 1850s, talk began to surface about the possibility of a federal union of all the British possessions in North America, to get around the difficulty. In such a union, the French would be swamped.

In 1858, Sir Edmund Head, the governor general, prorogued Parliament with a promise to "communicate with Her Majesty's Government, and with the Governments of the sister colonies, on another matter of great importance. I am desirous of inviting them to discuss with us the principles on which a bond of a federal character, uniting the Provinces of British North America, may perhaps hereafter be practicable."

Population growth had swung the balance in favour of Canada West (English Canada), and a great many English Canadians, who had hitherto seen the virtues of dual-majority government when the English were in the minority, began to fight for a unitary system in which only the sum of all votes would be counted, now that they were a majority. What had amounted to a French veto based on bloc voting would disappear. In Canada East, the fear of submergence was raised once more, and prevented any move to a union of the provinces. It was not until 1864 that the continuing problems of trying to govern a united Canada torn apart by two majorities led to the Charlottetown and Quebec Conferences of 1864, and the launch of Confederation.

When the British North America (BNA) Act was finally passed in 1867, it became clear that the Fathers of Confederation had rejected John A. Macdonald's original plan, a legislative union that would bind all four of the joining provinces together, and had instead accepted a federal union that allowed each of the four to preserve its own traditions and culture, its own uniqueness.

It is laughable to suggest that the Canadas, Nova Scotia, and New Brunswick would ever willingly have consented to handing over control

*"Of course we still need you, Eric — uh — can you drive a truck?"*

Yardley Jones of the *Toronto Telegram* drew this nifty cartoon after I was relieved of the Postmaster General portfolio. He gave it to me when we met in Toronto in 1970. You can see his note at bottom left.

When things got too worrisome, Terry and I liked to take off on a cruise. Despite the happy smiles in the picture above, at this time, in 1969, I was already wondering if I could stay in the Trudeau cabinet, considering how strongly I disagreed with some of the government's centralist policies. The picture at right is a poignant one for me; it shows the life-size statue of René Lévesque outside the National Assembly building where we fought so many battles together.

Walter Stewart

Here I am gazing somewhat bemusedly at a mock-up of the Anik satellite that would get me into so much trouble. Despite the fuss, the project was completed on time and on budget. I resigned from Vandenberg air force base three weeks after the successful launch.

Three generations of Kierans gather, in 1980: Terry (left), my daughter Cathy, Inta, Tom's first wife, me, and my mother, then a youthful 95.

I just had to show you one picture of one of my plants. This is the Canadian Adhesive factory in Montreal.

My daughter Cathy —
psychiatric nurse,
administrator, strong
personality, and dog
fancier. The Kerry blue
terriers are Maggie and
Murphy. At left is the
house in Hampstead
that held so many
memories, and
adventures, for us.

Our glasses are charged and our smiles likewise on the occasion of our 60th wedding anniversary, on November 12, 1998. From left are granddaughter Julia, her father Tom, me, Terry, Renata, Julia's sister, and Cathy. In the picture at right are my brother Hugh and his wife; Hugh was a priest for many years, but left to marry. He was professor emeritus of English literature at York University when this picture was taken.

Here is Terry, hard at work on one of her sculptures, on the deck just below our Halifax home. That is the Northwest Arm in the background. At right, the end product.

At Rideau Hall, Governor General Roméo LeBlanc presents me with the Order of Canada on October 19, 1994.

of their communities, traditions, language, and culture to an unknown and untried proposal of legislative union. What they would, and did, approve was to be "federally united into one Dominion."

This was a far cry from what Macdonald wanted, which was "a powerful Central Government, a powerful Central Legislature, and a decentralized system of minor legislatures for local purposes."

Nevertheless, the financial settlement that accompanied the union wound up with each province being heavily dependent on the newly created federal government, through grants and subsidies. In 1874, seven years after Confederation, federal subsidies accounted for 47 per cent of revenues for Ontario, 48 per cent for Quebec, 81 per cent for Nova Scotia, and 92 per cent for New Brunswick. Financially, the provinces were dependent on Ottawa, and their leaders had become what Macdonald had always wanted them to be — mere caretakers.

Not surprisingly, reaction set in. Slowly, power and control over fiscal resources began to be reclaimed by the provinces. A series of decisions by the Privy Council in London, Canada's ultimate court of appeal on constitutional matters, helped the process along, led by a pronouncement of that body in 1892 that

> The aspect of the [BNA] Act was neither to weld the provinces into one, nor to subordinate the provincial governments to central authority, but to create a federal government...each province retaining its independence and autonomy.

The gradual reassertion of provincial powers reflected the reality that Canada, by its history, by its huge geography, its clearly distinct regions, varying resource bases, and differing economic challenges, cannot prosper under centralized policies. By 1939, the nation had gradually assumed the shape of the federated system that was inherent in the BNA Act of 1867. In the period 1926 to 1929, the federal government collected an average of 39 per cent of all revenues, with the provinces and municipalities collecting the other 61 per cent. Subsidies to the provinces averaged 8.2 per cent, a fraction of the figure in 1874.

However, this more balanced role for all three levels of government came apart when the Second World War broke out, and an all-out and united war effort demanded that fiscal and monetary levers and all economic activity be centralized within the federal government, and directed to the war effort. A huge federal bureaucracy sprang up to accomplish this. To which there was some objection, until the federal government gave a solemn undertaking that the status quo would be restored after the war.

Specifically, on second reading of the Dominion-Provincial Taxation Agreement Act of 1942, the legislation that embodied this abrupt change of affairs, the minister of finance, J.L. Ilsley, "stated that what the provinces were required to do was to vacate the personal income and corporation tax fields for the duration of the agreement which will run one year after cessation of hostilities unless a province terminates its agreement sooner, that is, at the end of any fiscal year."

By 1943, Ottawa was collected 76.2 per cent of all revenues, while the provincial and local governments collected, respectively, 11.3 per cent and 12.4 per cent.

## THE SOURCE OF OUR TROUBLES

The Canadian bureaucracy, proud of its achievements during the war and still equipped with full legislative authority and control of revenues to match, decided that it wanted a centralized Canada to continue, and put forward a Keynesian program in the postwar period. This was embodied in a White Paper on employment and income, released in 1945, which required a centralized structure for implementation. Mitchell Sharp later commented on "the remarkable degree of consensus among the government's tightly-knit group of advisors as to the desirable direction of future policy."* Then the federal government simply tore up its promise.

We had been a federal state with a workable division of powers; now we were to be plunged back into the unworkable arrangements of the last century, aided and abetted by a centralizing bureaucracy led by Bank of Canada governor Graham Towers and the Department of Finance.

The war's end had brought a series of meetings to try to straighten out new fiscal arrangements between Ottawa and the provinces, meetings that produced more frustration than progress. At the Dominion-Provincial

---

* Quoted in D.C. Smith, *Economic Policy Advising in Canada* (Montreal: C.D. Howe Institute, 1981), 216.

Conference on Reconstruction in August 1945, C.D. Howe, the minister of everything in Mackenzie King's government, told the conference that increased payments to the provinces would hinge on the under-governments mounting projects only with the approval of the Dominion government and on timetables laid down by the Dominion government.

It was an arrogant and humiliating performance and a political blunder that echoes to this day. Ottawa turned Canada away from federalism and into a centralized state without benefit of any constitutional discussion or amendment; indeed, such amendment was specifically rejected. The Dominion government had control of the spending power, and intended to keep it, notwithstanding the BNA Act of 1867 and the Dominion-Provincial Taxation Agreement Act of 1942. Not surprisingly, the under-governments rebelled, and no agreement could be reached.

The conference collapsed nine months later, as Nova Scotia, Quebec, and Ontario firmly and finally refused the federal proposals. Premier Angus L. Macdonald of Nova Scotia stated crisply why:

> Provincial autonomy will be gone. Provincial independence will vanish. Provincial dignity will disappear. Provincial governments will become mere annuitants of Ottawa.

An English Canadian myth has it that Quebec premier Maurice Duplessis was the one who killed the conference, by slamming the door and taking the train back to Quebec City. In fact, Duplessis was at every plenary session and Quebec was represented at all the coordinating committee meetings from August 6, 1945, until the conference was adjourned *sine die* on May 3, 1946.

After this failure, seven provinces were forced, one by one, into tax rental agreements on Ottawa's terms. In their desperate need for funds, they had no choice in the end but to give way. Two other provinces, Ontario and Quebec, held out as best they could. Ontario collected its own corporation taxes, but rented out personal income taxes to Ottawa. Quebec collected both taxes, refused subsidies, and for fourteen years — from 1946 to 1960 — operated on the minimal tax room left to it by the central government. Quebecers call this period *La Grande Noirceur* (The Great Darkness).

Today's leaders in Quebec grew up and lived through these years,

years when the very core of society — health, education, and welfare programs — were starved for funds. Those are the years when separatism was born.

The separatist movement did not begin with the Quiet Revolution, but with the unilateral, illegal, and unconstitutional takeover of Quebec's financial resources and responsibilities by a determined Ottawa bureaucracy in 1946. This effort reached its peak when the St. Laurent government, under C.D. Howe's impetus, presented the Defence Production Act of 1955 to Parliament. This was a bill seeking to extend the arbitrary powers conferred on Ottawa during the war years, ten years after that war was over. It died only because it became caught up in a general repugnance of the arrogance of the ruling Liberals, a sentiment that led to the party's defeat in 1957.

There has always been an elitist cast to federal Liberalism, supported by a swollen bureaucracy and driven by the view that only Ottawa knows what is best for Canada. Whether the slogans were "co-operative federalism," in Pearson's day, or a "just society," in Trudeau's, made little difference. The arbitrary imposition of medicare without provincial assent in 1965 represented the former; the fraudulent imposition of a 3 per cent surtax, called a "social development tax" to get around the fact that it violated federal-provincial agreements, represented the latter.

The issues between the federal government and the provinces have, at bottom, never been anything other than this question of the division of powers, with the resources to match. Ask Manitoba, which had to wait sixty years after Confederation to gain control over its own resources. Or ask Saskatchewan and Alberta, which were created provinces in 1905, but denied rights over their own lands for decades.

## THE CASE FOR MEECH

The Meech Lake Accord was a commendable attempt to reduce the role of the Ottawa mandarins and return the nation to something like the federation that our ancestors originally agreed to. It recognized that the centralized control of a John A. Macdonald or a Pierre Elliott Trudeau left no significant role for the provinces to play. Provincial premiers and their cabinets are forced to wait patiently for the terms and conditions of policies and decisions in which they have not shared, and can only rubber-stamp.

This was the essence of the case I laid before the joint parliamentary committee in August 1987, where it was received politely, but not enthusiastically. Needless to say, my explanations and expostulations did not generate many headlines in Ottawa. These were devoted to Trudeau's views.

Even prior to attention generated by Pierre's attendance at the committee, my mother had already given me her take on his involvement. I still travelled from Halifax to see her every second or third Wednesday in Montreal, but the week before my trip to Ottawa for my committee appearance, I telephoned her up to say, "Look, Nanny, I won't be there next Wednesday, but I will be there on Thursday."

She said, "Oh, that's all right, as long as you stay more than ten minutes." This was the thumb, the German thumb, coming down on her son.

I said, "You cut out that stuff; I'll be in to see you on Thursday."

I was about to hang up when she said, "Hey, wait a minute."

I said, "Yes?"

"What is Trudeau up to?"

"Well…"

"I know what he's up to."

"All right, Nanny, what is he up to?"

"He wants to come back, and you've got to stop him."

That Saturday night, I got a call from the hospital that she was slipping away, and not likely to get through the night, but I couldn't get up to Montreal in time. My sister Kathleen was able to get down from Ottawa just before she died. She had recently celebrated her 102nd birthday.

## A PROPOSAL FROM THE PREMIER

The eventual failure of the Meech Lake Accord, when the provinces of Manitoba and Newfoundland declined to ratify, threw us back into the constitutional mess that had dogged us for decades, and leaves us today in much the same position. In the circumstances, it is not remarkable that I was drawn into the rumpus in Nova Scotia, although it happened so gradually that I hardly noticed. Donald Cameron succeeded John Buchanan as Conservative leader in 1991, and the very next morning he called and asked me to come over to his office in the legislature. I went down to that magnificent old building in downtown Halifax, in a state of considerable bemusement. I had never met Cameron, knew very little about him, was not a Conservative, and had very little regard for his predecessor, who had resigned abruptly when it became apparent even to him that he was unable to cope.

I was not left long in suspense. When I got to his office, he told his secretary, "Leave us alone for at least an hour and a half." Cameron, a forthright, bluff man, who had been a successful farmer near Pictou, faced an imminent federal-provincial conference in Ottawa.

"Now, Mr. Kierans," he said, "I am going to be sworn in as premier in a couple of days, and then I am off to this conference. I know very little about Quebec, but I know that you know quite a lot, and I need your help."

He said that his aim as premier was to cut out the patronage that was crippling the province, and to make Nova Scotia stop wasting its time dreaming about transfer payments from Ottawa, and instead get to work to support itself. Well, that appealed to me, of course, so we talked for quite a while about what could and should be done.

Later, I received another call, and again went to see Cameron, who by now was installed in office. He told me he wanted to prepare for another constitutional round by finding out what Nova Scotians felt about these issues. "What I'm thinking of doing is forming an official commission, and I have pretty well decided who should be members, but what I really need is a chairman. Do you have any ideas on who we could get?"

I mentioned two or three names, and he suddenly said, "How about you?"

"Look," I said, "I'm seventy-seven years old."

He laughed and said all the usual things about hoping he would be in such good shape at that age and he kept at me in such a way that before I knew it, I had agreed to act as chair of the Nova Scotia Working Committee on the Constitution (NSWCC). The committee's first meeting took place on June 22, 1991, and then we were off on a hectic series of public meetings, consultations, and presentations all across the province.

The bulk of the organizing, I am happy to say, was done by Brian Lee Crowley, the secretary and executive director, and an associate professor in the Political Science Department at Dalhousie. He did 90 per cent of the administrative work, and if I had let him he'd have done it all.

The point of the exercise was not to try to force any point of view, but to listen to what the people of the province themselves had to say. Quite a lot, it turned out. The fifteen public meetings we held, from Dartmouth to Yarmouth, from Shubenacadie Reserve to Sydney, were well attended, and produced a number of excellent submissions. There were ten committee members, besides myself and Brian, representing a broad cross-section of the community, ranging from government employees and fisherfolk to pensioners and the Aboriginal community, and we got along together. The opposition leaders in the legislature, Vince MacLean for the Liberals and Alexa McDonough for the NDP, quickly agreed that party politics had no place in these discussions.

The result was that we were able to produce our report on time on November 28, a scant five months after the NSWCC was established. Perhaps its most important finding was the following:

> Nova Scotians will no longer tolerate the exclusion of women's groups, aboriginal nations, the disabled, ethno-cultural groups from constitution-making and economic policy formation. The exclusive process is dead and public participation will be mandatory from now on. All these groups will be heard from in the years and elections ahead. Empowerment flowing from the Charter of Rights and Freedoms adds force to their efforts to make rights meaningful and our political institutions accountable.

The government did not have to take any specific action on the report; the purpose was not to try to sort out the Constitution but to make sure that Nova Scotians had their say in the next round.

That turned out to be the Charlottetown meeting of the summer of 1992, which resulted in another accord, this time including recognition of Aboriginal rights to self-government and a guarantee to Quebec that its representation in the Senate would never fall below 25 per cent. However, when Prime Minister Mulroney put the Charlottetown Accord to a nationwide referendum, it was defeated — and all that weary work to do again.

This naturally gave encouragement to the Parti Québécois, and Parizeau, now premier, released his draft bill on the sovereignty of Quebec in December 1994. When it was put to a provincial referendum on October 30, 1995, it lost by a hair's breadth. Then we passed into a lull, brought on by an onset of economic prosperity and a feeling everywhere in Canada that nothing could be more enervating than another round of constitutional fury.

## BACK TO MONTREAL

Halifax is a lovely city, with many lovely people, but it is the most lawyer-ridden city in Canada. Nothing, it seems, moves without the imprimatur of one of the great law firms, who dominate business, politics, finance, and even society, as well as their own profession. They seem to be thicker on the ground in Halifax than anywhere else, no doubt because the city is a capital, where lawyers and lobbyists, often the same people, come into their own. I served for one three-year term as a lay member on the Discipline Committee of the Nova Scotia Barristers' Society, and before long had many of the legal backs up by insisting that cases in which lawyers abused the trust of clients should be dealt with more severely. The normal practice seemed to be to place much more emphasis on defending the profession than the victim, and I said so. This was not well received, and I was not invited back for a second term.

One day, after I came back from my routine afternoon walk, I stood in the entryway of our house taking off my coat, and I said to Terry, "Would you like to go back to Montreal?"

She said, "How long have you been thinking about this?"

I replied, "Oh, about a couple of years."

She waved her hand in dismissal. "I've been thinking about it longer than that," she said.

And so in October 1998, we uprooted once more and went back to Montreal, back to the hillside that overlooks the bustling, fractious old city, close to the scenes of our childhood and youth. Back home.

My days are spent now in thinking, reading, and writing. I have slowed down some, I grant. I do not go for the long-striding walks of my youth; I do not plunge into every passing controversy with quite the same zest that I did half a century ago. I very much enjoy my life with Terry, with Cathy nearby, Tom dropping in from his busy round in Toronto from time to time, and our granddaughters coming to call and go shopping with their grandmother. The city is still full of interesting people, abubble with the ferment of ideas, as well as memories. I continue to work on the theory and practice of the corporation, on constitutional issues, on political questions. I still have much to learn, and something to say, I hope.

As I look over the last few pages of this manuscript, around the book-crowded walls of my den, I say to myself: Right, there, that's done. What comes next?

## Thirteen

# THE CAIN CULTURE

*And the Lord said unto Cain, Where is Abel thy brother?*
*And he said, I know not: Am I my brother's keeper?*

— GENESIS 4:9

ONE OF THE ACCUSATIONS levelled at me with regrettable frequency is that I have never kept at anything, that I am constantly starting one career or job or position, only to turn around a few years later and quit, usually leaving behind a strong letter of remonstrance. I protest, mildly, that I have been a life-long Liberal, a life-long Roman Catholic, that I spent half a century as a businessman, and taught for more than twenty years. However, what I suspect is really in people's minds has to do, mainly, with politics; I jumped from Quebec to federal Liberalism, and then quit to become, from time to time, a critic of the Liberal party with a capital *l*. In my defence, I would argue that what really happened is that the party of my choice abandoned the principles of reform and social liberalism that drew me to it in the first place, and has become, instead, just another piece of political machinery in the service of corporatism.

For decades, since I first began to learn the rudiments of economics, I have been a critic of the corporate agenda, and I haven't changed one whit from that position.

In the 1930s, I lived in two communities. The depression in Montreal was visible and everywhere — tremendous numbers of unemployed, soup kitchens, poverty, a sense of hopelessness and despair. In the Maritimes, when I moved there, the conditions in terms of numbers of unemployed and average incomes were worse, but the despair was not as visible. Sharing was a part of living, and was maintained until the crisis lessened. Simply providing for oneself was not the end of one's day.

Now, in good times, for some, that attitude seems to have vanished.

It was not, and is not, easy to develop and broaden one's horizons when working in a corporate environment. The advantages of living under the corporate umbrella have long since disappeared, but even in earlier times there was a recurring fear and anxiety in the face of an uncertain future. For these and other reasons, I was obsessed with the desire to be "my own boss." As we saw in chapter 2, November 1945 was the happy month.

In the late 1940s and early 1950s, I continued to live in two worlds. Security for the family demanded success in the commercial and technological challenges of practical living and provided, at the same time, a springboard for the study and evaluation of the world beyond individualism.

On May 19, 1960, I was introduced to the Canadian financial community as the new president of the Montreal and Canadian Stock Exchanges. Members of that community from across the country were on hand to witness and judge what was then a curiosity in Canada: a president from outside the exchanges, and a university professor at that. It was time to say where one was coming from. A public persona should not be a mask. In my inaugural address — to which I am going to refer often in this chapter, to underline the argument that my basic positions have not changed over four decades — I wanted to make clear that social programs were an intrinsic element of an economic system. That system could survive only if it provided a basic standard of living for all its citizens. Social programs did not grow out of the self-serving politics of either the left or the right. They were the matter of the social consciousness of each one of us. We are not only individuals, but social beings.

I said, "A wealthy and prosperous nation cannot permit want and poverty in the midst of abundance. Public assistance, welfare payments, social security are all called for and involve a redistribution of incomes." My argument was that since the free market did not supply the funds for this redistribution, either practically or in theory, then governments had to do so in its stead. The more the private sector supplied, the less need for state interventions.

Economic theory has no answers, I said, since it has no theory of distribution. As in the work of Adam Smith — in whose *An Inquiry into the Nature and Causes of the Wealth of Nations* there was no integration of the unemployed or the poor — an economics that continued the Malthusian opposition to relief for the poor could not call itself either a science or a social study.

## WE HAVE NO ECONOMIC DEMOCRACY

During my years at McGill, I had completed a study of the sources of funds of 603 major corporations in Canada, and I cited this in my speech before the stock exchanges:

> Over a period of sixteen years, 603 corporations financed 82.2 per cent of their growth by internal funds, 9 per cent by bonds, 8 per cent by common stock, and 1 per cent by preferred [stock].

I pointed out that praising capital markets might be more persuasive if corporations used them more. Internal investment leads to overinvestment, and the misallocation of funds. I inveighed against double depreciation, depletion allowances, and other government measures, which distorted the investment decisions of Canadians. (Most of my criticisms were later addressed by the Carter Commission, and we know what happened to that report.)

The point in these remarks was that I had believed in a liberal capitalism and free markets all my life — that is, from the time when I began to understand the meaning of such terms. The problem is that while we have political democracy in Canada, we do not have the economic democracy to match it.

In Adam Smith's time, there was much more turnover in partnerships and family enterprises, and much more opportunity for the new generations and new entrepreneurs to enter the commercial arena. Since the recognition of corporations as a never-ending succession with limited liability, firms have been able to grow without constraint, and in time are merged into larger and larger units. Governments — Canada being one of the guilty ones — showered corporations with tax privileges, subsidies, etc., not realizing that every dollar in corporate tax reduction discriminated against the use of labour.*

---

* Innumerable studies have shown that these giveaways result in more capital being put into machinery to increase productivity, with concomitant cuts in jobs: the creation of unemployment by government subsidy.

Worse, by building the corporation to its present greatness, governments failed to take the measures to control the firms thus created and force them to integrate the social purposes and cultural goals of the community into their operations.

I further pointed out that when the corporate community financed 82.2 per cent of its investment needs from internal sources, the Canadian economy was in danger of becoming sclerotic, rigid, and unresponsive to the surging dynamism of our neighbours to the south.

The challenge to the financial community was clear. Encourage and advise its corporate clients to distribute a larger percentage of their profits to their shareholders, and look to the financial community for investment funds. This address went over well, but as Doug Chapman of A.E. Ames, dean of the underwriting fraternity, said to me, "A very good speech, Eric, but, of course, it will never happen."

## WE ARE HEADED FOR FASCISM, OR CHAOS

We are not born to live in a corporate globe, yet that is the world that we are moving towards. Moreover, we have created a society in which so much of the world's riches are accumulated in so few hands — a curve that grows steeper every year — that we are headed for fascism, or chaos. The controls of a civil state will no longer apply, and when that happens the inevitable outcome is an uncivil state, either because it is controlled by tyrants or because it lacks any controls at all.

When we add 2 billion more people to the global population, as we will over the next few years, while, in order to feed the insatiable maw of corporate culture, we remove more and more support from the 6 billion of us here already, something has to give. Either the few will control the many by force of arms — the example of old South Africa springs to mind — or the mob will rule — consider the land confiscations in Zimbabwe, where the state is either complicit or helpless. When people have nothing to lose, as more and more of them are plunged into poverty for the enrichment of others, they must either subside or rebel; and there is an end to community, responsibility, and society.

If this sounds too extreme, I am not the only one to hold such a view. James Wolfensohn, president of the World Bank — a staid and conservative institution if ever there was one — had this to say just prior to the annual meeting of the International Monetary Fund and the World Bank in September 2000:

> Today, you have 20 per cent of the world controlling 80 per cent of the Gross Domestic Product; you've got a U.S.$30 trillion world economy, and $24 trillion of it is in the developed countries…These inequities can't exist. So if you are talking about systemic breakdown, I think you have to look in terms of social breakdown.*

When the Elizabethan Poor Laws were passed at the beginning of the seventeenth century, it was not because the ruling classes had suddenly discovered compassion. What they had discovered was fear. The countless thousands of vagabonds and "sturdy beggars" produced by an inequitable distribution of the national wealth were on the move, with nowhere to go, and nothing to lose. As society evolved from feudalism into capitalism, as the national population grew, and as thousands of former church servants were rendered homeless by the breakup of the monasteries, the numbers of the poor mushroomed far beyond anything the local parishes, the sole source of civil succour, could handle. The mobs took to the road, or were thrust there, and bid good riddance. The result was that England lived in terror of the tramp.

## THE RISE OF THE SECURITY STATE

It is no accident that the United States, current temple of the doctrine of the wicked poor, jails more of her own people per capita than any other advanced nation; eleven times more than the Scandinavian countries, seven times more than Germany or France, five times more than Canada.† The world's richest nation is one of the most violent, and sees no connection between the two. The United States, abandoning the civil society erected by Franklin Roosevelt, has gone instead to what Paul Chevigny, a professor of law at New York University, calls "the security state," brought about by what he calls "the populism of fear." The welfare state reduced crime by alleviating the conditions that produced criminals, and so, as that state was dismantled to make room for corporatism, it

---

* Quoted in the *Toronto Star,* 24 September 2000, B8.

† In 1999, the American rate of imprisonment was 649 people per 100,000. *Toronto Star,* 19 August 2000, K5.

became an important part of the populism of fear to assert that "crime is not caused by poverty and other social conditions, but instead is the result of choices made freely by criminals."[*]

Today's giantism, with its single-minded concentration on its own growth and coupled with the shuffling off of social and economic responsibility, is creating a new and uninhabitable world for the very reason that it rejects the very values that make life bearable for most of mankind. This has been obvious since Berle and Means (whom we met in chapter 3) described the corporation as the end of politics and the beginning of the economic state, back in 1932. They had this to say about the substitution of economic for political power:

> The rise of the modern corporation has brought a concentration of economic power which can compete on equal terms with the modern state — economic power versus political power... — where its own interests are concerned it even attempts to dominate the state... The law of corporations, accordingly, might well be considered as a potential constitutional law for the new economic state... The future may see the economic organization, now typified by the corporation, not only on an equal plane with the state, but possibly superseding it as the dominant form of social organization.[†]

We can't say we weren't warned.

The warning was repeated in 1968, when A. Wedgwood Benn, then Britain's minister of technology, said in the House of Commons, "As the international companies develop, national governments, including the British Government, will be reduced to the status of a parish council."[††]

The corporations have been quiet, but not subtle, as they went about the business of persuading us to leave the direction of society to them. Corporations have nothing to do with values, and they know it, and sometimes say it. Here is Milton Friedman, the economist who validated the triumph of mindless accumulation:

---

[*] Ibid.

[†] Gardiner Means and Adolf Berle, *The Modern Corporation and Private Property* (New York: Columbia University Press, 1932), 18.

[††] *The Times* (London), 28 November 1968.

> There is one and only one social responsibility of business — to use
> its resources and engage in activities designed to improve its profits so
> long as it stays within the rules of the game, which is to say, engages
> in open and free competition, without deception and fraud...
>
> ...Few trends could so thoroughly undermine the very founda-
> tion of our free society as the acceptance by corporate officials of a
> social responsibility other than to make as much money for the
> stockholders as possible. This is a *fundamentally subversive doctrine*
> [emphasis added].

Friedman, of course, is perfectly right, given the nature of the impersonal, a-personal, depersonalized legal institution that man created in the
corporation.

But think for a moment about what this approach implies in the
modern world. If one corporation gives money to a charity and another
does not, the directors of the first are at fault, because they have suc-
cumbed to the subversive doctrine that something other than maximum
profit is part of the corporate goal. (Unless they are able to argue that the
amount given was so minimal that it was defensible as a public-relations
tax write-off.) Going further, a firm that does not pollute the stream near
its pulp mill is reprehensible, because only by polluting can it keep its
costs down, and avoid being engulfed by another and dirtier firm. (This
is a serious argument, seriously advanced by an American professor of
economics in a paper produced for the Law and Economics Center of
the University of Miami.)

**THE ROOTS OF THE COMMUNITY**

The trouble with this argument, besides its moral obtuseness, is that it
assumes that the only legitimate motive for humankind is greed. But neither experience nor common sense supports this view. We develop,
change, move, make decisions, prodded by all sorts of spurs, not all of
them monetary. Why did we come to Canada in the first place? My
parents came from Ireland and Germany in the first decade of the twentieth century, in that great wave of immigration that led Laurier to
exclaim that the twentieth century belonged to Canada; they were
searching for a better future than could be found in their homelands.
The people who come to Canada have a variety of reasons for coming

here — a simple search for new opportunities and directions, a flight from discrimination and prejudice, a move towards preferred institutions and freedoms. They bring with them their hopes and their expectations, their values and their purposes. They have founded a unique community, a community that, until recently, believed in sharing as their only basis for survival.

They knew this, that the roots of any community are only two: the land and the people who come to that land. Everything else stems from these two fundamental factors — capital, knowledge, entrepreneurship, and technology are all derivative and secondary. If the land is not attractive or yields but little, few will come and stay. If the land yields much and if this is retained, the community will grow and prosper. If, however, the surpluses are drained away, the community will stagnate in an accelerating dependence. If the land itself is thrown on the market and cashed in, the people then have no place to stand. Where there is no solid attachment to one's environment, to one's region, to one's land, there can be no community, no nation. Whoever owns the land controls his or her future. As it is with people, so it is with nations.

My sense of the contemporary is this: that we (men and women) no longer believe in ourselves, in our essential worth as humans, in the essential dignity of all human beings. The worst thing that can be said about the argument for corporate greed, then, is that we are beginning to believe it. We believe in money. George Santayana said it achingly:

> My heart rebels against my generation,
> That talks of freedom and is slave to riches,
> And, toiling 'neath each day's ignoble burden,
> Boasts of the morrow.

It is my belief that the original sin, in Christian theology, is not the sin of Adam but rather the sin of Cain; and that Cain's sin was not primarily the murder of his brother, Abel, but his belief that he was *not* his brother's keeper, which led him to the murder. Cain, in other words, was the first secularist, the first materialist, the first to say, "I want it all." Not content with being the tiller of the soil, he wanted also to be the keeper of the flocks.

The single most important question that has ever been asked is, in my view, "Am I my brother's keeper?" It is not a religious question only;

it is a question that covers all aspects of living and meaning, all spheres of activity — the political and the economic, the social and the cultural, and, of course, the spiritual and the moral.

Cain had already answered the question before he committed the murder. No, he was not his brother's keeper. He had no responsibility for his brother, no sense of fraternity. He was for himself and no one else; his instincts were purely selfish.

The question divides society and the future in two. There can be no quibbling with the answer. One either is or is not one's brother's keeper. A "no" answer, of course, is antisocial, the denial of community and responsibility; it is every person for himself or herself — competition, conflict, and chaos.

The truest and most complete sense of community, and my favourite, is that of Moses ben Maimon (Maimonides), who outlined eight degrees of charity, laws of moral behaviour and justice, of which the eighth:

> The highest type of charity is the prevention of poverty by provid-
> ing a poor man with a means of livelihood.

There could be no truer interpretation of the meaning of "brother's keeper" than this law. There can be no excuse for failing to provide the poor man with work so that he can maintain himself in dignity by being self-supporting. In the twelfth century, unemployment was, as it is today, the overriding evil. The difference is that where our policy-makers treat unemployment as an economic statistic, Maimonides in the *Mishneh Torah* saw it for what it was, a social evil of the highest order and a human tragedy depriving man of his dignity by making him a disposable element in his society. Make no mistake, unemployment is the greatest of all social evils.

The Cain culture, that is, his negative response to his own question, demands individual freedom and the absence of social restraint, a self-determination that defies and denigrates the concept of community. The question itself posed a false choice, a choice between a personal ethics and a social ethics. There is no such choice. We live in society, whether it is the family of Cain or the billions in our own time. The freedom that Cain claimed by his act is a freedom equal to that of God. Similarly, it is the freedom that Jean-Paul Sartre claims when he puts man over and above society. "L'homme se définit par une exigence." Man, being intelligent and accepting change, grows to fulfillment:

> (a) en décrivant la réalité dans sa laideur, son absurdité et son obscénité, (b) en répétant toutes ces formes qui restreignent sa liberté, et (c) en s'engageant.

One looks at society and changes it.

This is nihilism rather than individual freedom. Man becomes completely free and is so in every association. There is no law in society above him that can limit or direct him. This is what Alexis de Tocqueville saw and feared when he wrote *De la démocratie en Amérique* (published in English as *Democracy in America*). Putting the individual above society was the doctrine of Ralph Waldo Emerson, who spoke of "the infinitude of the private man." It was the sin of Cain. It is the sin that endures in our own day — *original, continuing,* and *always with us.*

Individualism crested and has remained with us since the last half of the nineteenth century. The industrial and machine age, the economies of scale, administration and management, the accumulations of wealth, the land clearances of Britain, and the limits of the American frontier — all combined with an integrating technology to create the instrument of corporate concentration and accumulation. The problem was that the fear of the state persisted — the fear of evil, dominating governments that could prevent the operation of those natural laws that alone could create the ultimate level playing field. Bigness was more efficient, concentrations of capital were clearly more productive, and the consolidation of corporate power would lead to the blasting open of the markets of the world. However, individualism and corporate style would need the same kind of protection from the state that the self-sufficient entrepreneur had enjoyed in earlier times.

## WE TOOK THE CAIN SOLUTION

How did we get this way? The answer is that we came to a fork in the road, and took the Cain solution. People found they could reject community and come out on top. Individualism, in Adam Smith's view, meant that each person doing his or her own thing in a competitive world would ensure the well-being of all. Emerson rejected society as an artificial order — "Every man takes a place which leads out from the common centre, and every step separates him further from all the rest" — on the grounds that there existed a "natural order," which would provide harmony and congruity to a world of individuals. Today we believe in neither. Nor do we believe in the self-sufficiency of the individual. Despite the last spasms of deregulation fever, it is certain that the future will bring an insistence on institutions, community, and social values. *For the present, we are living on the knife-edge of instability and widespread disorder.*

The Industrial Revolution drove the world output of goods and services to unparalleled heights. Its continuous appeal for the need for more growth, and still more growth, meant that the important goals of distributing wealth and balancing growth were put forward to an indefinite future. Thomas Robert Malthus argued that the poor should be left to the punishment of nature, the punishment of want; and Marxists have generally approved the violent dispossession and destruction of the peasant class of the English enclosure movement as providing the basis for the modernization and development of the industrial class. This amassed the capital needed to build the factories. Production was not for a standard of living, it was for accumulation. Few besides Oliver Goldsmith saw the issue for what it was, one where "wealth accumulates, and men decay."

Today, that accumulation has become the locomotive driving the economies of the world. Capital, never concerned with distribution, is now less and less concerned with production. Capital is driving for power, for the control over markets, lands, resources. Capital, in corporate hands, can move anywhere and thus demand and get the utmost in concessions and privileges as well as the freedom to operate in the interest of ever-increasing wealth and assets. Capital generated from the control of markets in one nation can be used to finance expansion in other nations — by the purchase of their property, lands, resources, and markets. Capital in money form has no citizenship. It is fungible, an asset capable of moving from place to place in a nanosecond, capable of extending its reach from the immediate to the distant future. Money capital searches for heartlands, avoids peripheries. Existing capital assets, as ghost towns testify, can be easily liquidated and moved to other sectors, leaving behind residues of unemployment and empty factories.

## THE WORLD ECONOMY IS DRIVEN
## BY CAPITAL MOVEMENTS

The world economy has changed. Once agricultural, then industrial, it is now driven by capital movements alone. The purpose of economic activity in the past was to create a standard of living; production was for consumption and involved an appropriate and just dispensation of what was produced. But this is no longer the case. Capital movements are no longer necessarily related to the production of goods and services. Through the financial markets of the world, capital movements today are overwhelmingly concerned with the capture of and trade in property rights, the ownership of assets that magnify a corporation's wealth, power, and control. It is what John Maynard Keynes described as "a casino world" — wealth without worth.

When a Canadian company such as Nortel can acquire other corporations worth $30 billion in less than three years, there is no new production of anything; it is simply a change of ownership via the monetization of the future surpluses that will flow from the monopoly control of markets over the next ten or fifteen years. This is the standard procedure for corporate growth these days; one company buys up another on loans that are floated on the basis of future earnings, and the monopoly or oligopoly created in this way produces the necessary funds by squeezing out competition, and passing the costs along to the consumer. The bucket that holds the new wealth is called a corporation.

### PROPERTY HAS BECOME DEPERSONALIZED

Whereas Hegel held that "property is the embodiment of personality," property rights have become depersonalized. Property, once considered the necessary basis for freedom, for defence against a bureaucratic state, as a life-support system and entitlement to secure employment, now takes on the responsibility of ensuring its own economic growth as its first and only priority. Thus property becomes separated from its original function of ensuring freedom, justice, and a personal standard of living — that is, removed from the realm of individual rights — and is transferred to an impersonal entity that is then endowed with the title and rights of persons, while remaining exempt from personal responsibility (compare this with Milton Friedman), and exempt from moral substance.

The corporation is the dominant and dominating institution of our time. Governments identify growth and development with commercial corporations and shower them with subsidies, tax privileges, and appropriate labour legislation and market support to attract a commitment and investment. Peter Drucker has accurately reflected the euphoria with which we have covered corporate institutions when he wrote:

> Multinationals, whether corporate or communist, put economic integrity ahead of political nationality; the multinational corporation is by far our most effective economic instrument today and probably the one organ of economic development that actually develops. It is the one non-nationalist institution in a world shaken by nationalist delirium. *It puts the economic decision beyond the effective reach of the political process and its decision-makers, national governments* [emphasis added].

However much one may be appalled by Drucker's justification of corporate domination over the political process, what he is saying is for all practical purposes the simple truth. When the act of incorporation for commercial purposes became a simple right in the nineteenth century, few suspected that the chartered company would ever attain its present importance and strength.

However, the basic flaw in Drucker's reasoning is the notion that the institution of which he is so enamoured somehow rises above nationalism. Corporations, especially American corporations, have been deliberately turned into battering rams for the national policies of the United States. Witness the changes demanded by Congress as the price of U.S. support for the International Monetary Fund, as recorded by Robert Gilpin, Eisenhower Professor of Public and International Affairs Emeritus at Princeton. Gilpin's most recent book notes, among the conditions laid down by Congress, the following: "The U.S. Treasury must certify that IMF loans do not subsidize industries that compete against American industry." Gilpin adds, parenthetically, "What more can be said than 'economic nationalism is alive and well in the U.S. Congress?'"*

Encroaching corporations do not bring a magic and nation-neutral

---

* Robert Gilpin, *The Challenge of Global Capitalism* (Princeton: Princeton University Press, 2000), 334.

boon to the countries where they land. It is in the very character of the commercial corporation, large or small, to drain a market or an environment. Just as plants suck up moisture from the earth, so do corporations draw out and drain the surpluses inherent in the contributions of labour and the resources of nature. The corporate invader's primary objective is to increase its own wealth and assets, not the level of community income. When communities enter into arrangements with corporations, it is important that the nature of this institution be clearly understood.

## HOW THE UNITED STATES MOVED TO HEGEMONY

Following the Second World War, the United States faced a serious challenge. Its power to produce a tremendous output of goods and services met up against a Europe and Great Britain bankrupt from the costs and destruction of the five-year conflict. Out of the need to rebuild and restructure the stricken economies of the Allies evolved the Marshall Plan, designed to promote their recovery and at the same time to contain the growing influence of the Soviet Union in Eastern Europe, as well as in France and Italy. Some $12 billion was spent under the program, which was deservedly proclaimed a major contribution to European revival.

The American corporate economy was then operating from a position of enormous strength and with the capacity to produce goods and services far beyond the economy's capacity to consume. In response, and in short order, former president William McKinley's old policy was revived:

> We want our own markets for our manufacturers and agricultural products; we want a *foreign* market for our surplus products [emphasis added].

This revived doctrine worried American business. Resources were in finite supply and there was the distinct possibility that the United States would run short. President Harry Truman responded by creating the President's Materials Policy Commission, under William Paley, chair of the Columbia Broadcasting System. His report, released in 1951, admitted that resources were becoming more expensive, and while there was no imminent danger of running out there was serious cause for concern. Nations at the height of their power have a long perspective.

The report in effect threw a second Monroe Doctrine over the resources of Canada and other nations. In velvet terms, it declared:

There is no such thing as a purely domestic policy towards materials that all the world must have; there are only world policies that have domestic aspects.

The overall objective of a national materials policy for the United States should be to ensure an adequate and dependable flow of materials at the lowest cost consistent with the national security and with the welfare of friendly nations.*

The United States accepted this approach with enthusiasm, and takeovers in Canada took a marked swing upwards. Soon I was debating the heavy percentages of our mining, forest, and oil industries that were being swallowed by American investment. The net effect was that American corporations became an arm of the State Department, political instruments, under the self-serving argument that economic developments are somehow above politics. So, acting apolitically, American corporations took over the policy-making apparatus of the world; and as other nations returned to prosperity, their corporations joined in the game. To say that General Motors, or Mitsubishi, has no politics is to ignore the fact that the corporate decisions made by these giants have direct impacts on the way of life in the dozens of nations in which they operate, as well as on the world as a whole. Indeed, it seems evident that the triumph of U.S. corporations around the world is provoking direct political response, with protest meetings springing up around almost every so-called global conference. It seems evident, too, that our continental neighbours stand in great danger of arousing such dislike that the old phrase about the "ugly American" will be recalled and reused with all the old bitterness of the 1960s.

Despite the evidence, the corporate system that we are dealing with still claims to be independent from the political sphere and from the demands of a society of brothers and sisters. When economics separated itself from political science, it died from want of purpose. A cost accountant serves society better than an economist without social goals.

George Ball, once the U.S. undersecretary of state and later a corporate manager, was right when he declared, "Commerce has been in advance

---

* Quoted in Eric Kierans and Walter Stewart, *Wrong End of the Rainbow* (Toronto: Collins, 1988), 142.

of politics." That is the problem. Commerce is meant to find a need and then to fill it. Today, commerce does not attempt to satisfy the palpable stress of the poverty-stricken and unemployed, but invests tremendous sums in the creation of new needs. What we truly need is more schools and hospitals, not more models of all-terrain vehicles, but guess what we are getting? It is not that the expectations of the poor have increased but that the poor are being ignored in the mad rush of a "new economy" that diverts attention from the concern of raising the standard of living of all nations to the creation of the baubles, entertainment, and other divertissements. In the new economy, we trivialize ourselves and our culture as we produce fewer and fewer useful goods and services and more and more gadgets and novelties.

## THE PRETENCES OF MANAGERS

Complicating this development is the fact that on paper, and in economics textbooks, the corporation is still the creature of its shareholders; but in reality the modern corporation pays little or no attention to shareholders. It has escaped the control not only of liability laws and state regulation, but even of its owners, with consequences that must be addressed, and soon. Such consequences affect the global aspects we have already discussed, as well as the operation of the corporation itself.

The economic structure of a managerial society is centralized. Except in rare instances of crisis, boards of directors follow the managers. There is no or little opposition to the managers, especially in this technological era. There is even less recognition of the rights of shareholders, who are entitled to receive the profits of their investments.

Effective ownership of capital in a corporation means that the shareholders have the absolute right to the net income from operations. And yet, dividends on average today do not exceed 1 to 3 per cent of profits; the balance is retained for managerial reinvestment.

This is not necessarily the best investment. Moreover, the investment is restricted to the existing enterprise, which may or may not be the most appropriate use of funds. In a dynamic economy, new savings and investment must examine a wide range of alternatives, not just the existing enterprise.

I have long held these views. In the 1960 speech to the Montreal exchanges, which I mentioned earlier, I said that governments should concentrate on increasing personal savings. "Personal savings are new savings; as such they are tremendously mobile, not committed to any specific industry or firm." Nor are they restricted to private enterprises; instead, they are also available for investment in municipal, provincial, and federal works through the purchase of bonds.

When managers talk about the glories of the marketplace, they are pretenders. They do not expose their own internal flows of business savings to a market test. They fear that the market would quickly expose the misallocation of their investment decisions.

The large corporation is not respectful of shareholders' rights. Shareholders learn of new uses of their funds after the decisions have been taken — taken sometimes by a small group of insiders, sometimes by the leader alone. Witness some of the recent mergers, where the first the shareholders knew that their investment had been entirely transformed, perhaps even moved half a world a way, was when they read in their newspaper that the change had already taken place, and their money was no longer in oil, or broadcasting, but was now churning up the Internet, about the dodgiest field for investment imaginable.

It is time to take a look at the concept of managerial trusteeship, if that is the phrase. Management's interests are not to distribute the profits of the corporation but, by their retention, to increase the enterprise and so increase their own incomes and justify the issuance of stock options, pension plans, bonuses, etc. This is contradictory to the private-property theory of our economy. The company must be operated in the interests of the shareholders, who invest for incomes and not in the interests of management. The essence of our economic system is that there be a full distribution of what is earned. Promising capital gains in the future is gambling, and the exchange becomes a casino; meanwhile, the corporation puts its own future ahead of the current needs and rights of its shareholders.

By withholding income from shareholders, we do not build the economic power of households to consume rationally as we build the industrial capacity to grow. We promote the concentration of wealth and production at the expense of current consumption. The imbalance forces investment in plant and machinery to the detriment of employing labour. In the process, we have spoon-fed the large corporations with so many deductions that a large percentage of them pay no corporate taxes at all. Our nominal measures of corporate tax are meaningless (for the obvious reason that so many of our dominant firms are able to avoid the imposts altogether), although the Business Council on National Issues uses them to complain about high corporate taxes. This is pure hypocrisy, and the leaders of business who support such statements should be ashamed of themselves.

## MAKE CORPORATIONS DISTRIBUTE ALL THEIR PROFITS

The beginning of economic freedom — to match the political freedom that we have — would be to force corporations to distribute 100 per cent of their profits yearly to their shareholders, who would then have an improved chance to invest in better opportunities elsewhere, in their particular social and cultural interests, in standard of living, or to reinvest in the original corporation. Capital, including the corporation's internal sources, should rotate, eternally searching for the most promising returns as needs change.

The corporation is an instrument, a tool to facilitate the amassing of capital to pursue profitable activities. Holding back the distribution of profits from shareholders is the negation of a private-property, free-market theory of our economy as a system. It also destroys the idea of economics as a science, for there must be a principle of distribution of all that is produced to match the production itself.

In France, the limited company is called a *société anonyme* (a literal translation: anonymous society). There is a peculiar and apt resonance to this term, which reflects the disconnection of this form of commercial enterprise from the community in which it operates.

A corporation claims the right to be a person. Yet it refuses the responsibilities of that person. Since it does this, it should be forced to distribute all its income to the shareholders, who in turn accept the responsibilities of the increased income. The corporation would then become the strictly commercial instrument that it really is, and the logic of the private-property economy would be preserved. There can be no income or property without responsibility to one's brother or sister — that is, to the entire community.

Since progress does not develop by leaps, a period of adjustment is called for; my proposal is that corporations would be required to distribute at least half their profits in the first year, increasing to reach 100 per cent distribution over five years. The distributed profits would be tax-free at the corporate level, and taxed at the personal level; that is, the corporation would not have to pay on the funds distributed, but the shareholder would be required to take the amount into his or her income for the year.

## A CORPORATION MUST BE A SOCIAL ORGANISM

We are going too fast. Markets cannot fix the problems of our schools and universities, nor provide all our people with the health care and employment that they need. Governments have had to broaden their activities to provide housing, help for the poor, and money to clean the environment. We organize ourselves, our land, and people, to meet the needs of all members of the community. An economy is a social organism.

If the world is instead considered to be the basic economic unit, then the technical principles of industrial location theory will assign resources according to the demands, real or forced, of the global economy, rather than the needs of nations. This global vision is based on money flows, emptied of values, principles, or purposes. Regional influence will not count and the political region (i.e., the nation) makes no economic sense. Economically, a nation will be defined as a source of cheap labour, a supplier of capital, or a reservoir of raw materials. Global allocation will put aside the natural desire of a community for balanced growth and ignore regional priorities and policy preferences. As employees, we will be free to move with the geographical flow of capital, but this is a very peculiar definition of freedom in that it takes no account of the costs of giving up one's heritage, culture, and community of friends and family.

An increased world output? This is the claim. An unobjectionable goal, but could it be attained? If it were, who would decide how the annual global output is to be divided? What proportion would go to an improvement in the standard of living of Canada, or other nations? How much would be saved to invest in a better tomorrow? What happens to regional politics if a supranational body makes the crucial investment-consumption choices for a whole host of countries scattered across the globe and in various stages of development? Can anybody do this? Can any international institution? Will not each society's demands for a level of social security, justice, and an adequate standard of living conflict with capital's demands for increasing returns and asset growth? Which countries will share now? Which will be told to wait another year?

I am no fan of this thrust to global markets. The financial system, it is true, has become international, or global, as they like to say. But that is a paper world in which the multiplication of financial products creates an arena for gambling, not investment, and in which speculation on sunspots and time periods replaces real investment in the production of goods and services. In the 1930s, John Maynard Keynes foresaw the waste of speculation and proposed a transfer tax on such transactions, which would have brought the excesses to a dead halt then, and would do so now. The notion of a tax on "day trades" or other speculative swaps was revived in recent years,* but has been studiously ignored by all our purveyors of conventional economic wisdom. That is because we have been persuaded, against logic, and moral sense, that the institution that most needs our support these days is not society, nor the human community, but the global corporation.

Let us repeat with Professor Rahman, professor of Islamic thought at the University of Chicago: "There is no such thing as a society-less individual." Human beings, their activities, and their institutions are meaningful only in a community context.

As a liberal, I reject any global order or commercial worldview. Globalism and corporatism block intellectual growth and cultural and political freedom. An open-ended future for humankind demands the pluralism and diversity that are the hallmarks of a true liberalism.

---

* James Tobin, Sterling Professor of Economics at Yale, proposed in 1978 a small tax on any capital changed from one currency to another as a way to curb some of the international flows of speculative money. He suggested a rate of 0.2 per cent — $200 on $100,000 of capital — which would not interfere with any legitimate investment, but would become a burden if money was simply being flipped from currency to currency in search of a quick profit. He made his proposal in the form of his presidential address to the Eastern Economic Association, in front of a group of high-powered economists. His own summary of its reception was succinct: "One might say it sank like a rock."

## *Appendix*

———•✦•———

# LETTERS

**1.** *My letter to Prime Minister Trudeau, resigning from cabinet the first time. He never opened it.*

March 17th, 1970

The Right Honourable Pierre Elliott Trudeau, P.C., M.P.,
Prime Minister of Canada,
Ottawa.

My dear Prime Minister;

Last evening, the Cabinet reversed its direction of September 24th last to the Postmaster General, authorizing him to proceed to open tenders for transportation services in the Montreal area. The new Cabinet instruction requires me to inform the successful contractors that they must release those whom they have already hired and that they will only be permitted for the purposes of their contracts, to employ drivers according to seniority from a list furnished by the C.N.T.U. [Confederation of National Trade Unions]. The government, recognizing the serious constraints it is imposing, is prepared to revert to one year arrangements on a cost plus basis, i.e. the situation which has existed in Montreal since 1954.

I registered my dissent with the decision, after presenting fully my reasons to Cabinet. I will not repeat those reasons here except to say that I cannot consciously impose upon the new contractors conditions which take away their freedom to choose those employees who, they believe, will contribute to the success of their enterprises. Such a precedent will effectively destroy the tender system, as we now know it, not only for the Post Office but throughout the public and private sectors. The damage to the Canadian economy will be, I firmly believe, pervasive and enduring.

Acquired rights to employment (and the conditions thereof) are exercised with respect to a given employer. They are not transferable. Perhaps they should be but such a fundamental proposition should come about through appropriate legislation based on principle and not as an 'ad hoc' response to violence. When a union, or any other group, believes that violence will achieve its objectives, then the responsibility of government is to repudiate that violence. Unless it can be shown that violence won't work, then there will be continued violence.

As you know, I have all along recognized that the government had a moral obligation to these workers because of their long service and because of the peculiar circumstances of the Montreal mail system. To fulfill that moral obligation, I proposed the assurance of job security for those drivers with more than five years services [*sic*], as well as ex gratia payments. However, this is entirely different from the imposed situation now decided upon.

Therefore, I must ask you to accept my resignation as Minister of Communications, effective immediately. I leave with real regret.

I fully support the national policies of your government and I am certain that these will achieve a better and a united Canada. In my own sphere of activity, I have greatly enjoyed the challenge of the portfolio of the Post Office, and am confident that the reforms now initiated will produce an institution as good as any in the world. The Department of Communications is still in the process of developing its policies, but I am confident that the approach we have taken will result in a communications system that will not only serve the needs of Canadians, but far more important, the human and social needs.

Sincerely yours,


Eric Kierans

*2. My second letter of resignation. This one he opened, and accepted.*

April 28th, 1971

The Right Honourable P.E. Trudeau, P.C., M.P.,
Prime Minister of Canada,
Ottawa.

My dear Prime Minister;

I appreciated very much our lengthy discussion yesterday in which I expressed my concern about the economic problems, particularly employment, facing Canada in the seventies. Challenges, which did not exist ten years ago, now present themselves and demand a total reexamination of all elements of our economic policy. The rise of the international corporation, for example, is leading some economists and businessmen to talk in terms of Gross World Production as a better index of economic growth than the sum of national products. This may be, although I sense no similar concern with the distribution of that product. One can detect, however, the implicit assumption that Canada is to be assigned the role of supplier of resources presumably because we have them and also because we do not have a sufficient domestic market to justify their conversion into finished or semi-finished products here at home.

Economic policy is put together from a variety of elements but the overriding objective of all nations, in the seventies, must be the attainment of full employment, however defined, as the best guarantee of political, social and economic stability. To this end, all elements of policy — monetary, fiscal, commercial, energy and resources, agricultural, regional development — must be interconnected to ensure that they do not work at cross purposes and at the expense of overall objectives.

It is in this realm of ideas and policy that I wish to concentrate my efforts. Economic growth is not unlimited. Even with an exponential increase in capital and population — three billion now, six billion people by the year 2000 — a diminishing supply of non-renewable resources will restrain world growth. Canada is fortunate in its resource base and can insist on exports with a higher labour content. Tax concessions that force the pace of our raw material exports or favour the overemployment of capital, which we have to import, at the expense of labour which is in surplus would not be consistent with long-run Canadian growth and employment objectives. If Canada is to be an industrial force in the 1980s, we must be prepared now to husband our resources and to select those areas in which we can be internationally competitive and to manage and invest in the resources, physical and human, that will give us a compelling position.

To challenge openly long-established policies and practices would be embarrassing to my colleagues and to you, and unfair, if I were to remain in the Cabinet. Therefore, I ask you to accept my resignation as Minister of Communications, effective immediately. I leave with real regret.

I fully support the national unity policies of the government and I am certain that these will achieve a better and a united Canada. In my own sphere of activity, I have greatly enjoyed the challenge that you entrusted to me as Minister of Communications.

With my warmest personal regards, I am

Sincerely yours,


Eric Kierans

**3.** *My letter to Premier René Lévesque, resigning from the Caisse.*

Le 5 mai 1980

Monsieur René Lévesque
Premier Ministre
Gouvernement du Québec
Edifice "J", 3e étage
Hôtel du Gouvernement
Québec G1A 1A2

Monsieur le Premier Ministre,

En 1965, vous et moi avons appuyé la formation de la Régie des rentes du Québec et de la Caisse de dépôt et placement comme deux instruments clés qui pourraient servir à assurer le développement de la province.

De concert avec M. Lesage et nos collègues, nous avons convenu que la direction de la Caisse devait être indépendante et, autant que possible, libre des pressions du secteur public comme du secteur privé. Seule une équipe de gestion compétente et autonome pouvait, disions-nous, assurer la sécurité des placements et un rendement maximal des épargnes que les travailleurs confieraient à la Caisse.

Malheureusement, l'indépendance que nous souhaitions insuffler à la Caisse n'existe plus. L'ingérence toujours croissante du ministère des Finances auprès de la Caisse est devenue intolérable. La haute direction ne peut établir des politiques d'investissement équilibrées et diversifiées ni même assurer le meilleur rendement possible de ses actifs.

Après l'annonce d'un déficit de 2,3 milliard de dollars, le ministre des Finances a déclaré dans son discours sur le budget que le financement de nouveaux emprunts seraient facile à assurer puisque "la Caisse disposera en effet, en 1980, de 2,22$ milliards de ressources à investir à long terme." En réalité, la Caisse ne pourrait prêter un tel montant qu'à la condition de vendre quelques certaines de millions de dollars de ses actifs actuels. M. Parizeau a-t-il l'intention de vider la Caisse pendant les années à venir pour financer ses déficits?

Quand le gouvernement s'approprie environ 60 pour cent de

l'accroissement des fonds de la Caisse pour financer ses déficits, qu'arrive-t-il à l'objectif d'un porte-feuille équilibré et diversifié? Et si la chose se répète l'année prochaine? Et encore? Est-ce ainsi qu'on garantit la sécurité des sommes que les cotisants mettent de côté pour assurer leur retraite? Est-ce cela que nous avons promis en 1965?

M. Parizeau attend de la Caisse qu'elle prête 1,5 milliard $ au gouvernement et à Hydro-Québec en 1980, soit 83 pour cent de l'accroissement des fonds prévu [*sic*] (1,8 milliard $). Et il n'a pas l'intention de payer le prix courant pour ces emprunts. Le ministère des Finances est prêt à payer le prix courant aux investisseurs étrangers ou aux investisseurs indépendants mais il exigera des taux préférentiels de la Caisse. Je définis une telle politique, où la Caisse est appelée à subventionner l'Etat, comme une exploitation flagrante des employés qui contribuent à la Régie des rentes.

Je conteste formellement la déclaration suivante de M. Parizeau à l'Assemblée nationale (11-4-80): "La Caisse de dépôt…c'est l'instrument par excellence d'un gouvernement souverain." Si l'on s'apprête à dépenser les fonds confiés à la Caisse aux aventures constitutionnelles ou aux politiques de grandeur, il faut accepter qu'une retraite confortable pour ceux qui ont créé ce réservoir de capitaux ne pourra se réaliser que par la bonté des contribuables dans les années à venir.

Quand on utilise nos dépôts pour financer les déficits du gouvernement, on ne peut pas en servir de ces fonds pour financier la croissance économique de la province. En conséquence, le Québec dépendra de l'importation de capital durant biens des années.

Puisque je ne suis pas d'accord ni avec la politique ni avec l'ingérence du gouvernement dans les activités de la Caisse, je désire vous informer que je quitterai le 12 mai mon poste au conseil d'administration de la Caisse de dépôt et placement.

Veuillez agréer, Monsieur le premier ministre, l'expression de mes sentiments les meilleurs.

Eric Kierans

## 4. *René's reply.*

> In my resignation letter, I had charged that the government was, in effect, raiding the savings of Quebecers to meet its own financial needs by forcing the Caisse to lend money to it at below-market rates. You will see that René's defence is that I was at the meeting on March 17, 1980, that unanimously approved such a policy. That meeting took place six weeks before I resigned, and he thus saw my resignation as being tied to the referendum campaign then being waged, rather than as being a matter of principle. I was able to prove that the item that was approved was never on the agenda, and was introduced only after I left the meeting, and without my knowledge. I resigned and made my public complaint as soon as I was aware of what was happening. I don't know whether René ever accepted this. His memoirs avoided the entire series of events.

Monsieur Eric W. Kierans
5631 Queen Mary Road
Hampstead, QUEBEC

Monsieur,

C'est avec regret que j'ai pris connaissance de la lettre que vous m'avez écrite hier et que vous avez rendu publique le même jour m'informant de votre décision de quitter le Conseil d'administration de la Caisse de dépôt et placement du Québec, auprès duquel le présent gouvernement vous avait nommé en octobre 1978.

Je suis autant plus peiné que les raisons que vous invoquez peuvent porter atteinte à l'intégrité des autres membres du Conseil d'administration qui, bien que très respectés dans leur milieu pour leur esprit d'indépendance, laisseraient le gouvernement s'ingérer indûment dans l'administration de la Caisse. Cela est très injuste pour vos collègues et pour les membres du personnel de la Caisse.

J'aimerais vous rappeler que le programme d'emprunt du gouvernement et de l'Hydro-Québec auprès de la Caisse, qui sera de 1,5 milliard $ cette année, a été approuvé formellement par le Conseil de la Caisse <u>avant</u> le discours du budget; cette approbation s'est faite à l'unanimité lors d'une séance où vous étiez présent, le 17 mars dernier. Je comprends mal que se soit plus d'un mois et demi après, et moins de deux semaines avant le référendum, que votre conscience vous dicte aussi tardivement une aussi bruyante démission. Tenant compte de votre allusion aux "aventures constitutionnelles," je ne puis donc m'empêcher d'être un peu troublé par la façon dont vous motivez votre geste.

Quant à la décision de la Caisse de prêter au gouvernement et à l'Hydro-Québec aux conditions dont jouit, sur le marché public, la province ayant le meilleur crédit, elle refléte uniquement la valeur de nos institutions et leur capacité de rencontrer en tout temps leurs obligations. On ne saurait donc parler de taux préférentiels sans faire de démagogie. D'ailleurs, cette politique de placement a été approuvée, malgré votre opposition, par la très large majorité des membres du Conseil et il est évident qu'elle ne met aucunement en danger la capacité de la Caisse de rencontrer ses obligations à l'égard des retraites. C'est, à mon avis, une décision pleinement justifiée, qui est dans le meilleur intérêt des citoyens du Québec.

Veuillez agréer, monsieur, l'expression de mes sentiments distingués.

René Lévesque

# INDEX